Teaching Fantasy Novels

From
The Hobbit
to
Harry Potter and the Goblet of Fire

Phyllis J. Perry

TEACHER IDEAS PRESS
Portsmouth, NH

For

all those students, teachers, librarians, and parents

who have a love for the fantastic!

Teacher Ideas Press
A division of Reed Elsevier Inc.
361 Hanover Street
Portsmouth, NH 03801–3912
www.teacherideaspress.com

Offices and agents throughout the world

Library of Congress Cataloging-in-Publication Data

Perry, Phyllis Jean.
    Teaching fantasy novels: from The Hobbit to Harry Potter and the goblet of fire / by Phyllis J. Perry.
      p. cm.
    Includes index.
    ISBN 1-56308-987-4
    1. Fantasy fiction, English—Study and teaching. 2. Children's stories, English—Study and teaching.
  3. Fantasy fiction, American—Study and teaching. 4. Children's stories, American—Study and teaching.
  5. English fiction—20th century—Study and teaching. 6. American fiction—20th century—Study and teaching.
I. Title.
PR888.F3 P47 2003
823'.08766'071—dc21   2003013594

Editor: Suzanne Barchers
Production Coordinator: Angela Laughlin
Typesetter: Westchester Book Services
Cover design: Joni Doherty
Manufacturing: Steve Bernier

Printed in the United States of America on acid-free paper

07 06 05 04 03 VP 1 2 3 4 5

❖ Table of Contents

❖ Introduction

Teaching Fantasy Novels: From The Hobbit to Harry Potter and the Goblet of Fire is designed to assist busy educators who are enriching the upper elementary and middle school curriculum by including excellent fantasy literature to ensure that they are at the same time addressing the national standards.

In the twenty-first century, educators and parents are perhaps more aware than ever before of the need to provide a challenging and appealing curriculum that helps students to meet standards that have been developed across the various disciplines. This is certainly the case for those whose primary concern is with the Language Arts/Reading Standards.

These standards have been developed at each grade level in the broad areas of reading, writing, listening, speaking, viewing, literature, the English language, and accessing and processing information. At each level, students apply learnings and skills previously mastered to tackle more complex materials, and they experience, respond to, appreciate, and self-select from an increasingly wider range of literature.

For each of the twenty titles discussed in this book, the reader will find a detailed synopsis, a list of major characters, a vocabulary exercise, a set of comprehension questions with answers, some open-ended discussion questions, a set of suggested research activities for individuals or small groups to pursue, and some extension activities. There is also an explanation showing how each of these books, read in conjunction with the exercises, questions, and activities, helps to meet the 12 NCTE/IRA English Language Arts Standards.

As they progress through their education, students will read from a variety of genres and are almost certain to explore fantasy literature. The twenty novels that were selected for inclusion in this book represent some of the finest fantasy literature written. This estimation of quality is drawn from professional journal reviews; from recommendations of writers, readers, librarians, and educators; and by their inclusion in accelerated reader lists, lists of Newbery Honor Books, or lists of recipients of the prestigious Newbery Medal.

Although all of the books discussed here are classified in the broad genre of "fantasy," it should be recognized that this genre is often further subdivided into groupings about which there is little agreement. Many scholars recognize a category called "high fantasy," which includes those books that deal with kingdoms, magical creatures, a struggle between the powers of good and evil, and often a quest carried out by one of the characters. Some of the books included here such as *The Hobbit* and *The Dark Is Rising* fit neatly into this classification of high fantasy. Others do not.

Some scholars argue that "low fantasy" takes place in the rational, physically familiar world and can be contrasted with high fantasy, which takes place in a secondary world. Perhaps *Tuck Everlasting* by Natalie Babbitt would fit this definition of low fantasy.

Other books, like Avi's *Poppy* or Brian Jacques's *Redwall* are sometimes found listed in a subcategory called "animal fantasy." *Ella Enchanted* by Gail Carson Levine is often included in a subcategory called "light fantasy" or "humorous fantasy." Philip Pullman insists that his books, such as *The Amber Spyglass,* are not fantasy at all but are examples of stark realism, though many would not agree with his assessment. Fairytales, folklore, and myths are often included in the broad genre of fantasy, as are "dream fantansies" such as *The Wizard of Oz.* And many would argue that the boundaries between fantasy and science fiction are very fuzzy, indeed, and that all science fiction is a part of fantasy literature.

It is not possible, and there is no intention in this brief introduction, to adequately define the genre of fantasy literature and its various subgroupings. It is sufficient for the purpose of this book to assert that although fantasy literature may be difficult to define, it has recognizable attributes that to a greater or lesser extent are displayed by each of the examples included for discussion here.

Clearly a work of fantasy literature represents a deliberate departure from reality. Or it might be said that it presents an "alternate reality" containing events, places, and creatures that could not occur or exist in the rational world. Nonrational phenomena play a significant part in the fantasy story. Using this broad approach, each of the books included for discussion here represents an outstanding example of this elusive genre, fantasy literature.

The High King

Lloyd Alexander

New York: Henry Holt & Co., 1999, rev. ed., ISBN 0-8050-6135-5

Detailed Synopsis

There are five books in the Chronicles of Prydain. *The High King* is the fifth and final book in this series of high fantasy.

The High King begins with Taran, the Wanderer, returning home. With him is his faithful servant, Gurgi. Stopping to rest in a grove of ash trees, they tether their mounts, build a fire, and eat. Kaw, the crow, arrives to tell them that Princess Eilonwy is waiting for them. That information is enough to cause Taran and Gurgi to remount and ride again until they reach Caer Dallben.

At Caer Dallben, Taran, Gurgi, Eilonwy, and Dallben, a wizard, greet each other. King Rhun and Glew, a grumbling former giant, are there, too. They learn that Fflewddur Fflam and Prince Gwydion are expected shortly.

Fflewddur Fflam arrives carrying Gwydion, Prince of Don. Fflewddur explains that Huntsmen attacked, wounding Gwydion and taking from him the enchanted blade, Dyrnwyn. He suspects they have already taken the sword to Arawn, Death-Lord of Annuvin.

Fflewddur insists that he saw Taran at the battle, and Achren, the former evil queen, comes out of the shadows to explain that what Fflewddur actually saw was Arawn in the disguise of Taran. Achren explains that Arawn can assume any form and that while he is in another form, Arawn is vulnerable and can be slain. She insists that the face of Arawn cannot be hidden from her, and she volunteers to go and try to kill Arawn.

But Gwydion refuses her offer. He says she would be slain immediately in Annuvin. Dallben gets out the letter sticks and calls on Hen Wen, the white pig, to make a prophecy for them. Instead of cheerfully running up to Taran, Hen Wen crouches in a far corner of her pen. When she finally approaches the sticks, they shatter into splinters. Gurgi comes racing out of the house to announce that Achren has taken one of King Rhun's horses and left for Annuvin.

Dallben tries to decipher the partial message from Hen Wen, but the splintered sticks offer little encouragement in recovering the sword. The signs suggest that the sword will not be recovered until night turns to noon, rivers burn, and rocks talk, and that even then, the flame of the sword will be quenched.

Gwydion insists he must go seek the sword. He plans to go first to King Smoit's castle and there await a report from Kaw as to what he has learned about Annuvin. While Kaw flies off toward Annuvin, the other companions escort Gwydion to Smoit's stronghold at Caer Cadarn.

Eilonwy rides Lluagor and carries her golden sphere. Taran rides Melyngar. Fflewddur rides his giant cat, Llyan; King Rhun and Coll, a friend, ride horses, and Glew, the one-time giant, rides behind Gurgi on his shaggy pony. Around the campfire that night, Rhun talks about the seawall he wants to build and Taran offers suggestions.

The companions break into two parties. Eilonwy, King Rhun, Fflewddur, and Glew will go to the harbor to advise the shipmaster of their change in plans. The others will ride to Caer Cadarn. The two groups plan to meetup again at midday. When the appointed time comes, Fflewddur's group does not appear, and the others go on alone to Caer Cadarn.

When they reach the castle, instead of finding King Smoit, they find Magg, who was formerly chief steward in the Court of Mona and is now serving Arawn. Warriors quickly capture the small band, and Magg locks the companions in the larder along with King Smoit, who was overpowered earlier by Magg's men.

When Fflewddur and the others near Caer Cadarn, Eilonwy wonders why the House of Don banner isn't waving over the castle to denote their distinguished visitors and why no honor guard awaits them. With his concerns raised, Fflewddur agrees to go alone like a traveling minstrel to the castle to check things out. When he returns, he tells the others that Magg is in power and has imprisoned King Smoit and their companions.

Eilonwy spies Gwystyl of the Fair Folk lurking about and asks him to help. He carries a bag filled with strange things including eggs filled with smoke and toadstools that make puffs of flame. The companions take several of these items to use in their attempt to free their companions.

At dawn, the little band heads for the castle. Gwystyl scales the wall followed by Glew, Fflewddur, Rhun, and Eilonwy. While Fflewddur is trapped in the courtyard, Eilonwy sets the prisoners and Smoit's warriors free. Then Rhun rushes in shouting orders as if he is commanding a whole army. Magg's men fall into confusion and are routed, but Rhun is killed in the attack.

Gwydion decides to abandon the search for the sword and to gather a force to fight against Arawn. Gwystyl goes on to King Eiddileg to get help, and word is sent to King Pryderi at the West Domain to raise troops. All fighting forces are to assemble at Caer Dathyl. Fflewddur goes to gather help from the Northern Realms while Taran is to raise a band of warriors from the folk of the Free Commots.

In the meantime, Kaw, nearing Annuvin, is attacked by gwythaints. Kaw manages to get to Medwyn and tells him what is happening. Medwyn cures Kaw and sends his eagle and wolves to stir up every wild creature to turn against Arawn.

Taran gathers the Commot Folk to serve as soldiers for the House of Don. Llonio and Hevydd turn as many common objects as possible into weapons. The Weaver Woman and others weave warm garments to outfit the soldiers. As he goes from place to place, Taran must constantly fight marauders. Eventually he arrives at Caer Dathyl and confers with Gwydion and King Math.

When Pryderi arrives with all his men, everyone thinks he has come to join Math in safeguarding Prydain. But in the Great Hall, Pryderi announces he has come to demand King Math's surrender. Pryderi is ordered to leave, and the next day a battle begins. Toward sundown, the Cauldron-Born, or deathless, warriors of Annuvin appear with an iron-capped battering ram. They kill Math and capture Caer Dathyl.

The companions gather in a makeshift camp in the hills east of Caer Dathyl. With the death of Math, Gwydion becomes King of Prydain. Gwydion decides that now, while the Cauldron-Born are far from Annuvin, is the time to attack.

Gwydion divides his men into two groups. One group will try to slow the Cauldron-Born and prevent their quick return to Annuvin. Taran will lead this group. Gwydion will lead the second group in an attack by sea. Both groups set off on their assignments. Taran tries to slow the Cauldron-Born at the Red Fallows by turning them to the Hills of Bran Galedd. In this battle, Coll, a dear friend of Taran's, is killed and Eilonwy and Gurgi go missing.

A group of Fair Folk, sent by King Eiddileg, joins the companions. Doli, the dwarf, leads them on a shortcut through an old abandoned cavern. In the cavern, Glew causes a cave-in while hunting gemstones. This forces all the men to turn back and retrace their steps, losing precious time.

Meanwhile, Eilonwy and Gurgi are taken prisoner by marauders, but they are rescued by wolves. The wolves lead Eilonwy and Gurgi back to Taran. Using her golden bauble, Eilonwy lights up the area and reveals to Taran and his men the imminent danger from the nearby Huntsmen. After the Huntsmen make camp, Doli comes up with a plan to climb high in order to divert the lake and waterfall, to come straight down onto the enemy camp.

At home, Dallben and Hen Wen are visited by horsemen. They are all turned back by Dallben's magic except for Pryderi. He comes into the cottage, threatens Dallben, and tries to take the Book of Three. He is killed by a lightning bolt.

The companions and Doli continue through the mountains. Gwythaints appear and are seen attacking something at a distance. A black cloud of crows appears and drives off the huge birds. Kaw, the crow, appears to tell Taran that the once-powerful Queen, Achren, is nearby and has been injured by the gwythaints. They find Achren unconscious and put her on Llyan's back.

It begins to snow, but the companions continue on their way. They take shelter and are near freezing. Fflewddur smashes his harp for firewood and Doli lights it. All night the harp sings and the fire burns. Achren grows stronger and guides them on a hidden trail over Mount Dragon.

As they struggle up the mountain, Kaw returns with the message that Gwydion is at Annuvin. Taran slips from the trail and a gwythaint swoops down on him. It turns out to be a bird that Taran had once helped, and instead of attacking, the gwythaint carries Taran safely back to the peak of Mount Dragon.

As the Cauldron-Born rush to attack, Taran dislodges the stone at the peak of Mount Dragon and sends it crashing down on his enemies. Taran finds Dyrnwyn, the black sword, hidden there, and he picks it up. He drives the weapon into an attacking warrior's heart. With the death of this one warrior, all the other Cauldron-Born warriors fall.

Taran rushes onward until he reaches Gwydion, who demands the sword. Taran realizes that Arawn has disguised himself as Gwydion. He tries to slay the Death-Lord, but Arawn escapes. Magg appears at the throne and puts on the king's crown, which glows red-hot and kills him.

Gurgi and Glew, separated from the others, come upon the treasure house of Arawn. Flames leap out at them, but they manage to make their way to their companions. Arawn appears in the form of a serpent and strikes and kills Achren. Taran uses the sword to kill the serpent. The shape of the serpent blurs and a man appears and then sinks like a shadow into the earth. The brilliant fire of the sword dies and it becomes only a dull blade. As the companions leave Annuvin, the towers crumble and flames shoot up.

The companions return to Caer Dallben. Dallben explains that this is a time for farewell. To fulfill the prophecy, the Sons of Don must leave Prydain and return to Summer Country, a land without strife or suffering and where death is unknown.

Eilonwy, Dallben, Fflewddur Fflam, and Gwydion will all go to Summer Country. Doli will return to the realm of the Fair Folk with Kaw. Medwyn closes his valley to men and allows only animals to come in. Gurgi, Hen Wen, Glew, and Taran are to be rewarded by being allowed to also journey to Summer Country. Taran asks Eilonwy to marry him, and she agrees.

That night, three figures appear and give Taran the tapestry of his life. In the morning, Taran announces that he will stay and that he has much work to do in Prydain. Then Dallben explains that in the Book of Three, it is written that when the Sons of Don depart, Taran will become High King of Prydain.

His friends give Taran farewell gifts. Glew hands him a small crystal from the cavern of Mona. Doli gives him an ax. Fflewddur gives him the harp string he took from the fire. Gurgi gives him a box of parchments from the treasure house, which contain secrets of forging and tempering metal, shaping and firing pottery, and cultivating. Dallben gives him the Book of Three. Eilonwy gives him her golden bauble.

Dallben helps Eilonwy give up her magical powers so that she may stay in Prydain and marry Taran. They will rule Prydain as king and queen.

List of Major Characters: Taran is the Assistant Pig Keeper who becomes High King and is the main character in the book; Gurgi is Taran's faithful, hairy servant; Hen Wen is an oracular pig; Eilonwy is a princess with magical powers; Gwydion is a Prince of Don who becomes king of Prydain; Kaw is a crow; Dallben is a wizard who raised Taran; Gwystyl is one of the Fair Folk; Glew is a one-time giant; Arawn is Death-Lord and ruler of Annuvin; Doli is a friendly and helpful dwarf; Achren is a once-powerful queen now helping to destroy Arawn; Coll is a gardener who turned into a warrior to assist his friend, Taran; King Rhun is the young king of Mona who meets a warrior's death; and Fflewddur Fflam is a comical bard of Prydain.

Vocabulary: The page numbers shown after the vocabulary words below indicate a page on which the word was used. Look up each of the words, find synonyms, and rewrite the sentence from the book using a synonym in place of the vocabulary word.

wretched (8) _____

grievously (13) _____

haughtiness (17) _____

paltry (20) _____

livid (47) _____

mewed (50) _____

riven (108) _____

panoplies (110) _____

implacable (127) _____

tidings (149) _____

unwonted (156) _____

deign (173) _____

Comprehension Questions

1. Since Arawn does not use the various treasures he has stolen from Prydain, what is his motive for keeping them?
2. The companions are willing to send Glew, the former giant, home on a ship. What makes Glew decide to come with the others on their dangerous trip to Arawn's realm?
3. Describe the banner that flies over Caer Cadarn.
4. King Math has been a good king, and he is tired and ready to die. What makes Math reluctant to die right now?
5. Hevydd the Smith puts the complaining giant, Glew, to work in Caer Dathyl. What job does Glew have to do?
6. When Doli becomes weak while traveling through the mountains, what does he do to strengthen himself?
7. What figure is on the banner that Eilonwy embroiders for Taran?
8. When Llyan grows difficult, what does Fflewddur do to calm her?
9. When they are freezing in the mountains, what does Fflewddur sacrifice for firewood?
10. Why doesn't the gwythaint kill Taran in the mountains?

Answers: 1) His purpose is to simply deprive men. 2) Glew hopes to get some of Arawn's treasures for himself. 3) The banner over Caer Cadarn is crimson with a black bear. 4) He hates to see blood spilled in a land where he has so long sought peace. 5) Glew works at pumping the bellows. 6) Doli makes himself invisible. 7) Hen Wen, the oracular pig, is on the banner. 8) Fflewddur plays his harp to calm Llyan. 9) Fflewddur sacrifices his beloved harp for firewood. 10) The gwythaint saves Taran because as a young boy, Taran had nursed the bird back to health.

Discussion Questions

1. Toward the end of the book, there are some clues to suggest that Glew is changing for the better. What are these clues? Do you expect him to be a much different person in Summer Country? Why, or why not?

2. Pryderi is summoned to raise troops to help Gwydion and Math in their battle against Arawn. Why do you think he chooses this time to turn against them and to demand their surrender?

3. Eilonwy does not speak glowingly of the time she spent in training to be a princess. Often she does not act like a princess at all, but more like a clever warrior. What effect does it have on the story that Eilonwy is not a "typical" storybook princess?

4. Although a prophecy declares that the royalty of Don return to Summer Country, others have the choice of whether or not to go there. If you were Taran or Eilonwy, would you have chosen to stay in Prydain or to go to Summer Country? Why?

5. *The Dark Is Rising* and *The High King* are both fantasy writings in which darkness, or evil, is being fought by the forces of good. Ask students who have read both books to meet and discuss the statement made by Gwydion near the end of *The High King,* when he says, "Evil conquered? You have learned much, but learn this last and hardest of lessons. You have conquered only the enchantments of evil. That was the easiest of your tasks, only a beginning, not an ending. Do you believe evil itself to be so quickly overcome? Not so long as men hate and slay each other, when greed and anger goad them. Against these, even a flaming sword cannot prevail, but only that portion of good in all men's hearts whose flame can never be quenched."

6. Taran is as much distressed by the deaths of Coll, the turnip grower, and of Annlaw, the Clay Shaper, as he is at the death of Rhun, the young king of Mona. Part of the reason he stays behind in Prydain is to finish tasks that they had begun. He is as comfortable with being an Assistant Pig Keeper as he is with being High King. Why is this lack of interest in station in life on the part of Taran an important part of the story?

7. Discuss why you think that Medwyn closes his valley to the race of men. With Taran as High King, do you think Medwyn may open the valley again? Why, or why not?

8. Gurgi is ready for the "floatings" and "boatings," but as soon as he learns that Taran is not going to Summer Country, Gurgi offers to stay behind with his master. Taran says that he must go to "find the wisdom" that he yearns for. Discuss what you think life will be like in the future for Gurgi.

Research Activities

1. The sword, Dyrnwyn, is very important in *The High King.* But a much more famous sword is Excalibur, the sword of the legendary King Arthur. Invite a pair of students to research the sword, Excalibur. They should prepare a written report using at least three sources of information. One place to look is at htttp://www.geocities.com/robinhood_tw/ arthur.html. Another source of information is *King Arthur* by Jeremy Roberts (Minneapolis, MN: Lerner Publications Co., 2001).

2. Lloyd Alexander spent time in Wales during World War II, and he says that his story grew from Welsh legends. Invite a small group of students to research Wales. Where is it? What is its history? How is it governed today? Ask these students to make an oral report

to the class. They should be encouraged to use maps, web sites, magazine articles, and books in gathering and in presenting their information about this interesting country.

3. Several authors of children's books, including Lloyd Alexander, have won a Newbery medal after having written a book that was named as a Newbery Honor Book. Invite a pair of students to research books that have been selected as Newbery Medal and Honor Book winners. They should list the authors and titles of the books for those authors who have had one of their books named in each category. This list of distinguished authors who have had their books named for *both* a Newbery Medal and a Newbery Honor Book could be posted in the classroom or the library.

4. Arawn appears toward the end of the book in the form of a serpent. Invite a pair of students to research the role of serpents in legends and literature. If there are ESL students in the class, or other students with an interest in other cultures, perhaps they can locate other countries' legends or tales in which serpents play a role. They should write a paper on their findings in which they include a bibliography of their sources of information. The paper should be posted in the classroom where others who are interested may read it.

5. Traditionally, the people of Wales spoke a native tongue that sounds very different from English. With the help of a music educator, try to locate some Welsh ballads and play these for the class so that they can hear examples of this language.

6. The individual countries that make up the United Kingdom do not have their own kings and queens. They are bound in allegiance to the ruling king or queen in England. Ask a pair of students to learn more about the current English monarchy. Have them make up a family genealogy tree showing how the present monarchs are descended from earlier monarchs and indicating which people are next in line to the throne when the current queen dies or retires.

Extension Activities

1. Gurgi has a very distinctive way of speaking. Invite a pair of students to write a page of dialogue in which Gurgi tells Taran that he doesn't want to leave him and move to Summer Country and in which Taran tries to persuade his faithful friend to go. When both students are satisfied with their script, have them present the dialogue before the class.

2. Pages 35 to 37 of the book describe the major characters getting ready to ride with Gwydion on the first part of his journey to Annuvin. There is a description of each of the mounts. This scene might make an interesting mural. Invite a group of students to make a mural showing Gwydion on Melyngar, Taran on Melynlas, Eilonwy on Lluagor, Fflewddur on Llyan, King Rhun on his dapple gray steed, Coll on Llamrei, and Glew perched behind Gurgi on a shaggy pony. The students might use a variety of media in creating the mural and, with permission, could hang it in the library along with a few lines suggesting that others might enjoy reading *The High King,* an exciting high fantasy.

3. Imagine that a proclamation is sent out in Prydain inviting people to attend the coronation of King Taran and Queen Eilonwy. Use fanciful script and paper and appropriate language write the proclamation in the form of a scroll. Post it in the classroom.

4. In Summer Country, Fflewddur Fflam will become a well-known bard with a new lute. Write some verses in the style of Fflewddur Fflam commemorating the brave deeds that led to the death of Arawn and the destruction of Annuvin.

5. Choose a scene involving lots of dialogue and ask an interested group of students, perhaps working with a volunteer parent serving as director, to rehearse and present the scene for the class. Simple props and costumes might be used to enhance the production.

6. There is a small map in the book indicating where various places are located. Invite a pair of students to make a salt and flour map, showing on it the various places where the major events of *The High King* take place. They might use small figures and castles and build up the mountain ranges. Display the map in the classroom.

How does reading *The High King* and engaging in the various activities suggested above help students meet the 12 NCTE/IRA English Language Arts Standards?

1. *The High King* meets Standard #1 by serving as an example of outstanding fiction.

2. *The High King* meets Standard #2 because it is a representative work of the broad genre of high fantasy.

3. Discussion questions #1, #2, #4, #6, and #8 help students to comprehend and interpret text, and the vocabulary exercise increases knowledge of word meanings, helping students to meet Standard #3.

4. Extension activity #1, which suggests writing out a dialogue reflecting the unusual speech patterns of Gurgi, addresses Standard #4, which asks students to adjust written language and style to communicate effectively for different purposes.

5. Extension activity #3, which suggests that a student write up a proclamation in the form of a scroll announcing the coronation of a new king and queen of Prydain, helps meet Standard #5, which requires that students use different writing processes for different audiences and for a variety of purposes.

6. Extension activity #4, which suggests that a student write a heroic verse to commemorate the downfall of Arawn and Annuvin, helps to meet Standard #6 by requiring students to apply their knowledge of language structure and language conventions to create a print text.

7. Research activity #6, involving the genealogy of the current monarchs, helps to address Standard #7 by requiring students to gather, evaluate, and synthesize data from a variety of sources to communicate their discoveries.

8. Research activity #1, involving the history of King Arthur and his sword, Excalibur, helps to meet Standard #8 by encouraging students to use a variety of technological and information resources to carry out research and to communicate their knowledge.

9. Discussion question #6 about Taran's grief over lost friends who were kings, potters, and turnip growers helps to address Standard #9 by allowing students to develop an understanding of and respect for diversity in social roles.

10. Research activity #4, asking ESL students to compare and contrast the use of serpents in their ancestral literature with the use of serpents in this story, helps address Standard #10, which asks that students use their first language that is not English to develop a deeper understanding of the curriculum.

11. Discussion question #5 allows students to pool their knowledge in the form of a book discussion group and compare *The High King* with *The Dark Is Rising* in their depiction of the forces of "darkness" or "evil." It helps meet Standard #11, which asks that students

participate as knowledgeable, reflective, creative, and critical members of a literary community.

12. Extension activity #2 allows students to prepare a colorful mural from one section of *The High King* as a means of sharing their enthusiasm for this book with other potential readers. It addresses Standard #12, in which students are asked to use spoken, written, and visual language to persuade others.

Poppy

Avi

New York: Orchard Books, 1995, ISBN 0-531-08783-2
Recommended for grades 3 and 4

Detailed Synopsis

Poppy is an animal fantasy that is set near the edge of Dimwood Forest, where a great horned owl named Mr. Ocax perches on his watching post and keeps track of all that is going on. Mr. Ocax considers all the creatures who live in this place to be his subjects, and they are only allowed to move about with his permission.

One summer night when Mr. Ocax is looking for dinner, he spies two mice. They have come out on a romantic adventure without seeking permission. Ragweed, known to be a challenging and unconventional mouse, has brought Poppy out to ask her to marry him. She is hoping he is taking her dancing. When Ragweed finds a nut and begins eating it out in the open where he might be seen, Poppy is frightened. She begs him to take cover, but he scoffs at danger. Mr. Ocax plummets down, killing Ragweed instantly.

Poppy faints, and when she awakens, she worries about what to do. She knows that she should have gotten permission to move beyond the immediate area of Gray House, where she and her family live. She also knows that Mr. Ocax demands obedience in return for protecting the mice from raccoons, foxes, skunks, weasels, and especially porcupines. She is sickened by Ragweed's death and by the knowledge that she has done wrong, and she tries to sneak home.

But Mr. Ocax is still watching, and he swoops down as Poppy runs for cover. He almost catches her, but through good luck, she escapes with only a scratch on the nose. When she gets to Gray House, Poppy finds a red flag hanging from the end of the roof. This is a signal for the clan to gather in an emergency meeting. Her father, Lungwort, who is leader of the group, is advising everyone that due to the increase in their numbers, some will have to move to another dwelling.

Mr. Albicollis, a sparrow, has informed Lungwort that there may be a suitable place by a New House that has been built at the northern side of Dimwood Forest. When Lungwort asks for volunteers to go and ask permission from Mr. Ocax to move to New House, no one volunteers. After the meeting ends, Lungwort says that Poppy must go with him to seek permission. Poppy tells them what has happened to Ragweed, but she gets little sympathy and is still expected to go on the mission with her father.

Lungwort works in his study on a speech for Mr. Ocax. When it is ready, he and Poppy leave on their "permission party." Poppy carries a white flag. They set off down Tar Road to seek permission from Mr. Ocax. As Lungwort makes his request, Poppy stands in horror near the owl pellets at the foot of the watching post tree. In a pellet, she spies the earring that Ragweed once wore, and takes it.

Mr. Ocax denies the request of the mice to move. As an excuse, he says that his reason for denial is that Ragweed and Poppy disobeyed his orders. But Poppy feels that Mr. Ocax is agitated from hearing their request and thinks there is some other reason why he doesn't want them to go to New House.

Lungwort and Poppy trudge home. While her father goes to his study, Poppy informs the crowd that Mr. Ocax has denied permission for the move. She also tells them the reason he gave, and many of her relatives seem to be angry with her and to blame Poppy for their situation.

Poppy tries to go to sleep, but she keeps going over the conversation with Mr. Ocax. She finally decides that there must be a reason that Mr. Ocax is keeping from them that would explain why he doesn't want them to go to New House. She decides that she must go there and investigate for herself.

After telling her father and Basil, her cousin, of her plans, Poppy sets off for New House. She takes a route through Dimwood Forest. When she gets to Glitter Creek, the water is high from a recent storm. Poppy realizes she can't swim across. She decides to jump from rock to rock. Halfway across, Poppy slips on a mossy rock and falls into the water.

Poppy screams for help, and her cries are heard by Mr. Ocax. He watches her flounder and prepares to swoop down and eat her. Poppy is swept under the water. Thinking she has drowned, Mr. Ocax flies off to take another look at New House, but Poppy survives the near drowning and claws her way to the creek bank. As soon as she recovers, Poppy starts off for New House.

The sights and sounds of Dimwood Forest startle her. Poppy is chased by a fox and dives into an old log. Inside, she finds a smelly porcupine. It wakes up and tells Poppy that his name is Ereth. Ereth scares away the fox and talks with Poppy.

First, he assures her that he does not eat mice—he's a vegetarian who eats bark. Then he tells her that he cannot shoot his quills. When Ereth asks where she got her misinformation about porcupines, she tells him that is what Mr. Ocax tells everyone. Ereth explains that owls, not porcupines, eat mice. And he says owls fear him because he could hurt them with his quills. Ereth also confesses that the thing he loves most is salt, and he describes the big chunk of salt at New House that is up on a high steel pole where he can't reach it.

Poppy sleeps in Ereth's log. When she awakes, she is alone and sees that Mr. Ocax is nearby, so she waits for Ereth to come back. When he arrives, Ereth shouts up to Mr. Ocax and tells him what he has learned from Poppy. Poppy persuades Ereth to go with her to give her protection on the way to New House. In return, she promises she'll give him salt. When they start off for New House, Mr. Ocax follows them.

They arrive and Poppy sees the salt but can't figure out a way that she can get it for Ereth. She also sees the old barn where, on the roof, is an owl twice the size of Mr. Ocax. When Ereth leaves, Poppy stays behind and picks up one of his quills that has fallen out. She decides to keep the quill to use as a weapon.

In the morning, Poppy sees movement in New House. First, an old tomcat steps outside. Poppy watches, expecting the owl to pounce, but it doesn't move. Then a boy comes out with a fishing pole. The boy goes in the barn and opens an upper window. Poppy is amazed to see him move the owl around, and she wonders if the owl is real.

Later, Poppy talks to the old tomcat, who is too old to be dangerous to her, about the owl. He assures her that the owl is a fake. Then Poppy realizes that Mr. Ocax is afraid of the big fake owl. She starts for home and encounters Mr. Ocax. He swoops down to eat her and she fights him with the quill. She succeeds in sticking the quill into the owl's claw. The owl squawks and flies away with Poppy holding tight to the quill.

Out of control, Mr. Ocax slams into the block of salt while Poppy drops onto the grass. The salt shatters. Mr. Ocax falls to the ground, dead. Poppy picks up a feather and follows Ereth's scent back to the log, where she tells him that the salt is now scattered on the ground. He rushes off to get it.

Poppy sleeps in Ereth's log, then she goes back to Gray House where the red flag is again flying. Poppy goes to the meeting that is in progress, shows the feather, and tells everyone that Mr. Ocax is dead. They are free to move near New House, where there is enough corn to feed them.

In the final chapter of the book, Poppy and her husband, Rye, and their litter of young have started a happy new life.

List of Major Characters: Poppy, a deer mouse; Ragweed, Poppy's boyfriend; Lungwort, Poppy's father; Basil, Poppy's favorite cousin; Mr. Ocax, a great horned owl who rules Dimwood Forest; and Erethizon Dorsatum, a porcupine.

Vocabulary: See how each of the words below is used in the story by referring to the page number in parentheses. Look up each word in a dictionary and read its meaning. On the space following each word, write down what part of speech the word is.

dwelling (25) _____

multitude (36) _____

joshing (40) _____

deluge (41) _____

frailty (42) _____

flexing (45) _____

calamity (52) _____

ravenously (55) _____

effrontery (68) _____

whirligig (71) _____

richocheted (73) _____

contemplate (81) _____

Comprehension Questions

1. The mice in this story do not give applause by clapping their paws. How do they show their appreciation?
2. What unusual article of clothing does Lungwort wear?
3. What serves as a study for Lungwort in Gray House?
4. Poppy has her own unique room in the attic at Gray House. From what was her room made?
5. What was Poppy's secret desire that she had never told to anyone?
6. When she was lost in Dimwood Forest, what two clues did Poppy use that helped to give her a sense of direction?
7. What are some of the animals that Poppy encounters in Dimwood Forest?
8. Since cats eat mice, why wasn't Poppy afraid of the old tomcat at New House?
9. When Ereth wonders why Poppy was given such an idiotic name, how does she answer him?
10. Where does Ragweed's earring finally end up at the very end of the story?

Answers: 1) They applaud by tapping their tails upon the floor. 2) Lungwort wears a thimble on his head. 3) Farmer Lamout's old boot serves as a study for Lungwort. 4) Poppy's room in the attic is made from a tin Log Cabin Syrup can. 5) Poppy wants to be a ballroom dancer. 6) To give her a sense of direction, Poppy looks at the angle of slanting rays of sunlight and at the moss that grows on the north sides of trees. 7) In Dimwood Forest, Poppy encounters a porcupine, an owl, weasels, a raccoon, a ferret, a fox, and a bear. 8) Poppy doesn't fear the tomcat because he is too old to be dangerous. 9) Poppy explains that it's a family tradition to be named after flowers and fruits. 10) At the end of the story, Ragweed's earring is high on a hazelnut tree.

Discussion Questions

1. What evidence do you have in the beginning of the story that Ragweed is a different sort of mouse, one that questions authority?
2. Ragweed's speech is distinctive and different from the other mice's. Ereth, the porcupine, also has an unusual way of talking. What makes the statements of these characters stand out? What does their speech reveal about their characters?
3. Basil, Poppy's cousin, volunteers to go to New House with Poppy. Why do you think she refuses to let him come with her? Do you think Basil should have insisted on going? How might the story have been different if he went along?
4. In this story, all the mice fear porcupines although none of them has ever met a porcupine. People often fear what they do not know or understand. Can you think of someone

or something in your everyday life that you feared, but stopped being fearful of, after you had more information?

5. If you were a member of this clan of mice, would you want to stay at Gray House or would you want to move to New House? Why? Do you think that Poppy's father, Lungwort, will stay where he lives or make the move? Why?

6. Ereth says that he likes to be left alone, yet in a short time he seems to grow fond of Poppy. Why do you think Ereth likes Poppy? Are Ereth and Poppy respectful of one another? Do you think that Ereth and Poppy will continue to try to see each other in the future?

7. Gray House has been deserted for a long time. People live in New House. What sort of relationship do you think the mice will have with the occupants of New House?

8. In the beginning of the book, Poppy is meek and does what either Ragweed or her father tells her. She plays the conventional role of an obedient woman. But later in the book, Poppy shows a lot of spunk in fighting Mr. Ocax on her own. What made Poppy change from dependent to independent?

Research Activities

1. Ereth says that his name is Erethizon Dorsatum. This is the genus and species classification for the common porcupine found in North America. Invite a pair of interested students to research the porcupine. What is its geographic range? What are its physical characteristics? These students should learn as much as they can about the food and behaviors of porcupines and prepare a written report to share with the class. Possible sources of information include *Prickly and Smooth* by Rod Theodorou and Carole Telford (Crystal Lake, IL: Rigby Interactive Library, 1996) and *The Porcupine* by Victoria Sherrow (Minneapolis, MN: Dillon Press, 1991). Another useful source of information is http://animaldiversity.ummz.umich.edu/accounts/Erethizon/e._dorsatum.html.

2. Students in the class may come from different countries. If so, some students may be familiar with a different type of owl or another bird or animal that is common in their country and is used in the literature of their country as a symbol of evil power much as Mr. Ocax, the owl, was used in *Poppy*. Ask these students to make an oral presentation to the class sharing a piece of literature from their ancestral country that features a powerful and frightening figure that is a bird or animal.

3. Invite a small group of students to prepare a bulletin board on owls. They should draw or (with permission) cut from magazines pictures of various types of owls and perhaps could include some poems about owls. They should also include a short written report with information about some owls, being sure to include the great horned owl. Some sources of information include *Tiger with Wings: The Great Horned Owl* by Barbara Juster Esbensen (New York: Orchard Books, 1991) and *The Owl Book* by Laura Sterns (Minneapolis, MN: Lerner, 1983). A web site that offers pictures and information is http://www.petersononline.com/birds/month/ghow

4. Ask students to use a computer to carry out research about deer mice. They can print out pictures of the mice, their nests, and their footprints, then share the information with their classmates. Ask them to visit at least three web sites to gather their information. Possibilities to get them started include http://sevilleta.unm.edu/data/species/mammal/sevilleta/profile/deer-mouse.html and http://www.geocities.com/Yosemite/Rapids/7076/deermouse.html/. Another useful site is http://www.alienexplorer.com/ecology/m47.html.

These students might also want to check to see if a video recording on deer mice is available that might be shown to the class.

5. A common misperception is that porcupines can "shoot" their quills. This is incorrect. It is a fact, however, that porcupine quills were used by Native Americans in quillwork to decorate clothing, moccasins, containers, baskets, and bags. For information, see http://www.nativetech.org/quill/index.php. Ask a pair of students to research Native American quillwork and give an oral report to the class on what they learn. If possible, they should bring in pictures of some of the items decorated in this way so that the class can see the artistry involved.

6. Farmers and gardeners sometimes erect devices to frighten away birds that would otherwise damage their fruit trees and gardens. Sometimes they put up a scarecrow, sometimes they use a plastic owl or snake, and sometimes they use large whirligigs shaped like flowers that spin in the breeze. Other people string tin can lids or use aluminum foil flags to reflect light, make clattering sounds, and distract birds. If your students live in an agricultural area and know some fruit or vegetable gardeners, perhaps a pair of students can interview these people and ask what devices they have used to discourage birds and which appear to be more successful. The students should make an oral report to the class on what they learn.

Extension Activities

1. In the book, there are passages where Ragweed talks to Poppy and passages where Poppy talks with Ereth. Write a couple of pages of dialogue in which Ragweed, rather than Poppy, stumbles into the hollow log and meets and talks with Ereth. Be sure to try to catch the flavor of the special speech of each of these characters. With another volunteer, read the dialogue to the class.

2. Although each animal fantasy is unique, all have some characteristics in common. Gather together some students who have read both *Poppy* and a book from the *Redwall* series by Brian Jacques. Let them discuss how these books are alike and how they are different. Which book do they prefer, and why?

3. Lungwort goes to his study and writes out the appeal that he takes to Mr. Ocax, in which he explains why it is necessary for some of the mice to move and asks permission to do so. Lungwort even tries out parts of his speech on other mice and revises it until he is satisfied with it. Invite students to try writing this speech for Lungwort. It should only be one page in length, and it should be respectful, informative, and persuasive. When students have finished writing their appeal, ask for volunteers to share these with the class.

4. At a crucial time when Poppy needs to cross Glitter Creek, she cannot wade it because a recent storm has raised the level of the water in the creek. In some parts of the country, flooding is common. Invite a small group of students to do some research on precipitation in your area. This may involve consulting the local newspaper or other specialized resources to determine the average number of inches of rain in your area by month. Have the students construct a bar graph with months along the horizontal axis and inches of rain along the vertical axis. They should make an oral report to the class on rainfall in your area and should use their bar graph as a visual aid during their presentation.

5. A common science investigation involves examining owl pellets to learn more about the diet of owls Several science companies provide such materials. One source is

Owl-Pellets, Grades 3–8, Delta Education, P.O. Box 3000, Nashua, NH 03061-3000. The pellets hold bones and outer layers of three or more animals. These can be purchased for a single student or as a class set, and they come with a study guide. An ideal time to carry out such student investigations would be while the students are reading *Poppy*.

6. The battle between Poppy and Mr. Ocax is an exciting one, but no one is there to observe it. Invite students to pretend that they are reporters for the *Dimwood Gazette* and that they see the battle in question in which Poppy wields a porcupine quill as a weapon. They should write up the story as a feature news article that might appear in a newspaper. If important details such as time and date are missing, students should supply these in order to have a complete article that tells who, what, why, when, and where.

How does reading *Poppy* and engaging in the various activities suggested above help students meet the 12 NCTE/IRA English Language Arts Standards?

1. *Poppy* meets Standard #1 by serving as an example of outstanding fiction.
2. *Poppy* meets Standard #2 because it is a representative work of the broad genre of animal fantasy.
3. Discussion questions #1, #2, #3, and #8 help students to comprehend and interpret text, and the vocabulary exercise increases knowledge of word meanings and parts of speech, helping students to meet Standard #3.
4. Extension activity #3, which suggests writing out the speech that Lungwort will present to Mr. Ocax to persuade him to let some of the mice move to New House and which must not only be persuasive but also very respectful, addresses Standard #4, which asks students to adjust written language and style to communicate effectively for different purposes.
5. Extension activity #6, which suggests that a student write up the exploits of Poppy fighting off Mr. Ocax using a porcupine quill in the form of an article for a modern newspaper, helps meet Standard #5, which requires that students use different writing processes for different audiences and for a variety of purposes.
6. Extension activity #1, which suggests that a student write two pages of dialogue featuring a conversation between Ragweed and Ereth, helps to meet Standard #6 by requiring students to apply their knowledge of language structure and language conventions to create a print text.
7. Research activity #1 on porcupines helps to address Standard #7 by requiring students to gather, evaluate, and synthesize data from a variety of sources to communicate their discoveries.
8. Research activity #4 involving deer mice helps to meet Standard #8 by encouraging students to use a variety of technological and information resources to carry out research and to communicate their knowledge.
9. Discussion question #6 about the conventions involved in the treatment of Poppy by Ereth and her role as a guest in his log helps to address Standard #9 by allowing students to develop an understanding of and respect for diversity in social roles.
10. Research activity #2 asking ESL students to compare and contrast the use of Mr. Ocax as a symbol of evil power with a figure from their ancestral literature helps address Standard #10, which asks students to use their first language that is not English to develop a deeper understanding of the curriculum.

11. Extension activity #2 allows students to pool their information knowledge in the form of a book discussion group and compare and contrast *Poppy* with novels by Brian Jacques from the *Redwall* series. It helps meet Standard #11, which asks that students participate as knowledgeable, reflective, creative, and critical members of a literary community.

12. Extension activity #3 allows students to creatively write a respectful petition for Lungwort to read to Mr. Ocax in an attempt to persuade him to let half the mice move to New House. It addresses Standard #12, in which students are asked to use spoken, written, and visual language to persuade others.

Tuck Everlasting

Natalie Babbitt

New York: Farrar, Straus, & Giroux, 1975, ISBN 1-55736-050-2

Detailed Synopsis

Tuck Everlasting opens in a rural setting with a description of a meandering road that leads to the first house in the village before veering off to go around a small wood. The reader learns that the wood is private property and belongs to the Fosters. Since no one goes through the wood, people never notice the little spring that bubbles up near the great ash tree in the middle of the grove.

At dawn, in the first week in August, Mae Tuck wakes up and tells her husband, Angus, that she's going to ride on horseback to the outskirts of the village to meet their sons who are coming home for a visit. She takes with her a music box. Angus simply rolls over and goes back to sleep.

At noon on that same day, Winnie Foster, whose family owns the wood, sits on the grass in front of her house watching a toad on the road. She complains to it about her dull life and admits she is thinking of running away. But Winnie is called and obediently goes inside to eat her lunch.

At sunset, when Winnie is out in the yard catching fireflies, a stranger comes along and talks to her. He asks if she's lived there for a long time and says he is looking for someone. Winnie's grandmother comes out, cuts the conversation short, and brings Winnie back in the house. Before they go inside, they hear faint music from the wood, which the grandmother describes as "elf music."

In the morning, Winnie decides that she won't run away because she is afraid to do so, but she does decide to go into the wood. She bumps into the toad again, and she sees something else moving. She creeps closer, thinking it may be elves, and hopes to get a look at one. Instead, she finds a boy. She watches as he takes a drink from a spring, and then he turns and sees her. They talk, and Winnie asks questions. The boy is Jesse Tuck and at first says he's 104, but then admits to being 17 years old. Winnie is hot and thirsty and wants to drink from the spring, but Jesse won't let her.

Then Jesse Tuck's mother, Mae, and his brother, Miles, appear. They put Winnie on Mae's horse and leave the area. When they come out of the wood onto the road, they pass the stranger that Winnie met the night before. They finally reach a stream where they rest. Mae plays the music box and she tells Winnie their family history. They arrived here years ago planning to settle. They stopped near the wood and camped. Except for the cat, everyone, including the horse, took a drink from the spring.

Once they settled on their farm, they began to notice strange things. Jesse fell from a tree and wasn't hurt. The horse was shot by careless deer hunters and lived. And as the years passed, they realized, they were not getting older. Miles married, and he and his wife had two children. But his wife left him when she realized that Miles was not aging. She feared he may have sold his soul to the Devil. Angus Tuck finally pointed a shotgun and shot himself in the heart to prove that they are immortal. The gunshot had no effect on him.

Unknown to Mae, while she tells this story to Winnie, the stranger is listening. When Mae and her sons take Winnie home to allow Angus to try to persuade her to keep their secret, the stranger follows them.

The Tuck house is comfortable but untidy. The boys work at odd jobs and bring money home. Mae and Angus make handcrafts to sell. That night after dinner, Angus takes Winnie out in a boat and talks to her. He explains to her how important it is to keep the spring a secret. While they are out on the lake, someone steals their old horse. Winnie quickly becomes very fond of the Tuck family. She even entertains Jesse's idea that she might drink from the spring when she's 17, and then the two of them could marry and live together forever.

While Winnie spends the night with the Tucks, the stranger, who has stolen the horse, goes back to Treegap and tells Winnie's family that she's been kidnapped and he alone knows where she is. He says he will lead the constable to Winnie and rescue her if the Fosters will deed the wood to him. They agree, and the constable and the stranger head off for the Tucks' home together. The stranger rides on ahead.

The next morning, while the Tucks are eating breakfast, the stranger arrives at the house. He explains that he now owns the wood and offers the Tucks a role in advertising the wonderful spring. When they refuse, the stranger says he will have Winnie drink the water and he'll use her in his advertising. All the Tucks are angry, and Mae hits the stranger over the head with the shotgun just as the constable rides up.

The stranger is unconscious. The constable takes Mae to jail and Winnie back to her family. A doctor arrives, but the stranger dies, and it appears that Mae will be hung for murder on the town gallows. Jesse comes to tell Winnie that his family is going to break Mae out of jail at midnight. He brings her a vial of the spring water so that she can drink it when she is 17 and then join him.

Winnie offers to take Mae's place in the jail so that the constable won't find out so quickly that Mae is missing. At midnight, Winnie sneaks out, and goes with Jesse to the jail. Mae escapes, and Winnie takes her place. The Tucks make their getaway.

Later that month, the toad returns. Winnie is watching when a dog comes along the road and begins to attack it. She runs inside, gets the vial of spring water, and pours it on the toad, giving it everlasting protection. She thinks she can always return to the spring in the wood if she wants to drink some water when she is 17.

Years later, Mae and Angus Tuck come back to Treegap. Angus visits the cemetery and learns that Winnie lived a long life. She had married, had children, and died. The wood is gone, burned up in an electrical storm, and the big tree and the spring have been bulldozed away.

As the Tucks leave Treegap, they notice an old toad on the road, and the melody of a music box trails after them.

List of Major Characters: Winnie Foster, 10 years old, a member of the family that owns the wood near Treegap; her family, consisting of her mother, father, and grandmother; the Tucks, consisting of Angus and Mae and their sons, Jesse and Miles; the stranger; and the Treegap constable.

Vocabulary: Look up the following words on the pages indicated, and rewrite the sentence in which each word appears. Substitute a synonym or explanatory phrase in place of the vocabulary word.

elated (45) _____

receded (45) _____

colander (47) _____

indomitable (50) _____

camphor (62) _____

cahoots (77) _____

gander (80) _____

petulance (98) _____

plaintive (116) _____

sedately (127) _____

constricted (128) _____

Comprehension Questions

1. What words and phrases does the author use to portray the first sight of the Foster house as an uninviting place?
2. What interesting question does the author ask about ownership of the land?
3. Why is it that Winnie has never been curious and explored the wood?
4. Describe two instances the author uses to show that Winnie respects life and does not like to kill creatures.
5. Why didn't the Tucks' cat live forever like their horse?
6. What did Winnie like to do at home when she had a problem of some kind to think over?

7. What seemed unusual to Winnie about the way in which the Tucks ate their meals?
8. What was distinctive about the stranger's suit of clothes?
9. Why did the other children take more time to talk with Winnie after she spent the night in jail than they had done before?
10. What happened to the magical spring in the wood?

Answers: 1) The house is described as being square and solid with a touch-me-not appearance and an uninviting fence. 2) If you own land, how deep do you own it? 3) Nothing seems interesting when it belongs to you—only when it doesn't. 4) She remembers being sad when she killed a wasp, and she makes Miles put the fish he catches back into the pond. 5) The cat didn't drink from the spring. 6) Winnie sat and rocked in her too-small rocking chair. 7) They didn't talk while they ate and they didn't sit at the table. 8) His suit was yellow. 9) Winnie seemed more interesting and romantic after her adventure. 10) It was bulldozed away when the wood burned and the old tree was removed.

Discussion Questions

1. For the most part, people in this story play the conventional roles of men and women. Why, then, do you suppose the author had Mae Tuck rather than her husband or one of her sons hit and kill the stranger?
2. In the very first sentence of the book, the symbol of the wheel is introduced. It comes up several more times in the book. Discuss each appearance of this symbol and its function in the book.
3. When Winnie is taken by the Tucks, she alternates between thinking that they are criminals and wanting to get away from them and thinking that they are wonderful people that she wants to stay with. How do you think you would have felt with the Tucks—mostly frightened or mostly comfortable? Why?
4. If it had not been bulldozed away, do you think that Winnie would drink from the spring on her seventeenth birthday and go off and marry Jesse? Why, or why not?
5. If you had a chance to drink from the spring and live for time everlasting, would you do it? Why, or why not?
6. Angus tells Winnie that the "pond has answers." He explains that although it looks the same each day, it isn't. The water is moving on and changing, the way things are supposed to. Is this a good way to describe the strange situation in which the Tucks find themselves?

Research Activities

1. The explorer, Ponce de Leon, who was a companion of Columbus on his second voyage and who served as governor of Puerto Rico, is remembered for his search for the Fountain of Youth somewhere among the Bahama Islands. Invite a pair of students to research and write a report about Ponce de Leon. One source of information available on the Internet is http://www.publicbookshelf.com/public_html/Our_Country_Vol1/whowaspo.bf.html. Another source of information is *Juan Ponce de Leon* by Ruth Manning (Chicago: Heinemann Library, 2001).
2. The toad that Winnie often finds and talks to throughout the book would make an interesting research project. It may be an American toad, and if so, it is the most musical of the amphibians. Invite a pair of students to research the toad. At http://www.cmnh.org/

research/vertzoo/frogs/americanus.html, they will be able to hear the call of this toad. Another source of information is *Frogs and Toads: The Leggy Leapers* by Sara Swan Miller (Danbury, CT: Franklin Watts, 2000). Ask them to make a report to the class sharing what they learn. If possible, they should share with the class the sound made by the toad.

3. Natalie Babbitt, the author of *Tuck Everlasting,* has written a number of other books for children. Ask two interested students to research this topic. Once they know the titles of her other books, ask them to design and print bookmarks for the library encouraging students to check out and read some of her books. Include on the bookmark an interesting quote from *Tuck Everlasting.* Follow up with the media specialist to see if the bookmarks increased interest in checking out copies of Babbitt's books.

4. In this story, August is a very hot month indeed. Ask a pair of students to research the high temperatures in your town or city. What is the average high temperature for July, August, and September? What was the highest recorded temperature for last year? On what date was that temperature recorded? Ask the students to graph the results of their temperature study and to share the data with the class.

5. The prologue begins with mention of a Ferris wheel. Some students in the class will have ridden on a Ferris wheel, whereas others may not have done so. Invite two students to research the Ferris wheel. Who was Ferris? When and where was the first wheel used? Ask the students to share what they learn with the class in an oral report. One source of information on the Internet with a picture of the original wheel is http://users.vnet.net/ schulman/columbian/ferris.html.

6. Although people who travel in space cannot expect to live forever, scientists have seriously explored hibernation as a possible means of having people sleep through long space voyages. They found that blood has a substance in it, which they call HIT (hibernation inducement trigger). Scientists have taken blood from a hibernating squirrel and injected it into a different squirrel in the spring, causing it to begin hibernation. Invite an interested pair of students to do some research on HIT and write a report with at least three sources of information sharing what they learned. One site on the Internet with information about hibernation inducement trigger is http://www.sciencemadesimple. com/animals.html. It is also discussed briefly in *Animals that Hibernate* by Phyllis J. Perry (Danbury, CT: Franklin Watts/Scholastic, 2001).

Extension Activities

1. If the Tucks had not succeeded in getting Mae out of jail, she would have gone on trial for murder. Invite a small group of students to write the script and act out this trial. Two students can be prosecutors, two can be defense attorneys, and others can play the parts of the constable, Mae, and the witnesses. As the students present this trial scene to the class, the rest of the class may serve as a jury and render a verdict.

2. There would have been quite a stir in Treegap when the constable discovered that a suspected murderer (Mae Tuck) has escaped and that jailed in her place is Winnie Foster, recently kidnapped by the Tucks. Ask a pair of students to work together to write a feature article for the *Treegap Tribune* newspaper in which they report on this story. The article should include some quotations from Winnie and from the constable. Post this article on a bulletin board to share with the class.

3. Ask students who wish to do so to add a chapter to the book just before the Epilogue. In

this chapter, have Winnie, now grown up, married, and with children of her own, play a music box for her two young daughters and tell them a story about "elf music."

4. If there are ESL students in the class, explore with them stories from their culture that deal with eternal life or a fountain of youth. If there are such stories, discuss them and see in what ways they are similar to or different from this fantasy. Ask the students to share their ethnic stories with the class.

5. Arrange for a group of students who have read both Natalie Babbitt's *Tuck Everlasting* and Avi's *Poppy* to compare and contrast the two books in terms of the heroines, Winnie and Poppy. Both tend to do as requested by their parents. Both have a wild adventure in a wood. Both display bravery. Both eventually marry and raise young. How are these two heroines different?

6. Although there are vivid descriptions, the book is without illustrations. Invite class members to draw a picture for the book and to indicate on which page their illustration should appear. Possibilities include Winnie talking to the stranger in front of her house, Winnie with the toad, Mae on her old horse going to meet her sons, Jesse at the spring in the wood, Angus and Winnie in the boat on the pond, Winnie in her too-small rocking chair, or the jailbreak. Post these drawings to stimulate interest in reading the book.

How does reading *Tuck Everlasting* and engaging in the various activities suggested above help students meet the 12 NCTE/IRA English Language Arts Standards?

1. *Tuck Everlasting* meets Standard #1 by serving as an example of outstanding fiction.
2. *Tuck Everlasting* meets Standard #2 because it is a representative work of the broad genre of fantasy literature.
3. Discussion questions #1 through #6 help students to comprehend and interpret text, and the vocabulary exercise increases knowledge of word meanings, helping students to meet Standard #3.
4. Extension activity #1, which suggests writing out the script of a trial for Mae Tuck for murder, addresses Standard #4, which asks students to adjust written language and style to communicate effectively for different purposes.
5. Extension activity #2, which suggests that a pair of students write up the jailbreak for the *Treegap Tribune* newspaper, helps meet Standard #5, which requires that students use different writing processes for different audiences and for a variety of purposes.
6. Extension activity #3, which suggests that a student write a new chapter to be added to the book just before the Epilogue, helps to meet Standard #6 by requiring students to apply their knowledge of language structure and language conventions to create a print text.
7. Research activity #2 on the American toad helps to address Standard #7 by requiring students to gather, evaluate, and synthesize data from a variety of sources to communicate their discoveries.
8. Research activity #2 involving the background of the American toad and the sounds that this animals makes helps to meet Standard #8 by encouraging students to use a variety of technological and information resources to carry out research and to communicate their knowledge.
9. Discussion question #3 about the alternating views Winnie holds of the Tucks and the conventional roles played by men and women in this book helps to address Standard #9

by allowing students to develop an understanding of and respect for diversity in social roles.

10. Extension activity #4, which refers to stories from different cultures relating to the theme of a fountain or youth or to life everlasting and asking ESL students to share and to compare and contrast these cultural stories with *Tuck Everlasting,* helps address Standard #10, which asks students to use their first language that is not English to develop a deeper understanding of the curriculum.

11. Extension activity #5 allows students to pool their information knowledge in the form of a book discussion group and compare and contrast the heroines of two fantasy novels. It helps meet Standard #11, which asks that students participate as knowledgeable, reflective, creative, and critical members of a literary community.

12. Research activity #3, in which students make bookmarks with intriguing quotes from the book to encourage others to check out and read Natalie Babbitt's books, allows students to creatively select and prepare a means of sharing their enthusiasm for this book with other potential readers. It addresses Standard #12, in which students are asked to use spoken, written, and visual language to persuade others.

The Lost Years of Merlin

T.A. Barron

New York: Philomel Books, 1996, ISBN 0-399-23018-1

Detailed Synopsis

The Lost Years of Merlin is a quest fantasy. In the author's note that begins this book, Tom Barron points out that some scholars argue the myth of Merlin may be based on a Druid prophet who lived in Wales in the sixth century A.D. But Barron asserts that his book is not based on history but on imagination. He creates the youthful portion of Merlin's life, about which almost nothing has been written.

As *The Lost Years of Merlin* begins, a boy is tossed by waves onto the rocky shore of Wales. He bangs his head against the rocks and swallows seawater, but survives. He can remember neither his name nor his past. He hears a moaning and finds that a woman has been tossed ashore, too.

An enormous wild boar appears and seems ready to charge. The boy grabs the woman and drags her toward the hollow of an old oak tree. A stag charges at the boar, allowing the boy time to drag the woman to safety inside the hollow tree. When the boar charges, its tusk grazes the boy's face. The stag attacks once more and drives the boar away, and then it too leaves.

The story picks up again five years later. The boy, Emrys, awakens in a hovel made of twigs and clay. This is his home where he lives with the woman, Branwen, who is currently sleeping. The boy reflects that he does not believe Emrys is his real name, nor does he think Branwen is his real mother. He looks nothing like her. She refuses to tell him about the past. Only when she tells him stories does she reveal even a hint of her true self.

The hut is filled with bundles of herbs that Branwen uses to make various healing powders and pastes. The villagers view the two castaways with suspicion, but they still come when they are in need of a cure.

After Emrys wakes, he leaves the hut and walks into the village of Caer Vedwyd. Small events cause Emrys to suspect that he has some special powers, but he keeps such thoughts to himself. A village bully, Dinatius, tries to provoke Emrys to fight. Emrys runs away and climbs into a tree for refuge. Staying high up in the tree, Emrys rides out a storm before coming back down.

Going back into the village, Emrys stops to play with some boys who are throwing sticks and stones at what looks like a pile of rags. Dinatius reappears and beats on Emrys. Branwen comes and stops the fight. She and Emrys go home, where Branwen puts a paste and dressing on his bruises.

Then Dinatius and others come to the hut. They drag Branwen outside and act as if they are going to burn her. An angry Emrys wishes that Dinatius would burn, and in response to this wish, a large branch from a tree suddenly falls on Dinatius and pins him in the midst of the fire he has started. Feeling guilty, Emrys rushes into the flames to try to save Dinatius, and he falls unconscious.

When Emrys awakes, he finds himself in the Church of Saint Peter in the neighboring village of Caer Myrddin. He is not only badly burned, but he is also blind. Branwen cares for him. He gradually develops a second sight and is able to see things in a strange new way.

Emrys finally decides to go out on his own to try to learn his identity and past. Branwen gives him her pendant, called the Galator, and a small bag of herbs. Emrys makes his way to the sea, where he builds a raft and sets off. Emrys rides his raft until he is tossed up on the shore. When Emrys goes to a stream for a drink, he comes upon a small hawk, a merlin, fighting with two huge rats. Emrys rescues the bird, and using some of the herbs from his bag, he tends to the bird's wounds. Then he makes a nest of grass and puts the merlin safely in the nest in a tree.

Emrys walks into the forest, where he climbs a tree and looks around. He spies what first appears to be a bundle of leaves, but decides it is really a girl dressed in a leaf garment. On the girl's command, the branches of the tree wrap around Emrys and bind him. When Emrys mentions the Galator, the girl sets him free, and he learns she can speak with trees, birds, beasts, and rivers. Her name is Rhia. They visit a grove, which Rhia calls her garden and which is filled with fruit-laden trees.

While they eat delicious fruits, Emrys learns that his raft has brought him to a land called Fincayra. That is a name he has heard Branwen mention. Then the merlin that he saved earlier joins them and perches on Emrys's shoulder. The three of them journey to Rhia's house, where they are met by Cwen, the last of the treelings, a race that is part tree and part people. Rhia and Emrys eat and sleep.

In the morning, Rhia shares her dream with Emrys that the wooded area where she lives will die. She and Emrys go back into the forest. They think they see a beautiful and rare alleah bird and are surprised when the merlin, which they have named Trouble, attacks it. They learn that a shifting wraith has assumed the form of the alleah bird.

Rhia explains that once the lands east of the river were nearly as green as her beloved forest. Then a blight struck. Now shifting wraiths, goblins, and ghouliants live in the blighted land and are beginning to enter her beloved woods. They also guard Shrouded Castle. Stangmar, the king, lives there, far to the east in the Dark Hills, where he keeps all of the treasures of Fincayra except for the Galator.

Rhia and Emrys go to see the Grand Elusa. On their way, they cross a swamp and go through the Misted Hills. They come upon a broken tree and find a swarm of bees, where they stop to eat some honey and meet a very small giant named Shim. He joins them, and they finally stumble upon the cave of glowing crystals that is the home of the Grand Elusa.

The Grand Elusa, who appears as a small spider, says that Fincayra and the Druma are doomed unless King Stangmar is toppled. She explains that if Stangmar gets the Galator, he will win all of Fincayra. Then the Rhita Gawr, the most terrible spirt of all, who already has power over Stangmar, will control the bridge between Earth and the Otherworld, and he may eventually win Earth itself.

The Grand Elusa explains that if the castle is destroyed, the power of Stangmar and his army will end. The castle that appears so strong has a flaw. According to prophecy, if giants dance in the hall, the castle will fall. Rhia, Shim, and Emrys climb out of the crystal cave just as Cwen appears. She has led six warrior goblins to them in the hopes of being rewarded by being made young again.

The warrior goblins cut off Cwen's arm, and they threaten to kill the others. To save them, Emrys hands over the Galator, but an elm falls upon the goblin, and Emrys recovers the Galator. The Grand Elusa reappears as a hungry spider ready to eat them. During the confusion, Rhia, Shim, and Emrys escape and make it to the river that whisks them downstream to a sandbar.

The goblins catch up with them and are about to capture Emrys when Trouble begins to fight with them. One goblin knocks Trouble down, and then Emrys is knocked out and put into a sack. When Emrys wakes up, he finds himself in the woods with Shim. Shim tells Emrys that he was captured and carried off by goblins, but that Shim and Rhia followed them, and that when she could, Rhia switched places with Emrys, climbing into the sack to take his place.

Emrys is determined to rescue Rhia. He and Shim follow the trail of the goblins across the river to the blighted area. They come to a scrawny orchard, where they see a ditchdigger called Honn. Honn hides them from more goblins that come and also gives them a dagger for protection on their dangerous journey.

Emrys and Shim head for the Dark Hills. They arrive at Caer Neithan, Town of the Bards, and find that all have fallen silent there. Emrys and Shim leave the town and come upon a girl. They notice that she has webbed fingers and realize it is another shifting wraith. Emrys uses his dagger to kill it.

Finding a glowing tree stump, Emrys climbs down inside, and Shim follows him into an underground room that is filled with books. Cairpre, a poet, invites them to stay, eat, and rest. Cairpre tells Emrys about the past and about his mother and father.

He explains that Elen, now called Branwen, is really his mother. She once loved a Tree Climber. This man became part of the royal circle, which increasingly came under the power of Rhita Gawr, who offered to protect the king. The king made alliances with the warrior goblins and shifting wraiths, and he hunted down the giants and gathered all the treasures of Fincayra. Rhita Gawr built the Shrouded Castle and created the deathless warriors, called ghouliants, to guard it and the king.

Cairpre says the one person who may help Emrys is Domnu, or Dark Fate, who loves games of chance. To find her, Emrys must pass through the notch in the mountains. Domnu's lair is near the edge of Haunted Marsh.

Early the next morning, Emrys and Shim start off for the notch. They come upon two old people working in an orchard. They are T'eilean and Garlatha. Although the old people are pleasant to them, Emrys and Shim continue on their way and are caught in an ice storm. Then they are chased by goblins into the Haunted Marsh. By holding the Galator high, they manage to cross part of the marsh before collapsing.

When Emrys awakes, he and Shim are in a strange room with polished stone walls. The room contains bones, balls, bundles of sticks, and white cubes. Domnu invites Emrys to play a game of chess. Emrys finally makes a wager with Domnu. If she will get them to the castle, he will give her the Galator. But if Emrys or Shim returns alive, Domnu must give back the Galator.

Domnu shows them a cage that contains the missing little hawk, Trouble. Domnu shrinks Shim and Emrys so small that they can fly to the castle carried by Trouble. But when they arrive, they see that the castle is constantly revolving. They manage to enter by having Emrys steer Trouble through an open window.

Once inside the castle and back to their normal size, they go to the dungeon, where they find Rhia. They release her but are pursued by a ghouliant who cannot be killed by Emrys's dagger. They run up the stairs and find themselves in the throne room of Stangmar. There Emrys learns that Stangmar is his father. A warrior goblin is about to kill Rhia, so Emrys uses his special powers to cause a sword, Deepercut, to fly off the wall and kill the goblin.

Stangmar steps down from his throne to duel. Deepercut wounds Stangmar in the foot. Then Rhita Gawr appears, and the sword cuts Stangmar a second time. The second cut seems to put Stangmar back under the influence of Rhita Gawr again. Trouble breaks free from the guard that is holding him and attacks. Both he and the strange dark mass that is Rhita Gawr disappear.

Then Stangmar orders Emrys to be thrown into the Cauldron of Death. Before that can happen, Shim races out of the shadows and throws himself into the cauldron. The cauldron breaks, and Shim begins to grow. When Shim is giant-sized again, other giants come and join him. With the breaking of the cauldron and the dancing of the giants, the castle begins to crumble and the ghouliants die.

Shim, now a giant, reaches down through the ruins of the castle to rescue Rhia while Emrys gathers up the kingdom's treasures: Deepercut, Flowering Harp, Orb of Fire, Caller of Dreams, and six of the Seven Wise Tools. Shim then picks up the treasures, Emrys, and Stangmar and lifts them out of the rubble.

Among the ruins of the castle, Emrys and Rhia make plans to bring the blighted lands back to life. And Rhia gives Emrys a new name, Merlin, in memory of the brave hawk. Merlin says that he will try using the new name for a while.

List of Major Characters: Emrys, a young boy with magical powers, is the major character in the book. His mother is Branwen. Rhia is a girl about the same age as Emrys who lives on Fincayra. Cwen is a treeling who helps care for Rhia. Stangmar is king of the blighted lands and is the father of Emrys. Trouble is a small hawk that rides on the shoulder of Emrys. The Grand Elusa is a powerful spirit who appears as a spider. Rhita Gawr is an evil spirit. The Domnu is the powerful Dark Fate who loves to play games of chance. Cairpre is a scholar who reveals to Emrys much of his past.

Vocabulary: Using a dictionary and referring back to the page number in parentheses that indicates where in the text that word was used in the story, look up each of the ten words that appear below. Write a definition for the word that fits with how the word was used in the story.

daunting (2) _____

subsided (10) _____

winced (11) _____

undulating (39) _____

annihilate (76) _____

coalesce (97) _____

slogged (124) _____

irascible (141) _____

adamantly (144) _____

metamorphose (146) _____

Comprehension Questions

1. Why does Emrys give special importance to the number seven?
2. Why does Branwen refuse to go with Emrys or tell him how to get back to the land where he was born?
3. Out of what materials does Emrys construct his raft?
4. Who holds and protects Rhia much like a mother holds a child?
5. What makes the light and "fire" in Rhia's house?
6. What did Rhia say was the most beautiful sight in the forest?
7. What sort of marker does Domnu use to keep track of the various scores for games played in her lair?
8. Name the five treasures of Fincayra that Stangmar held within his castle.
9. For how long had the old couple, Garlatha and T'eilean, lived on their land and tended their garden?
10. What is the rarest of trees in the Druma wood?

Answers: 1) Seven was the number of fingers Branwen held up to determine if Emrys could see after he was burned in the fire. 2) Because Branwen was human, and it is forbidden for humans to be born on Fincayra, she knew she would be putting Emrys in danger if she helped her son return to his birthplace. 3) Emrys constructs his raft from limbs of the ancient oak, shreds of bark, and strands of kelp. 4) The tree, Arbassa, holds Rhia like a child. 5) Thousands of tiny beetles light up Rhia's house. 6) The most beautiful sight in the forest was the long-tailed alleah bird. 7) Domnu spits on her index finger and uses it as a paintbrush. 8) Deepercut, Flowering Harp, Orb of Fire, Caller of Dreams, and the Seven Wise Tools are the treasures. 9) The old couple had lived there for 58 years. 10) The rarest of trees is the shomorra.

Discussion Questions

1. Gather together interested students who have read both *The Hobbit* and *The Lost Years of Merlin* and have them compare the scene in each book where giant spiders play a major role. Which scene is more effective, and why?
2. A sword with special powers is used in both *The Lost Years of Merlin* by T.A. Barron and in *The High King* by Lloyd Alexander. Invite students who have read both books to talk

about the swords, Deepercut and Dyrnwyn. In what ways do they play the same role, and in what ways are their roles different?

3. Emrys does not believe that Branwen is the real name of the woman who cares for him, and he also doesn't believe that she is his mother. What makes Emrys so doubtful?

4. Cwen betrayed Emrys and Rhia by leading the goblin warriors to them. This seems like a strange action from someone who has cared for Rhia for so many years. Does this action seem justified? How do you explain it?

5. Early in the story, Branwen is almost burned like a witch, and she is regarded with suspicion by the villagers because of her healing powers. People have been accused of being witches throughout the years. Why do you think that women like Branwen cause fear in people?

6. Cairpre says that although no one truly understands the Galator pendant, he believes that its powers respond to love. Have the students look back on the use of the Galator in the story. Do they think that a review of these incidents suggests that Cairpre's theories about the pendant are true or false?

7. Three seemingly ordinary characters play small roles in the book. These are a ditchdigger called Honn and two old people who tend their garden, T'eilean and Garlatha. What function do these "ordinary" people play in a book in which there are so many fantastic creatures like ghouliants, wraiths, Arbassa, and the Grand Elusa?

8. Trouble, the young merlin, plays a major role throughout the story. Although not given any special powers, the hawk is crucial in many ways. Discuss the major events that hinge upon the actions of the merlin.

Research Activities

1. Branwen tells Emrys many stories. One of these is the story of the winged horse, Pegasus. Invite a pair of students to research this topic and to write a paper to share their findings with the class. They should include a bibliography and list at least three sources of information. Among the resources might be *The Flying Horse: The Story of Pegasus* by Jane B. Mason (New York: Grosset & Dunlap, 1999); *Pegasus, the Flying Horse*, retold by Jane Yolen (New York: Dutton Children's Books, 1998); and http://wings.avkids.com/Book/Myth/advanced/pegasus-01.htm.

2. Rhia's tree house is lit by beetles. This is possible through bioluminescence. Invite a small group of students to investigate bioluminescence and to make an oral report to the class on what they learn. Possible sources of information include *Creatures that Glow: A Book about Bioluminescence* by Melvin Berger (New York: Scholastic, 1996), *Animals that Glow* by Judith Janda Presnall (New York: Franklin Watts, 1993), and http://lifesci.ucsb.edu/~biolu/forum/vvivani2.html, which presents an article on bioluminescence in beetles by Vadim Viviani.

3. T.A. Barron uses the image of a hermit crab losing its shell, which it had tried so hard to claim for a new home, as a way of describing how discouraged Emrys is and how he feels about losing his dream of finding out about his past. (See p. 86.) Invite students to write a page similar to the one on page 86, using an animal other than a hermit crab to show the discouragement that Emrys feels at this moment of the story.

4. When Emrys thought of ancient seafarers, one of the names he thought of was Bran the Blessed. Most students will not be familiar with this name. Ask a pair of students to

research Bran the Blessed, sometimes called the King of Britain. They should report to the class orally on what they learn and especially point out any features in the legend that have found their way into *The Lost Years of Merlin* story (such as the sister Branwen, the magic cauldron, and the wounded heel.) Possible sources include http://www.geocities.com/RainForest/Canopy/1956/bran.html and http://www.britannia.com/history/legend/collection/legcol16.html.

5. Prometheus, another major figure discussed in this book, is a famous Greek legend. The myth is retold by Jacqueline Morley in *Greek Myths* (New York: P. Bedrick Books, 1998). Invite a small group of interested students to research Prometheus. They should write a short paper, using at least three sources of information and including them in a bibliography, and share what they learn with the class.

6. Many of the references in this book are to figures in Greek myths. These stories were staged in early Greek theater. Invite a pair of interested students to research Greek theater and to make a small model of one to bring into the class. They should have time to share their model and tell how such a stage was generally used and what sorts of plays were presented there. If there are ESL students in the class and they are familiar with Noh drama, Kabuki, puppet theater, shadow puppets, or some other dramatic form that is common in their home country, ask them to share their knowledge with the students in the class.

Extension Activities

1. Many students will be familiar with Homer's epic, *The Odyssey.* It appears on the Internet at http://www.mythweb.com/odyssey/ in a short version of 24 paragraphs, each telling part of the adventure and illustrated with a humorous drawing. An interested class might assign parts to each member, then have each class member print out and practice one of the 24 pages and make an illustration. Then the class could present this as a reading to another class, showing their illustrations as they tell an abbreviated version of the story.

2. Although the book has no picture of the Domnu, she is called a "hairless hag" and is described in detail on page 262. Ask an interested student to read the description and then to make a drawing of the Domnu. Display the drawing on a bulletin board.

3. Suppose you are a reporter for the *Druma Gazette,* a newspaper on Fincayra, and your assignment is to write up a factual news article on the destruction of Stangmar's castle. How will you write it? (You may make up interviews with the survivors to include in your article if you wish.) Post your article in the classroom.

4. Invite two interested students to add a few pages somewhere in the last chapter in the book in which Emrys talks with his father Stangmar. They have battled, seen the collapse of the castle, and survived. How do the two feel about one another? What role will Stangmar now play in Fincayra? Will Stangmar ask about Branwen? What will Emrys and Stangmar do in the immediate future? Once this new dialogue is written, have the two students read it to the class.

5. Ask two interested students to make a chart on a sheet of tagboard. The chart should be divided in half, with one half devoted to Emrys and one half to Rhia. In some ways these two characters follow the conventional roles of men and women. But in other traits and actions they do not follow the conventional roles. Record these traits and actions on the chart, and use this as the basis for a class discussion.

6. Except for the cover, there are no illustrations in *The Lost Years of Merlin*. Invite interested students to make bumper stickers with a phrase and a character from the book to serve as advertisements. Place these in the school library. Before hanging them up to attract attention and encourage other readers to enjoy the book, ask the students to show their bumper stickers in class and talk about the character and phrase they included on their bumper sticker.

How does reading *The Lost Years of Merlin* and engaging in the various activities suggested above help students meet the 12 NCTE/IRA English Language Arts Standards?

1. *The Lost Years of Merlin* meets Standard #1 by serving as an example of outstanding fiction.

2. *The Lost Years of Merlin* meets Standard #2 because it is a representative work of the broad genre of fantasy.

3. Discussion questions #3, #4, and #8 help students to comprehend and interpret text, and the vocabulary exercise increases knowledge of word meanings, helping students to meet Standard #3.

4. Research activity #3, which suggests rewriting a page of the book and substituting another animal metaphor in place of the hermit crab who has lost his home to show Emrys' deep discouragement, addresses Standard #4, which asks students to adjust written language and style to communicate effectively for different purposes.

5. Extension activity #3, which suggests that a student write up the destruction of Stangmar's castle as a newspaper article for the *Druma Gazette,* helps meet Standard #5, which requires that students use different writing processes for different audiences and for a variety of purposes.

6. Extension activity #4, which suggests that a student write a new section of dialogue to be included in the last chapter of the book, helps to meet Standard #6 by requiring students to apply their knowledge of language structure and language conventions to create a print text.

7. Research activity #5 on Prometheus helps to address Standard #7 by requiring students to gather, evaluate, and synthesize data from a variety of sources to communicate their discoveries.

8. Research activity #4 involving researching the history of Bran the Blessed helps to meet Standard #8 by encouraging students to use a variety of technological and information resources to carry out research and to communicate their knowledge.

9. Discussion question #5 about the general suspicion of witches and the healing powers of Branwen, which make her suspect in the community, helps to address Standard #9 by allowing students to develop an understanding of and respect for diversity in social roles.

10. Research activity #6 asking ESL students to compare and contrast the use of Kabuki, Noh, shadow puppets, or other dramatic forms with early Greek theater helps address Standard #10, which asks students to use their first language that is not English to develop a deeper understanding of the curriculum.

11. Discussion question #1 allows students to pool their information knowledge in the form of a book discussion group and compare and contrast the giant spiders of *The Hobbit* with the spider in *The Lost Years of Merlin*. Discussion question #2 compares the special

swords of *The High King* and *The Lost Years of Merlin.* Both of these help meet Standard #11, which asks that students participate as knowledgeable, reflective, creative, and critical members of a literary community.

12. Extension activity #6 allows students to creatively select and create a bumper sticker with characters and phrases to share their enthusiasm for the book and encourage other potential readers. It addresses Standard #12, in which students are asked to use spoken, written, and visual language to persuade others.

The Dark Is Rising

Susan Cooper

New York: Scholastic Inc., 1989, ISBN 0-590-43319-9

Detailed Synopsis

The Dark Is Rising is a quest fantasy. *The Dark Is Rising* sequence also includes *Greenwitch, The Grey King,* and *Silver on the Tree.*

The day before Will Stanton's birthday, and just four days before Christmas, Will and his brother, James, go out in the early evening to feed the rabbits and get some hay from Farmer Dawson. They see an old tramp called the Walker. Farmer Dawson gives Will a strange sort of buckle made of iron, which Will threads on his belt.

That night, the rooks bang into the skylight in Will's attic room, letting in the cold and snow. Will screams, and his brother Paul comes to help. Will

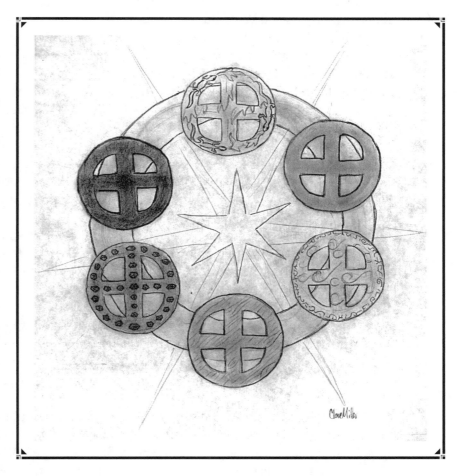

spends the rest of the night in the room with his brother, Robin. In the morning, Will wakes to a different world and finds his family asleep, as if under a spell.

Will goes out into the snow and comes upon a blacksmith shoeing a horse for a man called the Rider. Instinctively, Will distrusts the Rider. A white mare trots up, and the smith begins to shoe the horse. Will goes off on foot to find the Walker. When Will finds him, they talk, but the Rider appears, and the Walker hurries off. Will rides off on the white mare's back, chased by the Rider. They safely reach the Chiltern Hills.

The mare leaves Will standing in front of two carved wooden doors. Will enters and finds himself in a great hall. A Lady, Miss Graythorne, and a man called Merriman Lyon wait for him there. Merriman explains that Will has a gift, the power of the Old Ones. He must be trained to handle this gift and needs to find the six Signs of the Light to complete the Circle of the Old Ones. By finding all the signs, Will can bring to life one of the three great forces needed to vanquish the powers of the Dark.

As he tours the great hall, Will stumbles against a candlestick and the strange sign of the quartered circle is burned like a brand onto his arm. The forces of the Dark shriek through the hall. Will is almost captured when he breaks away from the Lady and Merriman, but the Lady manages to save them before she fades away.

Merriman leads Will to the grounds of Huntercombe Manor, which Will knows is not far from his own home. In this way, Will learns that for those of the Circle, all times coexist. In his own time again, Will returns home.

Will celebrates his birthday and goes Christmas shopping. On his way home, Will meets the Walker again and orders him to give Will the second sign. The Walker gives him a second quartered circle made of bronze. Almost immediately, Maggie Barnes, a dairy maid on the farm, appears. She has dark powers and freezes Will and the Walker in their tracks. She tries to take both of Will's signs but is driven off when Merriman reappears. Merriman releases Will and the Walker from the Dark's power.

On Christmas Eve, there is excitement in the Stanton house. Right after breakfast, some family members go out to get the Yule log and Christmas tree. They stop at Farmer Dawson's where Will learns that Maggie, the farm girl, has suddenly left. Old George, who works for Farmer Dawson, gives Will some special holly that he promises has protective power against the Dark.

The Stantons return home. Will puts holly everywhere, and they begin to decorate the Christmas tree. At the bottom of a box of ornaments, Will finds a lost box of alphabet letters carved at their birth for each of the Stanton children by Farmer Dawson. Will learns that he had another brother, Tom, who died at three days old.

That evening, some of the Stantons, including Will, go caroling. Their last stop is the manor, where Merriman is working as the butler. During the singing of the last carol, a spell renders them immobile. Merriman and Will leave to walk into another time and place. They find themselves at a party where Miss Graythorne shows Will the third sign, made of rowan, or mountain ash. She explains to Will that he will find this sign when he finishes his own particular learning.

Merriman and his man, Hawkin, take Will into a small library where Merriman hands him the oldest book in the world, the Book of Gramarye, which can only be read and understood by Old Ones. After Will reads the book, it is destroyed. Will and Merriman rejoin the others, and Will learns that Hawkin has joined forces with the Dark. The spell ends, and Will returns to the present time at the manor.

While the carolers sing, drink punch, and look at instruments, Will is able to retrieve the third sign, made of wood, and to withstand a sudden visit from the Rider and Maggie Barnes, who are both forces of the Dark. The carolers return home.

On Christmas morning, Will opens a big box from his brother, Stephen. It contains a letter and a strange carnival head from Jamaica. The other family members also open their gifts. There is a knock on the door, and the Rider, known as Mr. Mitothin to Will's father, enters on the pretext of delivering a package. Will recognizes him and freezes his family members in their moment in time to confront his enemy. He tells Mr. Mitothin that he recognizes him, but he takes no action. The Rider sets everyone back in motion before he leaves.

Several members of the family go to church through the thickly falling snow. After the service, when almost all have left, they are enveloped by an attack of the Dark. Will uses his new powers to protect his brother, Paul, and the rector. Farmer Dawson and the Old Ones stand in the doorway of the church, and Will uses the three signs on his belt to drive off the Dark. The signs glow and lead him to a spot in the church where Will retrieves the fourth sign, the Sign of Stone.

As they leave the church, a rook flies down and leads Will to a man in the snow. It is the Walker. They manage to get the sick man home to the Stantons. The storm continues, but that night Merriman comes and leads Will to a ceremony, the Hunting of the Wren, which is always performed on the solstice. Will sees the Lady of the manor in the procession and receives a warning from the boys.

The Stantons run out of food, so Will and his father and brother set out for the village for supplies. At the store, Merriman, as the butler of the manor, invites the villagers to come to eat and keep warm. Will's father refuses to go, but he does agree to take the Walker there to be seen by the doctor. Will helps move the tramp to the manor. The many guests prepare a concert, which Will begins by singing a song. The Rider appears at the door but is frightened off by the sign on Will's arm.

The Walker begins to call on the names of the Dark to come in. The Walker, under the influence of the Dark, attacks Will and tries to take the signs, but he is pulled off and sedated. When the Walker falls asleep, the Dark forces subside. The Old Ones grab candles to complete the circle of flame, and Will gets the Sign of Fire.

There is the sound of thunder and it begins to rain. The villagers are joyful that the rain will melt the snow. Will's brother arrives with the news that Mrs. Stanton has fallen down the stairs and is unconscious. When Will, his father, his brother, and the doctor go to care for Mrs. Stanton, they learn that their sister, little Mary, has vanished.

Will and Paul go out in the rain to look for their sister, but they become separated. Old George arrives and gives Will a ride on a farm horse named Pollux, and then leaves Will to go on alone, saying that he must raise the Hunt.

Will follows what is now a raging river. The white mare comes and drops him on an island in the water. There Will sees Hawkin, who demands that Will trade the signs for his sister who has been captured by the Dark. Will refuses to deal with Hawkin, so the Rider comes on his black horse. Although the Rider has Mary in his power, Will won't give away the signs. The Rider's horse is about to buck Mary into the river when Merriman arrives on the white mare and saves her.

The earth rocks, a great ship appears, and Will sees what looks like the body of a dead king on the ship. In the king's hand is the Sign of Water. Will takes this sign and climbs up on the white mare with Merriman. The ship is struck by a streak of blue light and burns as it floats off. Mary goes home, while Will and Merriman go to the Great Park near Windsor Castle for the Hunt.

Hern the Hunter, climbs on the white mare. Will holds up to him the strange mask that his brother had sent to him for Christmas and that was washed away from his house in the rainstorm. Hern becomes the antlered figure in the mask, and Will holds up the signs to show him. Then Hern and the hounds chase off the powers of the Dark.

Merriman takes Will to the blacksmith for the joining of the signs. Linked on a golden chain, they are given to Will by the Lady, who tells Will he has completed his quest but will need these signs in the future when the Dark is rising again.

Will and Merriman return home to find that Mary is safe, and Will's mother is recovering from her fall. Merriman delivers two gifts from the Lady of the manor. One is a musical instrument for Paul, and the other is a horn for Will to use in the future.

List of Major Characters: Will Stanton, the 11-year-old hero of the book; his father and mother, Mr. and Mrs. Stanton; his siblings, Stephen, Max, Paul, Robin, James, Barbara, Gwen, and Mary; Farmer Dawson and Old George, two Old Ones who live on the neighboring farm; Merriman, an Old One who assists Will throughout his quest; Miss Graythorne, the Lady of the manor; the Walker, who gives Will the second sign; and the Rider and Maggie Barnes, a farm girl, who are both in the service of the Dark.

Vocabulary: After the words below, the page numbers on which the words appear in the book are listed in parentheses. Look up the words in the book and look up their definitions in a dictionary. Rewrite the sentences in which each word appears by using a synonym for the vocabulary word.

clamorous (2) _____

spinney (16) _____

hummocked (22) _____

auspicious (24) _____

irresolute (29) _____

wizened (29) _____

disconcerted (40) _____

keened (48) _____

benison (50) _____

deferentially (93) _____

malevolence (105) _____

inexorably (107) _____

Comprehension Questions

1. What omens that appear in the first chapter of the book suggest that this is not an ordinary evening for Will Stanton?
2. Will wakes up to strange music on his birthday. Then he discovers something still stranger about his house. What is it?
3. What is unusual about the horseshoes that John Smith, the blacksmith, puts on the white mare?
4. What are the first two tasks that Merriman Lyon uses to have Will test his newfound powers?

5. When the reader first meets Maggie Barnes, she seems to be a sweet dairy maid who has a crush on Will's brother, Max. But what does the reader later learn about Maggie Barnes?

6. When the Rider, posing as Mr. Mitothin, comes to the Stantons', he takes one of Mary's hairs and he takes one of the carved wooden ornaments from the tree. What mistake does Mr. Mitothin make in taking the ornament?

7. During the snowstorm, when the Lady of the manor, Miss Graythorne, invites all the villagers to come to the manor for food and warmth, why doesn't Will's father want to go there?

8. During the flood, before Old George leaves Will, he gives Will two pieces of advice. First, he tells Will that if he remains where he is for the count of 100, he will have enough light to find his way. His second piece of advice is to remember something about moving water. What is Will to remember?

9. What was the figurehead on the curving prow of the ship that appeared to Will during the flood carrying the body of a dead king from long ago?

10. What were the six signs that Will had to find on his quest?

Answers: 1) The rabbits act oddly, rooks are disturbed and flying about, a weird-looking tramp scuttles behind a tree, a usually friendly farm dog snarls, and Farmer Dawson gives Will a strange present. 2) Everyone in the house is asleep and won't wake up. 3) The horseshoes are shaped like Will's belt buckle, a cross-quartered circle. 4) Will's tasks include transferring an image of Will's father's shop to Merriman's mind and putting out and relighting the fire in the hearth. 5) Maggie Barnes has strange powers and is part of the Dark side. 6) The "M" ornament for Mary is hanging upside down on the tree, so Mr. Mitothin mistakenly believes he has taken the letter "W" for Will. 7) Mr. Stanton's pride keeps him from being willing to go there for assistance as if he were still part of a feudal system. 8) Will is to remember that moving water is free of magic. 9) The figurehead is a stag. 10) The six signs are iron, bronze, stone, wood, fire, and water.

Discussion Questions

1. Hawkin is a complicated character. He is loyal to Merriman for a long time. Discuss the event that causes him to leave his service to the forces of the Light and go over to serve the Dark. When Hawkin finally dies, is he on the side of Darkness or on the side of Light? Justify your answer.

2. Will grows up in a family with eight brothers and sisters. Discuss what function Will's siblings play in the story.

3. The man Will meets beyond the great door teaches Will his first lesson. He says, "Nothing is what it seems. Expect nothing and fear nothing, here or anywhere." Discuss this first lesson and what it means to Will.

4. When Will is almost captured by the powers of the Dark, Merriman explains that they were able to seize Will through appealing to his impatience and hope. "They love to twist good emotions to accomplish ill." Discuss this, and give some examples from everyday life in which a good emotion might be twisted to accomplish ill.

5. Will receives from his brother a letter of explanation and a most unusual birthday/Christmas present. It is a West Indian carnival head. Once the gift is received, it pops up again several times in the story. What do you think is the significance of this carnival mask?

6. On his birthday, Will gets to choose what the family will have for supper. It seems that his siblings are seldom pleased with the choice made by the birthday boy or birthday girl. Does your family have a tradition of a special food or activity in celebration of birthdays? What is it? If you were in the Stanton family and got to pick a special birthday dinner, what would it be?

7. Many occupations are represented in this story including a blacksmith, a jeweler, farmers, shopkeepers, a butler, a rector, and a sailor. Even the Old Ones have jobs. When Will grows up in this village, what occupation do you think he will choose, and why?

8. The Lady is an unusual character. Part of the time she is strong and protects the others. Sometimes she appears weak or even dead on a bier. Will has a hard time deciding if the current Lady of the manor is the same one that he sees when he moves back in time. In a book discussion group made up of students who have read both *The Dark Is Rising* and *The Castle in the Attic,* compare and contrast the Lady from *The Dark Is Rising* with Mrs. Phillips from *The Castle in the Attic.* What special roles in the stories do these two women play? How are they alike, and how are they different?

Research Activities

1. The blacksmith in the story shoes the Rider's black horse and the white mare. He also joins the signs together for Will. He explains that his anvil is made of iron and oak. Ask a small group of students to research anvils. How big are they? What are they usually made of? Are they still used today for some purposes? Ask these students to write a report sharing what they learn with the class. One source of information is *Anvil Magazine,* published in Georgetown, California. You might also want to consult http://www.anvilmag.com.

2. The snowstorm that hits during the Christmas season is the worst that anyone in the village can remember. Many statistics are available from various sources about the weather in any area. Invite a small group of students to learn more about "unusual" weather in your area. What was the driest year? What is the highest and the lowest recorded temperature for your town or city, and on what dates did those temperatures occur? If your area has lots of snow and rain, what was the year with the deepest snow and/or the most inches of rain? Are there "old-timers" in the community who can share photos or tell stories about a great snow storm, flood, drought, etc? Does the local newspaper have an archive of weather material? Ask these students to make an oral report to the class and to share their various sources of information.

3. Will's story takes place during the Christmas season in England. He and members of his family have special Christmas traditions. They decorate a tree and they burn a Yule log. Invite a small group of ESL and other interested students to research the December holiday traditions of other countries and to prepare a written report on what they learn about those traditions to the class. One source of information would be *Keeping the Traditions: A Multicultural Resource* by Phyllis J. Perry (Golden, CO: Fulcrum Publishing, 2000).

4. *The Dark Is Rising* is a Newbery Honor Book. Another book by Susan Cooper, *The Grey King,* won the Newbery Medal. Invite a pair of students to learn more about these book awards. Who was Newbery? How often are the Newbery Awards given? What book won the Newbery Medal last year? Were there also Newbery Honor Books named last year? What were their titles? Have the students share their information in the form of a poster

to hang in the classroom or library in which they encourage readers to sample some of the past Newbery Award books.

5. Invite a pair of students to find the answers to these questions and to share with the class what they learn. What does the word "solstice" mean? When is the winter solstice? Why does it occur? How many degrees is the tilt of the earth's axis? How did scientists determine this? One source of information is http://scienceworld.wolfram.com/astronomy/WinterSolstice.html. In making their class presentation, students might want to use a model or a video presentation.

6. Sometimes birds that are black or that fly in the night are viewed as omens of darkness. Rooks appear as omens early in this story. A rook leads Will to find the Walker out in the snow. The rooks that live in Rook's Wood are missing at the end of the story, although Merriman says they will return eventually but that they are not to be trusted. Invite two students to learn more about rooks. In what parts of the world do these birds live? How large are they? How do they nest? Do they have special markings? Ask these students to make a drawing of a rook and to orally report what they learn about this bird to the class. One source of information is *Birds of Britain & Europe* (London: HarperCollins, 1992). If there are ESL students in the class, ask them to report to the group if there is a special bird from their culture that appears in stories and that is viewed as an omen of darkness. What is its special significance?

Extension Activities

1. On page 131, there is a description of the carnival mask Will received as a present from his brother. Ask interested students to use this description as the basis for making a colorful drawing of the mask. You can post these drawings on a bulletin board for others to enjoy.

2. In the chapter called "Betrayal," Will imagines that he flies in the sky like an eagle and becomes familiar with the "patterns of the stars." Among the constellations and stars mentioned are the Herdsman, Arcturus, the Bull, Aldebaran, and the Pleiades. Invite a pair of interested students to research and learn more about these stars and constellations and report back to the class what they learn. Are any of them currently visible in your night sky? Possible sources of information include *Constellations* by E.M. Hans (Austin, TX: Raintree Steck-Vaughn, 2001) and *See the Stars: Your First Guide to the Night Sky* by Ken Croswell (Honesdale, PA: Boyds Mill Press, 2000).

3. Will's brother, Paul, is an accomplished musician. He is fascinated by the old flute that he sees in the manor and that is finally given to him on "permanent loan." He begins to play a well-known melody called "Greensleeves." With the help of the school music educator, have a student locate a recording of "Greensleeves" and bring it in to play for the class.

4. During the great cold spell, it is reported that it has never been this cold before and that "every port of England on the entire coast was iced in." Ask two students to make an outline map of the United Kingdom. On it they should show the section that is England, and along England's coast, they should identify and label the major seaports. Post the completed map on a classroom bulletin board.

5. At one point in the story, Will reflects that if he were to try to explain to someone about being an Old One and having special powers, he would probably talk to his brother, Paul. Have two students write out a section of dialogue for this part of the story. Then encourage the two students to role play such a moment before the class. What would Will say to

explain his powers? What questions would Paul have? Would Paul believe Will?

6. There is a poem or chant about the six signs that appears at the end of the chapter called "Christmas Day." Invite interested members of the class to write their own poems about the six signs. They might be long or short and could be rhymed or unrhymed. Post the poems on a classroom bulletin board.

How does reading *The Dark Is Rising* and engaging in the various activities suggested above help students meet the 12 NCTE/IRA English Language Arts Standards?

1. *The Dark Is Rising* meets Standard #1 by serving as an example of outstanding fiction.
2. *The Dark Is Rising* meets Standard #2, as a representation of the broad genre of fantasy.
3. Discussion questions #1, #3, #4, #5, and #8 help students to comprehend and interpret text, and the vocabulary exercise increases knowledge of word meanings, helping students to meet Standard #3.
4. Extension activity #6, which suggests writing a verse about the six signs that Will finds during his quest, addresses Standard #4, which asks students to adjust written language and style to communicate effectively for different purposes.
5. Research activities #1, #3, and #5 suggesting that student prepare written reports on different subjects help meet Standard #5, which requires that students use different writing processes for different audiences and for a variety of purposes.
6. Extension activity #5 asking students to write a section of dialogue before role playing the scene in front of the class helps meet Standard #6 by requiring students to apply their knowledge of language structure and language conventions to create a print text.
7. Research activity #2, which suggests using a variety of information including oral interviews, photographs, and print resources, helps to address Standard #7 by requiring students to synthesize data from a variety of sources to suit their purposes and audience.
8. Research activity #5 involving the tilt of Earth's axis and the solstice helps to meet Standard #8 by encouraging students to use a variety of technological and information resources to carry out research and to communicate their knowledge.
9. Discussion question #7 about the variety of occupations of people in the village, including the "Old Ones," helps to address Standard #9 by allowing students to develop an understanding of and respect for diversity in social roles.
10. Research activity #6 asking ESL students to compare and contrast the use of birds of the night from their culture with the rooks as omens of darkness in this story helps address Standard #10, which asks students to use their first language that is not English to develop a deeper understanding of the curriculum.
11. Discussion question #8 allows students to pool their information knowledge in the form of a book discussion group and compare and contrast a character from *The Dark Is Rising* with a character from *The Castle in the Attic*. It helps meet Standard #11, which asks that students participate as knowledgeable, reflective, creative, and critical members of a literary community.
12. Research activity #4 allows students to creatively select and prepare a means of sharing their enthusiasm for Newbery Medal and Honor Books with other potential readers. It addresses Standard #12 in which students are asked to use spoken, written, and visual language to persuade others.

Into the Land of the Unicorns

Bruce Coville

New York: Scholastic Inc., 1994, ISBN 0-590-45955-4

Detailed Synopsis

Into the Land of the Unicorns is book one of the Unicorn Chronicles. It is a fantasy that involves a quest, humans, and magical animals.

Cara and Grandmother Morris are walking home in the snow from the library when Cara notices a man following them through the streets thronged with holiday shoppers. Grandmother glances back at the man and becomes frightened. She leads Cara into a back pew of St. Christopher's Church. Grandma removes a chain from around her neck and gives it to Cara. It holds a gold and crystal amulet that contains a tightly coiled strand of white hair, which her grandmother said came from a unicorn's mane.

When they hear the church door open, Grandma drops down to the floor out of sight and motions Cara to do the same. They slip into a side foyer of the church, lock the door behind them, and race up a set of spiral stairs. Behind them, they can hear someone trying to break down the door. They reach a landing and Grandma says she will ring the church bell to summon help. Cara is instructed to climb to the roof, press the amulet to her chest, and on the twelfth bell stroke whisper, "Luster, bring me home," and then jump.

A frightened Cara leaves her Grandma and continues upward, climbing a ladder to the top of the bell tower. Her way is lighted by the glowing amulet. She flings open the trapdoor to the roof. Cara hears a voice cry out behind her, but on the twelfth chime of the bell, she throws herself from the tower. At first Cara stifles a scream, then she has a sudden, soft landing.

Cara realizes she has fallen into another world. She removes her winter coat and sweater and looks for a path to follow. She strikes off through the trees toward the sound of water. A manlike creature about three feet tall appears and tries to take her amulet. They struggle, and Cara falls unconscious into the stream.

Cara wakes up in a cave with a creature that appears to be a man-bear. Her amulet is gone. The man-bear gives her some tea, and Cara falls asleep. When she reawakens, a unicorn is in the cave. It walks up to her and with its horn pierces her chest.

This is followed by a moment of pain and shock. Cara sees a tiny star-shaped scar on her chest, and finds that inside her head she can now hear the unicorn speaking. The unicorn tells her she is in the Cave of the Dimblethum in the Forest of the Queen in the world of Luster, home of the unicorns. The unicorn, called Lightfoot, uses its horn to heal Cara's other injuries. Then they both rest.

When Cara awakes, she sees a foot-high creature that looks like a cross between a monkey and a squirrel with thick, gray hair. It is the Squijum. When the Dimblethum reappears in the cave, he returns to Cara the amulet that the creature, which he calls a Delver, had taken from her earlier.

The Dimblethum explains that many centuries ago, the Queen ordered the creation of five amulets to be used as rewards for those who had given great service to Luster. The amulets allow the bearer to pass between Earth and Luster.

Cara and her new friends decide to take the amulet and visit the Queen in the morning. Although the Dimblethum is a friend of Lightfoot, he blames unicorns for opening the gates between Earth and Luster and letting others come in. He also says that the Queen, a unicorn named Arabella Skydancer, is now so old and thin that sometimes you can see right through her. And he explains that the delvers, who live underground, are enemies of the unicorns.

At first light, they set off for the Queen. Cara is not lonely in the company of the Dimblethum, the Squijum, and Lightfoot. They stop at a stream to drink, and a dozen delvers approach them. One of the delvers, Nedzik, tells them that his king is searching for Cara and the amulet. The king plans to use the amulet to let unicorn hunters come into Luster. Nedzik believes the king's plan may destroy Luster, so he is risking his life to defy the king and to warn Cara.

Alarmed, Cara and her friends hurry toward the Queen, following the dragon path to Grimwold's Cavern. It is a shorter route but more dangerous because the dragon, Firethroat, might catch them.

They come upon a camp of delvers. Though Cara and Lightfoot escape, the delvers catch the Dimblethum and hold him prisoner. Cara hides the amulet while they try to rescue the Dimblethum. The Squijum comes along then with Thomas the Tinker and his cart. Thomas temporarily blinds the delvers when they gather around him. Cara cuts free the Dimblethum and helps him to hide in the magical cart belonging to Thomas.

Thomas pulls the cart with Cara, the Squijum, and the Dimblethum to a clearing where they are supposed to meet up again with Lightfoot. Lightfoot uses his magical powers to heal the wounds of the Dimblethum, and they all continue toward the Queen. They bed down for the night when it begins to rain.

The magical cart can expand to be big enough to carry them all or be small enough to fit into the Tinker's pocket. Once they are all safe together, they retrace their steps and retrieve the hidden amulet. Then, carrying the amulet with them, they head for the Queen again. Firethroat, the dragon, sees them but does not attack.

When they get to Grimwold's Cavern, Cara recognizes Grimwold as the little old man she has seen in a painting on her grandmother's dresser at home. They journey through the caverns to the story room. It is filled with books, paper, pens, and ink. Cara tells Grimwold the story of how she and her grandmother were pursued and chased up into the bell tower of St. Christopher's Church.

Grimwold tells them of a long-ago time when magic unicorns lived on Earth. Then man came to power. When a unicorn died, a man took the horn and told lies about how he had battled a fierce unicorn. He used the power of the horn to heal, and many people came to him. Other men went out hunting unicorns because they wanted these horns, too.

One man had a daughter called Beloved. When Beloved fell ill, the man hunted a unicorn hoping that its horn would save Beloved. A unicorn came along and was in the act of healing Beloved when the hunter, thinking the unicorn was hurting his daughter, killed it. Then the hunter was killed. Beloved buried her father, grew up, married, and had sons. Her sons and grandsons continued to hunt unicorns and viewed them as enemies. The unicorns fled to Luster, and the hunters continue to try to enter Luster, still questing for revenge.

Grimwold leads his guests into the room of the Unicorn Chronicles, which contains the history of the unicorns as told to him and written down by him. Then they go to the scrying pool. The pool begins to shimmer, but then, instead of connecting them with the Queen, the water darkens and a message appears that says, "Surrender the amulet." It is signed "Beloved."

They return to the writing room, and Grimwold says he will show his guests an emergency exit so that they may leave quietly and hasten to Summerhaven to see the Queen. Again they travel through the land of the dragon, but this time, Firethroat appears and snatches up Cara, Lightfoot, and the Squijum.

Firethroat flies to her cave in the mountains, and she explains that a man came to her cave while she was out and stole her heart, which she keeps hidden in a casket among her treasures. Firethroat explains that she must do the bidding of the one who holds her heart. Since the man bid Firethroat to bring Cara to him, she had to obey him. Then a man steps out of the darkness of the cave, and Cara recognizes him as her father.

Cara's father explains that he did not abandon his daughter years ago but that Cara's grandmother stole Cara from him because she feared he would use Cara to get at the unicorns. Her father, called Ian Hunter, wants Cara to give him the amulet. Then they will go home, and her father will use the amulet to bring hunters to Luster and destroy all the unicorns.

Instead of doing as her father bids her, Cara throws the amulet to the Squijum, who runs off with it. She and her father fall out of the cave and off the cliff with Cara holding the box containing Firethroat's heart. Firethroat saves them both. She returns Cara's father to Earth and Cara to the cave. Then Cara gives Firethroat's heart back to her.

As a boon, Firethroat pulls a scale from her neck and orders Cara to catch the drops of blood in a chalice and drink it. This act gives Cara the gift of tongues, the knowledge of the languages of all creatures.

Firethroat returns Cara, Lightfoot, and the Squijum to the place from which it had snatched them. The Dimblethum and Thomas are waiting for them, and they all travel for a week to reach Summerhaven and the Queen. When Cara meets the Queen, she gives her a message from her grandmother back on Earth, "The wanderer is weary."

The Queen asks if Cara would like to be the one to fetch her grandmother, and when Cara agrees, the Queen says, "Then so it shall be." And that is another story to be recorded in the Unicorn Chronicles.

List of Major Characters: The main character is a girl named Cara, who has been cared for on Earth by her grandmother; Cara is being pursued on Earth and in Luster by her father, Ian Hunter. The unicorn who befriends Cara is called Lightfoot; Cara is helped by the Squijum, a squirrel-monkey-like small animal, and by the Dimblethum, a man-bear. Thomas the Tinker, a man who has a magical cart, assists Cara and her friends in Luster. As Cara journeys to the Queen, she is captured and then assisted by Firethroat, a dragon.

Vocabulary: The page number in parentheses following each word below indicates a place where it was used in the book. Look up each word in a dictionary, and write the definition that fits with how the word was used in the story.

acceded (5) _____

abashed (94) _____

myriads (95) _____

tendrils (134) _____

flared (134) _____

burnished (134) _____

trifle (135) _____

wily (136) _____

whickered (143) _____

abyss (150) _____

boon (151) _____

chalice (153) _____

Comprehension Questions

1. When Cara first comments that she thinks a man is following them home through the snow, how does she think her grandmother will respond?
2. What kind of danger did Nedzik put himself in by telling Cara and the others about his king's plan to open the door from Earth to men and allow them to enter Luster and kill the unicorns?
3. What is the gift that, as a species, all unicorns possess?
4. What gift do the dragons, as a species, have?
5. What does Thomas the Tinker notice about chains when he mends the chain on which Cara's amulet hangs?
6. What does Thomas the Tinker think in general of things that cannot be broken?
7. When Cara asks about her mother, how does her father respond?
8. Since Cara's father has proved himself to be very dangerous, what prevents Firethroat from letting Cara's father fall to his death?
9. How many dragons does the world of Luster have?
10. Why didn't Firethroat carry Cara and Lightfoot to the Queen in Summerhaven?

Answers: 1) Cara thought her grandmother would say, "Don't be silly, child." 2) If the king found out about it, the king would take the delver's life for committing treason. 3) Unicorns have the gift of being able to heal. 4) Dragons have the gift of tongues. 5) The place where you fix a broken chain may end up being the strongest part of the chain. 6) Thomas thinks that things that cannot be broken are generally a bad idea. 7) Her father said that Cara's mother was waiting for her. 8) Firethroat must do as commanded by whoever has her heart, and Cara ordered her to save her father. 9) Luster has seven dragons. 10) Firethroat was not strong enough to fly all the way to Summerhaven carrying a human and a unicorn.

Discussion Questions

1. When Cara first arrives in Luster and doesn't know where she is, why doesn't she stay in one place and let others come looking for her?
2. If Cara's father, Ian Hunter, doesn't have an amulet, how does he get from Earth into Luster?
3. Instead of familiar animals, the Squijum is described as being like a combined squirrel and money, and the Dimblethum is like a combined man and bear. Why do you think that the author makes up combination animals instead of using familiar ones?
4. Why do you suppose Lightfoot doesn't want to go to Summerhaven and meet with his mother and the Queen?
5. All the characters in the book speak in a fairly normal way except for the Squijum. What does the Squijum's odd way of talking add to his characterization?
6. Firethroat, the dragon from *Into the Land of the Unicorns,* and Smaug, the dragon from *The Hobbit,* both have treasures. Ask students who have read both fantasy books to discuss the two dragons and their roles in these stories. Which of the dragons emerges as the stronger character? Why?
7. Thomas is an unusual character. He is the only "ordinary" human in the story. Why do you suppose he was included? What different dimension is added by having Thomas and his magical wagon play a role?
8. When Grimwold tries to use the scrying pool to contact the Queen, he fails. He says this is the first time it failed because the pool is a powerful magic set up by the Queen herself. Why do you think the pool failed this time? What added information does this give the reader about Beloved?

Research Activities

1. Many students will be especially interested in the character Firethroat, the dragon. Dragons appear in folk tales from around the world. A small group of students might choose to find a folk tale of interest, prepare it as a reading, and share it first with their own class and then perhaps with a kindergarten class. If there are ESL students in the class, they may have familiar tales to share from their own cultures, or students may choose a tale from any country of interest. Some suggestions are: *Tobias and the Dragon* by Val Biro (Hungarian); "The Dragon" from *Shadows from the Singing House,* Helen Caswell (Eskimo); *The Irish Cinderlad* by Shirley Climo (Irish); *King Krakus and the Dragon* by Janna Domanska (Polish); *Vasily and the Dragon* by Simon Stern (Russian); and *The Dragon Prince: A Chinese Beauty & the Beast Tale* by Laurence Yep (Chinese).
2. There is a long history in connection with unicorns. Invite a pair of students to study the history and mythology of unicorns and to report to the class what they learn in the form

of an oral report. One source of information is *The Truth about Unicorns* (Madison, WI: Turtleback Books, 1996) by James Cross Giblin.

3. Bruce Coville has also written *The Dragonslayers*. It has been produced as a musical and has been recorded in both CD and cassette versions. A group of students might be interested in researching this musical to see if, with the help of volunteer parents and working with the music educator, classmates might want to produce and perform this play for the school. For more information, write to Dragonpartners, P.O. Box 6110, Syracuse, NY 13217.

4. Cara wears an amulet. Amulets have a long history with evidence that they were even worn by prehistoric man and by ancient Egyptians as a means of protection from a God or a specific animal. Invite a pair of students to research some of the history of amulets, write a paper using at least three sources of information, and share it with the class. One source of information is http://me.essortment.com/whatisanamule_rldf.htm. If possible, students should bring in pictures from magazine articles or books showing famous amulets.

5. Thomas the Tinker has a magical wagon and is able to fix the broken chain of Cara's amulet. Cara seems to trust and respect Thomas without reservation. Thomas goes with Cara to the Queen, but he does not go inside to meet her. Tinkers, or tinsmiths, have an interesting history. As a type of traveling salesman, they are sometimes regarded with suspicion as gypsies. Invite an interested group of students to research the history of tinkers, prepare an oral report, and share with the class what they learn. The original tinsmiths or tinkers often mended spoons and traveled about in wagons. In the United States, some were known as Yankee Peddlers. In Ireland, they were called travelers. How were such people regarded? Some sites for information include http://www.local108. org/History/Trade_in_Passage/trade_in_passage.html and http://www.irish-society.org/ Hedgemaster%20Archives/travelers.htm.

6. The horn of the unicorn is considered to be magical. Horns of other animals have also been regarded with interest. Although most animal horns are made of bone, the horn of the rhinoceros is made of matted hair. Rhino horns have been used in traditional medicine and in making ornamental dagger handles. Invite a pair of interested students to study the rhinoceros and its horn and make a written report to share with the class on what they learn. Some possible sources of information are *Black Rhinos* by Melanie Watt (Austin, TX: Raintree Steck-Vaughn, 1998) and *Horns and Antlers* by Allan Fowler (New York: Children's Press, 1998). Information on the Web from a rhino preservation group is at http://www.savetherhino.com/index.php?ed=105.

Extension Activities

1. Invite a pair of students to write up a factual news article about what happened at St. Christopher's Church. They should report that the bells were rung and that one of the doors was broken down, and they should quote Grandmother. Some observers may even be quoted in the story as saying that they thought they saw someone fall from the roof, although no body was recovered. But do not include any "magical" elements in this news story. Try to explain what people saw and did in an ordinary, factual way. Post the news item in the classroom.

2. Thomas is an unusual character. He explains that he was rewarded for some service he performed by being allowed to drink from the Queen's pool. This drink allows him to live longer than an ordinary mortal. Invite a pair of students to write out a short original adventure that Grimwold will record into the Unicorn Chronicles detailing what service Thomas performed for the unicorns. Have these students read their story to the class.

3. The Squijum and the Dimblethum are "combination" animals. One looks like a cross between a monkey and a squirrel, and the other is described as a man-bear. Invite a pair of students to make a poster encouraging students to read *Into the Land of the Unicorns* and, with permission, to hang their poster in the library. Be sure that the poster contains a picture of both the Squijum and the Dimblethum.

4. Cara is placed in an unusual position. As a young girl, just reunited with her father after a long absence, she might be expected to follow the conventional role of being an obedient daughter. Instead, she defies him. Cara says, "Family isn't blood. Family is who loves you, who takes care of you." Invite four students to take part in a panel discussion. Have two of them take the position that Cara owes obedience to her father and two take the position that Cara is right in disobeying her father. What arguments can be mustered on each side?

5. Invite a pair of interested students to write a picture book to share with a first-grade class. The students may both write and draw or one may write and one may illustrate the picture book. Each page of the picture book should display a creative combination animal. The hippo-giraffe, for example, might show a long neck and giraffe head on the stocky body of a hippo. The text will then describe where the combination animals live and what they eat. The lion-oceros, for example, might have the body of a black rhino and a lion's head with a horn growing from its forehead.

6. The Queen has indicated at the end of this book that she will send Cara on a mission to bring back her grandmother to Luster. Suppose that the Queen puts her request in writing. Have a pair of interested students write two letters from the Queen. One will instruct Cara on what to do, and the other will instruct Grandmother on what to do. Both should be formal in tone and be in the form of a royal decree from the Queen to two of her subjects. These decrees should be posted in the classroom where other interested class members might read them.

How does reading *Into the Land of the Unicorns* and engaging in the various activities suggested above help students meet the 12 NCTE/IRA English Language Arts Standards?

1. *Into the Land of the Unicorns* meets Standard #1 by serving as an example of outstanding fiction.

2. *Into the Land of the Unicorns* meets Standard #2 because it is a representative work of the broad genre of fantasy.

3. Discussion questions #2 and #8 help students to comprehend and interpret text, and the vocabulary exercise increases knowledge of word meanings, helping students to meet Standard #3.

4. Extension activity #1, which suggests reporting the events at St. Christopher's Church in a factual manner and without any allusion to magic for a newspaper article, addresses

Standard #4, which asks students to adjust written language and style to communicate effectively for different purposes.

5. Extension activity #6, which suggests that a pair of students write up a royal decree telling Cara to bring her grandmother to Luster and advising Grandmother that her presence is required in an audience with the Queen, helps meet Standard #5, which requires that students use different writing processes for different audiences and for a variety of purposes.

6. Extension activity #2, which suggests that a student write a new chapter to be added to the Unicorn Chronicles in which Thomas the Tinker is featured, helps to meet Standard #6 by requiring students to apply their knowledge of language structure and language conventions to create a print text.

7. Research activity #2 on unicorns helps to address Standard #7 by requiring students to gather, evaluate, and synthesize data from a variety of sources to communicate their discoveries.

8. Research activity #4 involving amulets helps to meet Standard #8 by encouraging students to use a variety of technological and information resources to carry out research and to communicate their knowledge.

9. Research activity #5 about the role in society of tinkers, or Irish travelers, and considering how Thomas the Tinker was viewed by Cara, help to address Standard #9 by allowing students to develop an understanding of and respect for diversity in social roles.

10. Research activity #1 asking ESL students and others who are interested to share dragon folk tales helps address Standard #10, which asks students to use their first language that is not English to develop a deeper understanding of the curriculum.

11. Discussion question #6, which allows students to pool their information knowledge in the form of a book discussion group and compare and contrast the dragon Firethroat from *Into the Land of the Unicorns* with Smaug, the dragon from *The Hobbit,* helps meet Standard #11, which asks that students participate as knowledgeable, reflective, creative, and critical members of a literary community.

12. Extension activity #3 allows students to create a poster using two of the combination animals from *Into the Land of the Unicorns* as a means of sharing their enthusiasm for this book with other potential readers. It addresses Standard #12 in which students are asked to use spoken, written, and visual language to persuade others.

James and the Giant Peach

Roald Dahl

New York: Bantam Books, 1961, ISBN 0-553-15113-4

Detailed Synopsis

James Henry Trotter lives a happy life until he is 4 years old. Then his mother and father go shopping in London, where they are eaten up by an angry rhinoceros that has escaped from the zoo. James goes to live with his Aunt Sponge and Aunt Spiker. The two aunts treat James very badly. They live in an old house on a high hill in the south of England. James is never allowed to leave the yard, which holds one peach tree. He has no friends or pets to keep him company.

One summer when James is 7, he is chopping wood for the kitchen stove, and he is hot and tired. He asks the aunts if they may take the bus to the seaside. The aunts shout at him, and he goes and hides in the laurel bushes. There he sees a very small old man in a dark green suit. The man pulls out a little bag that has tiny green crystals in it. The crystals are moving, and the man says there is more magic in them than in all the rest of the world.

The man gives the bag to James and tells him to put the green things in a jug of water, add ten hairs from his head, and drink it. The man assures James that if he does this, marvelous things will start happening to him. As James eagerly runs toward the kitchen, he slips and falls, and the green crystals scatter and sink into the soil.

Suddenly a peach appears on the tree, which never bears any peaches. The aunts are about to ask James to go pick it for them when they notice it is getting bigger and bigger by the minute. The branch bends over but doesn't break, so the peach grows ever larger. By the time it stops growing and rests on the ground, the peach is as big as a small house.

Aunt Sponge wants to eat the peach but Aunt Spiker has a plan to use the enormous peach to make money. The aunts have a big fence built around the peach and sell tickets to everyone to come and look at it. As newsmen and visitors come to stare at the peach, James is locked in his bedroom and kept out of the way.

That night, after the crowds leave, James goes out into the yard to clean up the trash. The garden is alive with magic. James notices a hole in the side of the peach and crawls in it. He discovers a tunnel. When he reaches the stone in the middle of the peach, he sees a door. James opens it and walks in to find many strange creatures, all his size. There is Old-Green-Grasshopper, Miss Spider, Ladybug, Centipede, Earthworm, Silkworm, and Glowworm. They welcome James to their crew, and they prepare to go to bed. James helps the Centipede remove his many boots while Miss Spider weaves beds for them, and the Glowworm puts out the light.

The strange crew sleeps, and in the morning James awakens to great excitement. The Ladybug explains that they are about to roll away. The Centipede frees the peach from its stem, and the peach comes crashing through the gate and rolls right over Aunt Spiker and Aunt Sponge. The peach rolls through herds of animals, through a village, through a chocolate factory, over a white cliff, and into the sea where it floats. The crew climbs up a rope ladder to the top of the peach to look around. They are not too worried because they are floating, have plenty to eat, and are hopeful that they may be picked up by a passing ship.

Then two sharks appear in the water. Soon others come, and they attack the peach. James comes up with a plan to use strong string made by the Silkworm and the Spider to slip around the necks of flying seagulls, which will lift them safely out of the water and away from the hungry sharks. The Earthworm is left on top of the peach to lure the seagulls to come down. When a bird flies down, James slips a loop of silk around its neck as the Grasshopper and Ladybug pull the Earthworm safely out of danger.

After attaching threads to 502 seagulls, the peach is lifted and flown over a ship. While they are floating through the air, the Grasshopper makes music, and the other crew members share their accomplishments. The Earthworm explains how it helps improve soil. Ladybug describes eating insects that destroy the farmer's crops, and Miss Spider bemoans the fact that she does good but is not loved. The Centipede happily admits to simply being a pest. The Centipede is making up songs and dancing when he falls off the peach. James uses a silkworm cord to go down and rescue the Centipede.

Flying high on the peach that is being pulled by the seagulls, James and his crew watch night coming on. They see Cloud-Men making hailstones. The Centipede yells at the Cloud-Men who pelt the peach and crew. The peach passengers take cover down inside the peach.

When they come on top of the peach again, they see it is leaking from having been pelted by hail. As they float through the air, they see more Cloud-Men who are painting an arched bridge in the sky. The Cloud-Men begin to lower the rainbow on ropes, and it gets entangled with the peach strings being pulled by the seagulls. The rainbow snaps across the middle and breaks into two separate pieces.

The Cloud-Men release the rainbow from its ropes and it falls to Earth, freeing the peach. Then the Cloud-Men pelt James and his friends with paints, brushes, and ladders. A gallon of purple paint falls on the Centipede. As the paint dries, the Centipede finds it hard to move.

They hear a voice above them and then see an enormous rain cloud, which dumps a mass of water on them. They survive the deluge, which washes the Centipede clean. During the night, they fly past more Cloud-Men operating a snow machine, making thunder, working in frost factories, and manufacturing cyclones.

In the morning, James sees land below. It is a vast city. The Centipede bites through the strings to the seagulls, and as one after another of the threads is cut, the peach goes lower over New York City. The people of New York think the giant peach may be a bomb. A passenger plane flies by and slices through all the remaining strings, causing the peach to come crashing down. It lands on top of the Empire State Building. The pointed top of the building plunges right into the peach.

New Yorkers wonder if this is a flying saucer carrying creatures from outer space. Police and fire fighters rush into the building. At first as the creatures peer down, the fire fighters and police are terrified. Then James appears and introduces his friends. They are brought down and treated like heroes. The mayor gives a welcome speech, and they ride in a ticker-tape parade. The peach is carried in the parade in a large truck. Children swarm all over it and begin to eat it up. By the time the procession winds down, the peach has been completely consumed.

James and his crew remain in the city working at different interesting jobs. The peach pit is placed in Central Park, and James lives inside where he happily greets many visitors who stop in every day.

List of Major Characters: James Henry Trotter, a young boy, is the main character; his aunts are Aunt Sponge and Aunt Spiker: and his peach crew is made up of Old-Green-Grasshopper, Miss Spider, Ladybug, Centipede, Earthworm, Silkworm, and Glowworm.

Vocabulary: Look up each of the words below on the page number indicated in parentheses to see how it was used in the story. Then look up the words in a dictionary and write a synonym for each.

ramshackle (2) _____

slither (41) _____

colossal (41) _____

hysterics (43) _____

gossamer (44) _____

desolate (49) _____

repulsive (49) _____

dilemma (51) _____

perambulator (72) _____

pathetically (73) _____

exhorting (81) _____

malevolently (119) _____

Comprehension Questions

1. What few things does James carry with him when he goes to live with his two aunts?
2. What does Aunt Sponge think of herself when she looks in the mirror?
3. What happens as Aunt Spiker talks when she gets excited or angry?
4. How much do the aunts charge to come and see the peach?
5. Which creature is responsible for loosening the peach from its stem?
6. From where do the creatures get a rope ladder that enables them to climb to the top of the peach?
7. How many seagulls does it take to lift the peach out of the water?
8. How does the Earthworm think they might get a new outside skin for the paint-covered Centipede?
9. What do the Cloud-Men's wives cook them for supper?
10. What do the people of New York at first think the giant peach is?

Answers: 1) James brings a small suitcase with a pair of pajamas and a toothbrush. 2) Aunt Sponge thinks she is as lovely as a rose. 3) When Aunt Spiker gets excited, flecks of spit shoot out of her mouth as she talks. 4) The aunts charge one shilling. 5) The Centipede frees the peach from its stem. 6) Miss Spider weaves a rope ladder. 7) It takes 502 seagulls to carry the peach away. 8) The Centipede would have a new skin if they turned him inside-out. 9) The Cloud-Men's wives are frying snowballs. 10) At first, the people of New York think the peach is an enormous bomb.

Discussion Questions

1. This story begins in an unusual way by having a child orphaned through the death of his parents, who are eaten up in broad daylight by an angry rhinoceros that has escaped from the London Zoo. Although only a very few paragraphs are spent on this background, it plays an important function in setting the tone of the book. Have students discuss this.
2. What do you suppose might have happened if James had done exactly as the little old man suggested and drank all the green crystals himself instead of tripping and losing them in the ground by the peach tree? What changes might have occurred to James and his life?
3. Ask a small group of students to prepare a simple questionnaire that they will administer to the class in which students identify the character they like best (Old-Green-Grasshopper, Miss Spider, Ladybug, Glowworm, Earthworm, Centipede, or Silkworm) and which one they would prefer to lead an adventurous expedition. The students should prepare the results of the questionnaire in a chart form to display, and then lead a class discussion on their findings. Is there a clear favorite? Do students pick the character they like best to also provide leadership for an adventure?
4. Little James displays no sadness over the fact that the runaway peach has killed both Aunt Spiker and Aunt Sponge. Both aunts are unlikeable, but there are differences between them. In a discussion group, have members list the traits and distinguish between the two aunts.
5. Gather in a discussion group students who have read both *Dragonflight* by Anne McCaffrey and *James and the Giant Peach* by Roald Dahl. In one book, characters ride on dragons, and in the other they sail through the air in a giant peach pulled by 502 seagulls. Ask students to discuss which of these two types of rides they would prefer to take, and why.

6. Several times throughout the story, the crew of the giant peach faces danger: they go rolling and crashing through the countryside, they are attacked by sharks and Cloud-Men, and so on. In discussion, have students point out the four major dangers that are faced during the journey and the ways in which the voyagers avoided disaster.

7. The author has Cloud-Men making hailstones and painting rainbows while their wives were crouching over stoves preparing dinners of fried snowballs for their husbands. Discuss whether you think this reflects the author's view of the appropriate role and function of men and women. Is there anything else in this book or in other writings of Roald Dahl that supports your opinion?

8. Chapter 39 tells how each of the peach crew members found something to do in New York City. Reread the chapter and then, in discussion, come up with other jobs that take into account their special talents and that might be appropriate for James, Miss Spider, Glowworm, Silkworm, Centipede, Ladybug, and Old-Green-Grasshopper.

Research Activities

1. The Silkworm plays a major role in the story. Invite a pair of interested students to research silkworms in general, write a paper with at least three sources of information, and share this with the class. Possible sources of information include *Silkworms* by Sylvia Johnson (Minneapolis, MN: Lerner Publications, 1982), *Life Cycle of a Silkworm* by Ron Fridell and Patricia Walsh (Chicago, IL: Heinemann Library, 2001), the film *Silkworm Story* by Jennifer Coldrey (London: Oxford Scientific Films), and on the Internet at http://insected.arizona.edu/silkinfo.htm. Complete lesson plans, poems, songs, and so on appear at http://www.pclaunch.com/~kayton/.

2. The Centipede is active in getting the crew into considerable trouble. A pair of students may wish to find out more about centipedes and make an oral report on what they learn to the class. Information on the Internet can be found at http://www.enchantedlearning.com/subjects/invertebrates/arthropod/Centipde.shtml and at http://www.ent.iastate.edu/ipm/iiin/housece.html. More information is available in *Centipede* by Karen Hartley, Chris Macro, and Philip Taylor (Des Plaines, IL: Heinemann Library, 1999).

3. The Earthworm was used to entice the seagulls down to the peach, and the Earthworm brags about how much he helps farmers. Invite a pair of students to learn more about earthworms, write a paper with at least three sources of information, and present it to the class. Sources of information include *Earthworms* by Patrick Merrick (Chanhassen, MN: Child's World, 1999) and *Earthworms* by Elaine Pasco (Woodridge, CT: Blackbirch Press, 1997). Information is available on the Internet at http://www.mertus.org/gardening/worms.html and at http://www.nysite.com/nature/fauna/earthworm.htm.

4. A small group of students might want to prepare a presentation on weather information and arrange a time to give it to their own class as a rehearsal, and then to a primary grade class in the school. First they could read a section from *James and the Giant Peach* telling how the Cloud-Men created hailstones, rainbows, and thunder. Then they could use diagrams and discussion to explain why and how these three weather phenomena really do occur. Sources of useful information might be *Weather* by Chris Oxlade (Austin, TX: Raintree Steck-Vaughn, 1999) or *Blizzards! And Ice Storms* by Maria Rosado (New York: Simon Spotlight, 1999). Additional sites for information about

different weather phenomena on the Internet are http://www.chaseday.com/ hailstones. htm and http://www.usatoday.com/weather/tg/whail/wds9.htm for information and pictures of hail, http://www.usatoday.com/weather/tg/wismwhat/wismwhat.htm/ for thunderstorms, and http://www.unidata.ucar.edu/staff/blynds/rnbw.html for information on rainbows.

5. The adventures of the high-flying crew of *James and the Giant Peach* will cause some students to reflect on the dangers faced by various men in the last few years as they have tried to circumnavigate the globe in some type of balloon. Invite a pair of interested students to research this topic and the flights of such men as Steve Fossett, Bertrand Piccard, and Brian Jones and to present their findings to the class in an oral report. Among sources of information are http://www.launch.net and http://www.pbs.org/wgbk/nova/balloon. Book sources include Glen and Karen Bledso's eBook, *Ballooning Adventures* (Mankato, MN: Capstone Books NetLibrary, 2001) and *Ballooning* by Phyllis J. Perry (New York: Franklin Watts, 1996).

6. According to the story, this book had its beginnings in the fact that an angry rhinoceros escaped from the zoo and ate James's parents. Invite a pair of students to write a factual report on the five different species of rhinoceros including a bibliography of at least three sources of information. They should share their report with the class. Data for the report may be found at http://www.kidsplanet.org/factsheets/rhinoceros.html and at http://animaldiscovery.com/features/rhinoceros/rhinoceros.html. Other sources of information include *Black Rhino: Habitats, Life Cycle, Food Chains, Threats* by Malcolm Penny (Austin, TX: Raintree Steck-Vaughn, 2001), *Black Rhinos* by E. Melanie Watt (Austin, TX: Raintree Steck-Vaughn, 1998), and *Wild Animals* by Sarah Fecher (Princeton, NJ: Two-Can, 2000).

Extension Activities

1. The peach tree is especially beautiful in spring. With the help of the school art educator, perhaps students could have an art lesson on painting spring trees. The finished products could be put on display in the school. One site of interest would be http://www.vangogh-gallery.com/painting/p_0551.htm, which shows *Orchard with Peach Trees in Blossom* by the artist Vincent van Gogh. One picture might be developed into a poster to advertise the book, *James and the Giant Peach,* and be hung in the library.

2. Plan a brief news segment to present to the class in which a student role plays a radio broadcaster and pretends to interview people on the street who saw the giant peach come crashing down on the Empire State Building. Use the format of an "eyewitness" account. In addition to general spectators, the news broadcaster might also interview class members playing the roles of members of the police and fire departments, seeking information from them about what they found when they went up into the building to investigate. Record and play this news segment for the class.

3. Aunt Spiker and Aunt Sponge are representative of the scary "witch-like" women that are found in fairy tales from many different countries and cultures. If there are ESL students in the class or others with an interest in folk tales of the world, invite them to share a witch-like story book character in an oral report to the class. Maybe they could tell a familiar story or read aloud a section from a favorite tale. Among the possibilities are "Fair Vasilissa and Baba Yaga," retold by Charles Downing in *Russian Tales and Legends*

(New York: H.Z. Walck, 1964); *Snake's Toothache* (Guatemala) by Melinda Lilly (Vero Beach, FL: Rourke Publications, 2001); *Hansel and Gretel: A Fairy Tale* (Germany) by Jacob and Wilhelm Grimm (New York: North-South Books, 2001); and "The Fiddler and the Dancin' Witch" (Afro-Caribbean) from *Listen to the Storyteller* by Kristen Balouch (New York: Viking, 1999).

4. Since the people of New York were frightened by the appearance of the giant peach, have volunteers from the class write a declaration from the crew members to be read to the people of New York in which they explain that they come in peace. What style and tone should such a declaration have? Ask volunteers to read their declarations to the class.

5. A newspaper account of the fall of a giant peach onto the Empire State Building would make headlines around the world. Have students check local papers for the tone and style of such news stories. Then invite interested students to write such an account and post all the news stories on a bulletin board under the caption of **"GIANT PEACH HITS CITY!"**

6. Invite students to write a new chapter for *James and the Giant Peach* between Chapters 15 and 16 in which all the townspeople come running and watch in fascination as the peach crashes through the countryside to reach the sea. Invite volunteers to read their new chapter to the class.

How does reading *James and the Giant Peach* and engaging in the various activities suggested above help students meet the 12 NCTE/IRA English Language Arts Standards?

1. *James and the Giant Peach* meets Standard #1 by serving as an example of outstanding fiction.

2. *James and the Giant Peach* meets Standard #2 because it is a representative work of the broad genre of fantasy.

3. Discussion questions #1, #2, #4, #6, and #7 help students to comprehend and interpret text, and the vocabulary exercise increases knowledge of word meanings, helping students to meet Standard #3.

4. Extension activity #4, in which various students write "declarations of peace to the citizens of New York," addresses Standard #4, which asks students to adjust written language and style to communicate effectively for different purposes.

5. Extension activity #5, which suggests that students write up newspaper accounts of the landing of the giant peach as front-page articles for a modern newspaper, helps meet Standard #5, which requires that students use different writing processes for different audiences and for a variety of purposes.

6. Extension activity #6, which suggests that students write a new chapter to be added to the book, helps to meet Standard #6 by requiring students to apply their knowledge of language structure and language conventions to create a print text.

7. Discussion question #3, which requires that students conduct research; gather, evaluate, and synthesize data; and communicate their discoveries in a discussion using a chart format before the class, helps to address Standard #7.

8. Research activity #1 on silkworms helps to meet Standard #8 by encouraging students to use a variety of technological and information resources to carry out research and to communicate their knowledge.

9. Discussion question #7 about the conventional roles played by Cloud-Men and Cloud-Women in this book helps to address Standard #9 by allowing students to develop an understanding of and respect for diversity in social roles.

10. Extension activity #3 asking ESL students and others with an interest in folk tales of the world to share, compare, and contrast the use of witch-like characters in fairy tales and legends helps address Standard #10, which asks students to use their first language that is not English to develop a deeper understanding of the curriculum.

11. Discussion question #5 allows students to pool their information knowledge in the form of a fantasy book discussion group and compare and contrast the flight of the dragons in *Dragonflight* by Anne McCaffrey with the flight of the seagull-powered peach in *James and the Giant Peach* by Roald Dahl. It helps meet Standard #11, which asks that students participate as knowledgeable, reflective, creative, and critical members of a literary community.

12. Extension activity #1 allows students to creatively select and prepare a means of sharing their enthusiasm for this book with other potential readers. It addresses Standard #12, in which students are asked to use spoken, written, and visual language to persuade others.

Redwall

Brian Jacques

New York: Philomel Books 1986, ISBN 0-399-21424-0

Detailed Synopsis

The story, which is an animal fantasy, opens in June at Redwall Abbey in Mossflower Country. Matthias, a woodland mouse, dressed in an oversized novice's habit, trips and falls in front of Abbot Mortimer. While he and the Abbot talk, they walk past a tapestry depicting early Redwall history. It shows the figure of Martin the Warrior, considered by Matthias to be the bravest mouse who ever lived.

Even as Matthias and the Abbot are talking, Cluny the Scourge, a bilge rat, comes riding on the back of a hay wagon with his 500 followers. He doesn't know exactly where he is going, but Cluny is headed toward Redwall Abbey.

At the Abbey, preparations are under way to celebrate Abbot Mortimer's golden jubilee. Creatures of all kinds are coming to the feast. Afterwards, the Abbot sends Matthias and Constance Badger to see the Churchmouse family safely home. Halfway to the Church of St. Ninian, they see the cart carrying Cluny and the rats race by.

Cluny and the rats take over the Church of St. Ninian, and Matthias and the others return to the Abbey where all the mice are called to a meeting and told about the army of rats that has appeared. The next day, one of the rats arrives at the Abbey's gate house. The rat will not surrender his weapon, so the mice won't let him inside the Abbey walls, and he threatens to return with an army of friends. The hedgehog is sent out to tell the other animals in the area to come to the safety of the Abbey.

Cluny's army soon comes marching down the road. Cluny and Redtooth are admitted to the Abbey, and they read out the articles of surrender to the Abbot. Cluny and Redtooth are immediately escorted back outside, where Cluny calls on one of his followers, Shadow, to sneak back into the Abbey and cut out the figure of Martin the Warrior from the tapestry and bring it to him. Without their hero, Cluny feels the mice will be demoralized and surrender.

The Redwall mice organize and train to protect the Abbey. Matthias wishes he could find the sword of Martin the Warrior to use in battle, but Old Methluselah thinks it may have been stolen long ago by the sparrows.

Shadow enters the abbey and chews off the piece of the tapestry depicting Martin the Warrior. Matthias awakens while the theft is going on, and he raises the alarm. Constance and Mr. Fieldmouse try to stop Shadow, but he falls over the parapet with the precious fabric. Cluny snatches up the piece of tapestry and leaves Shadow to die.

Cluny uses the piece of tapestry in his war banner, and Matthias sets off for the Church of St. Ninian to try to get it back. On his way, Matthias meets up with the rat, Ragear, and ties him up in the wood. Then Matthias meets Basil Stag Hare, tells him about the rat attack, and shares with him what he is trying to accomplish. Basil shows Matthias how to secretly enter the church and creates a diversion to distract the rats. Cluny has already left the church to attack the Abbey, so all Matthias accomplishes is freeing a family of captured voles.

Cluny lays siege to the Abbey. Some rats try climbing the walls with grappling hooks, but they are knocked aside. While Cluny's men are searching in the wood for another way to attack, they come upon the adder, Asmodeus, who has made off with a soldier. Frightened, they come running back, but by that time another scout has found a tall tree that may provide entry to the Abbey.

In the Abbey, Old Methuselah spies the rats climbing up into the elm and sounds the alarm: when the rats try to cross from the tree to the Abbey walls, Constance sends them hurtling to the ground. Cluny is injured and his army retreats. Back at his camp, Cluny sends for a healer to help cure his wounds, and Sela, the fox, is brought to him.

Matthias, Constance, and Methuselah try to follow the instructions of a riddle to locate Martin's sword. They figure out that the sword was placed in the arm of the Abbey weather vane that points north. Jess Squirrel climbs up to get it, but she is attacked on the way by sparrows. The Redwall mice shoot arrows to help Jess, and one of the sparrows is hurt and captured. After making her dangerous trip and returning, Jess reports that the sword has already been taken from the weather vane.

Cluny allows Sela the fox, guarded by rats, to go to Mossflower Wood to get medicinal herbs. Cluny knows clever Sela will try to betray him, and he arranges that she will deliver the wrong attack plans to his enemies. Constance takes the attack plans, not knowing they are false, and uses them to plan a defense against the attack.

Matthias, thinking that the sparrows have Martin's sword, tries to use Warbeak, the injured sparrow, to help him retrieve it. They slowly make their way to the top of the Abbey attic. On their dangerous journey, they become friends. They reach the court of the sparrow king, King Bull Sparra.

Cluny orders the two foxes, Sela and Chickenhound, killed. Both are speared and tossed into a ditch, but Chickenhound survives and decides to take his knowledge of Cluny's revised attack plans to the Abbey in hopes of a great reward. He collapses in front of the Abbey but is taken inside, where he explains that the battering ram is only a diversion and that Cluny's main attack will be from underground.

High in the Abbey loft, the sparrow king gives Matthias as a prisoner to Warbeak and his mother, Dunwing. Matthias learns that the sparrow king has the scabbard but not the sword he seeks. The sword has been taken by the adder, Asmodeus, who also killed Dunwing's husband.

Basil Stag Hare and Jess Squirrel hatch a plan to take the tapestry back from Cluny. They run about on the rat's training field, just out of reach, and lure Cluny into coming after them. Although Basil twists his foot, he and Jess manage to take the stolen piece of tapestry and make their way back to the Abbey, where Methuselah sews the figure of Martin the Warrior back into the hanging tapestry.

Dunwing comes up with a plan for Matthias to escape the Sparra court. She will spread a rumor that the adder is dying, and when Bull Sparra and his warriors go to investigate, Matthias will run out on the roof and be helped down by Jess Squirrel. Matthias takes the scabbard and sword belt with him and goes out on the roof. But before Jess Squirrel can reach him, Bull Sparra comes back and attacks. Both the sparrow and Matthias topple from the roof.

Chickenhound, the fox, has recovered from his wounds and is roaming about the Abbey stealing. He puts all the valuables in a sack. Friar Hugo, the cook, sees the fox and gives chase. Brother Methuselah joins in and is struck in the head by the heavy sack of loot and killed. The fox races into the woods, then dives for safety into a hole in the hollow of an oak, where he is later killed by the adder, Asmodeus.

Search parties go out and finally find Matthias, still alive, after having fallen from the roof into the Abbey pond. Once Matthias is well again, he goes off to talk to a white owl named Captain Snow to learn what he can about the adder, Asmodeus, who probably has the sword of Martin the Warrior. Matthias meets up with some shrews who escort him to the barn near the edge of Mossflower Wood.

While Matthias is away, the invasion of Redwall by Cluny begins. The battering ram does a lot of damage until Jess Squirrel brings up a barrel with a hornet's nest inside it and two containers of vegetable oil. Both are dropped from the parapet. Constance Badger works on a plan to use a powerful bow to try to kill Cluny in his field tent. But at the time Constance shoots, it is not Cluny, but Cheesethief, who is in the tent, and Cheesethief is the one who is killed.

Matthias meets the barn cat, Julian, who takes him to a nearby hollow tree where Captain Snow, the owl, lives. Captain Snow tells Matthias that the adder, Asmodeus, lives in the stone quarry. He bets that the adder will defeat Matthias. Matthias sets off alone for the old sandstone quarry, and later the shrews join him. Matthais and the shrews spread out along the bank of the river hoping to see Asmodeus and to follow the snake to his lair. They follow the snake's trail through the grass and find the entrance to the adder's den.

Cluny and his rats build a siege tower on top of an old hay wagon. Cluny's plan is to leap from the tower onto the Abbey ramparts. Cornflower, while using a lantern to deliver food to the soldiers standing guard, discovers the siege tower. She throws her lantern at it, and the tower catches fire and burns. Cluny survives this attack but runs around ranting and raving as if he's gone mad.

Matthias and two of the shrews explore the tunnels of Asmodeus. One of the shrews is killed by the adder. When Matthias comes upon the sleeping snake, he spies the sword of Martin the Warrior, squeezes by the snake, and takes the sword.

Cluny's rats tunnel into the Abbey, but the moles are waiting. The rats Killconey, Darkclaw, and Fangburn lead this attack since Cluny is still behaving oddly as if out of his mind. When Darkclaw emerges inside the Abbey, boiling water is poured down into the rats' tunnel and many are killed.

Matthias and the shrew, Log-a-Log, accidentally awaken Asmodeus and the snake comes after them. Matthias uses the sword to sever the snake's head. Matthias returns to Julian, the cat, and the two go to find Captain Snow. Because Matthias has won the bet, the owl gives back to Matthias Basil's medal, swears not to kill another mouse or shrew, and apologizes to the cat.

Seemingly recovered from his sickness, Cluny gives his troops time to recuperate. Cluny then threatens the family of a dormouse unless the dormouse promises to go inside and open the Abbey gates. Plumpen, the dormouse, joins the Abbey work crew, gets inside the Abbey, and when it is dark, opens the door.

Matthias has feasted and celebrated with the shrews when Warbeak Sparra appears with the news of Cluny's latest attack on the Abbey. The sparrows and shrews join Matthias as he heads back to the Abbey, where Cluny's rats have captured Redwall. In the morning, when Cluny is ready to kill his prisoners, Matthias appears carrying the sword of Martin the Warrior.

The shrews, sparrows, and prisoners fight back against the rats. Cluny and Matthias battle for a long while until Matthias sends the Joseph Bell crashing down, killing the rat. Before Abbot Mortimer dies, he asks Brother Alf to take his place. The Abbot also makes Matthias the Warrior Mouse of Redwall, and with Cornflower for his wife, Matthias is to live in the gatehouse and guard the Abbey with the sword, which is now called Ratdeath.

List of Major Characters: The major character is a novice mouse at the Abbey named Matthias. Other major characters include Cornflower, a mouse who marries Matthias; Abbot Mortimer, head of the Abbey; Cluny, a bilge rat; Brother Methuselah, an old monk; Friar Hugo, the cook; Constance Badger; Jess Squirrel; Asmodeus Poisonteeth, the adder; Basil Stag Hare; Warbeak and Dunwing, two sparrows; and Log-a-Log, a shrew.

Vocabulary: The pages on which these selected words appear are listed in parentheses after each word below. Read the sentences in which these words appear, and then find these vocabulary words in a dictionary and study their meanings. Rewrite the sentences in which the words appear, using a synonym in place of the vocabulary word.

benignly (16) _____

gyrated (21) _____

legerdemain (21) _____

braced (31) _____

contemptuously (31) _____

insolently (52) _____

voluble (60) _____

curmudgeon (89) _____

ingratiatingly (137) _____

alacrity (163) _____

erudite (177) _____

filigree (241) _____

Comprehension Questions

1. How does Friar Hugo wipe away his perspiration generated by the heat of his kitchen?
2. How does the rat, Skullface, meet his death?
3. In the early scene of the book, what causes Matthias to keep falling flat?
4. What person in the Abbey can communicate in all animal languages?
5. What happens to Ragear after he is tied to a tree by Matthias?
6. When Warbeak, the sparrow, gives his word of honor, on what does he swear?
7. Among the shrews in Mossflower, what is the signal to show you want to speak?
8. Why are shrews and mice safe from the cat Julian?
9. How is the siege tower that was built by the rats destroyed?
10. How do Cluny's rats capture and hold Constance Badger?

Answers: 1) Hugo uses a dandelion held with his tail to wipe away perspiration. 2) Skull-face is run over by cartwheels after he falls off the horse pulling the hay cart. 3) The sandals of Matthias are too big and constantly trip him up. 4) Brother Methuselah can communicate with all animals. 5) Ragear frees himself from the tree but is killed by the adder. 6) Warbeak swears by his mother's egg. 7) To show they wish to speak, the shrews hold up a stone. 8) Julian eats no red meat. 9) Cornflower throws a lantern at the siege tower, which catches fire and burns. 10) They bludgeon Constance and throw a net over her.

Discussion Questions

1. Three of the major animal characters are female. Constance Badger is portrayed as a strong warrior and good strategic thinker. Jess Squirrel appears to be especially brave and daring. Cornflower Mouse portrays the more stereotypical female role of providing support by bringing and serving food from the kitchen to the soldiers on the ramparts. Do you think that the author set out deliberately to show females in very different roles? Is one more admirable than the others? Why, or why not?
2. Some birds think that Bull Sparra is mad. His troops believe that Cluny has gone mad. Discuss ways in which the leaders, Bull Sparra and Cluny, are alike and different.
3. There are many ways in which Cluny could have met his death, including being killed by Martin the Warrior's sword. Do you think that having him hit and killed by the falling Joseph Bell was a fitting end? Why, or why not?
4. Invite a group of students who have read both *Poppy* by Avi and *Redwall* by Brian Jacques to discuss the owls that appear in both stories. Mr. Ocax in *Poppy* and Captain Snow in *Redwall* are both feared by the mice. In what ways are the two owls alike and different?
5. Matthias spent quite a bit of time as a prisoner in the court of Bull Sparra. What valuable lessons did he learn there?
6. The animals portrayed in *Redwall* were governed in different ways. Those within the Abbey were governed by the Abbot. Bull Sparra ruled the birds firmly as a dictator. The shrews had their own strange code of conduct. The rats had to obey Cluny, who controlled

by brute power. Ask a group of interested students to discuss the strengths and weaknesses of each of these forms of governance and to interview others in the school and the community about which forms of government are most democratic, most effective, most oppressive, and so on. Then hold a panel discussion on various forms of government for the class.

7. Captain Snow and Squire Julian, the cat, are an unusual pair. Although each has apologized and the two go off together "wing in paw," do you think they will remain close friends for long? Why, or why not? What evidence from the text supports your opinions?

8. Before he died, the Abbot said that Matthias should not enter the Order as a Brother. Do you think this was a wise or unwise decision? What traits did Matthias possess that would have made him a valuable member of the Order? What traits did he possess that would have made it difficult for Matthias to enter the Order?

Research Activities

1. Matthias and Brother Alf catch a large grayling and bring it to the Abbey feast. Ask a pair of students to research graylings and write a report to share with the class that contains a bibliography with at least three sources of information. These fish are found in the northern hemisphere between 40 and 70 degrees latitude. There is a Grayling Society of Fishermen. Possible sources of information include the *Complete Book of the Grayling* by Broughton Richard (London: Robert Hale, Ltd., 2001) and http://www.daiwasports. co.uk/woa/species/grayling.htm.

2. Captain Snow is a snowy owl. Invite two interested students to find out more about snowy owls and orally report to the class what they learn. They should share a picture of the owl. Possible sources of information include *Snowy Owls* by Wendy Pfeffer (Parsippany, NJ: Silver Press) and *Snowy Owls* by Patricia Hunt (New York: Dodd, Mead, 1982). At http://www.owlpages.com/species/nyctea/scandiaca/Default.htm there are pictures of owls, and at http://www.zooregon.org/cards/Tundra/owl.snowy.htm there is additional information. There may also be available a video on different types of owls that might be shared with the class.

3. Asmodeus Poisonteeth is a fearsome enemy. He is an adder, or viper, the only poisonous snake found in Great Britain. Invite a pair of students to learn more about venomous snakes and to write and present what they learn in the form of an interview in which one student takes the part of radio interviewer and the other is an "expert" on snakes. What questions will the interviewer ask? What interesting information will the expert supply? The questions and answers might be written on three-by-five cards. When the students are ready, have them present their interview before the class. Possible sources of information include *Snakes* by Deborah A. Behler (New York: Benchmark Books, 2002) and *Snakes with Venom* by Lynn M. Stone (Vero Beach, FL: Rourke Book Co., 2001). Additional information on venomous snakes can be found at http://www.burmese.freeuk.com/ Snakes/viper.htm.

4. Brian Jacques is the author of *Redwall*. Students in the class might enjoy learning more about this author and the other books he has written. Invite a pair of students to research Brian Jacques and to report back what they learn. One possible source of information is http://www.mystworld.com/youngwriter/authors/brian_jacques.html.

5. The tapestry depicting Martin the Warrior was important to the story. ESL students and students from a variety of cultural backgrounds might be interested in exploring the topic

of tapestry. Tapestries go back to the Greeks; are found in the Song, Yuan, Ming, and Qing dynasties of China; and were especially famous in France, Holland, Belgium, and Italy. At http://www.quaker-tapestry.co.uk.the_tapestry.htm is information about a Quaker history tapestry. The famous Mystic Wine tapestry of 1500–1522 is discussed at http://www.christusrox.org/www1/vaticano/M-Tapestry.html. The well-known Bayeux Tapestry is discussed at http://www.sjolander.com/viking/museum/bt/bt.htm. And http://www.w.com/~tapestry/ gives a general history of tapestries. Ask students to share information about tapestries that they research.

6. When a messenger is needed to go outside the safety of the Abbey and warn the other small animals of the danger from Cluny and his rats, Ambrose Spike, the hedgehog, is chosen because when he curls up, nothing can touch him. Invite a pair of students to research hedgehogs and orally report what they learn. Possible sources of information include *Hedgehogs and Other Insectivores* by Steven Otfinoski (Chicago: World Book, 2000) and http://www.slider.com/enc/26000/insectivore.htm.

Extension Activities

1. Invite students to read the description of Cluny that appears in the last paragraph on page 49 of the book and then to make a picture of this character using any medium of their choice. Use this as a book jacket, advertising the book, and, with permission, display it in the school library media center.

2. Several students might want to contribute short newspaper articles, a comic strip, or a political cartoon to a publication of the *Mossflower Country Gazette*. Assume that this is a weekly newspaper and that this issue covers the recent attack on the Abbey by Cluny and the activities of the attackers and those under attack. There might be an obituary for Brother Methuselah and for Abbot Mortimer written in the appropriate style for such notices. There might also be a description of the wedding of Matthias and Cornflower. Arrange to have this edition printed and distributed to class members.

3. Basil and Constance proved to be great warriors. They would take a particular interest in the fact that Matthias has been made Warrior Mouse of Redwall and would no doubt have advice for him. Ask interested students to write a short new chapter to come near the end of the book after the Abbot's death, in which Constance and Basil pledge and support their future help to Matthias.

4. A group of students might want to make a bulletin board featuring some of the characters from *Redwall* by making a mask representing each character and labeling them. A hedgehog mask at http://www.janbrett.com/mitten_masks_thehedgehog.htm might provide a model for other figures from the book.

5. A group of students may wish to present a scene from *Redwall* as reader's theater, either for their own or for another class. Perhaps a parent volunteer would agree to work with the students and rehearse them for the performance. Needed are scenes with lots of dialogue between two or more characters. Pages 208 to 210 when Matthias is with the sparrows and pages 148 to 152 with Mathias and Methluselah would be good choices.

6. Often a great victory is celebrated by a poem praising the warrior who triumphs. A student may wish to try writing a poem about Matthias and how he defeated the adder, Asmodeus, or how he defeated Cluny. Allow time for the student to share his or her poem with the class.

How does reading *Redwall* and engaging in the various activities suggested above help students meet the 12 NCTE/IRA English Language Arts Standards?

1. *Redwall* meets Standard #1 by serving as an example of outstanding fiction.
2. *Redwall* meets Standard #2 because it is a representative work of the broad genre of animal fantasy.
3. Discussion questions #1 through #5 help students to comprehend and interpret text, and the vocabulary exercise increases knowledge of word meanings, helping students to meet Standard #3.
4. Extension activity #2, which suggests writing a special edition of the *Mossflower Country Gazette* complete with obituaries, battle descriptions, and a description of a wedding, helps to address Standard #4, which asks students to adjust written language and style to communicate effectively for different purposes.
5. Research activity #3, which suggests that students make note cards and conduct a mock interview between a radio commentator and snake expert to present to the class, helps meet Standard #5, which requires that students use different writing processes for different audiences and for a variety of purposes.
6. Extension activity #3, which suggests that students write a new chapter to be added near the end of the book giving advice and support to Matthias from Constance and Basil, helps to meet Standard #6 by requiring students to apply their knowledge of language structure and language conventions to create a print text.
7. Discussion question #6, which centers around forms of governance portrayed in *Redwall,* helps to address Standard #7 by allowing students to conduct research on issues and gather, evaluate, and synthesize data from a variety of sources and communicate information to an audience.
8. Research activity #2 on snowy owls helps to meet Standard #8 by encouraging students to use a variety of technological and information resources to carry out research and to communicate their knowledge.
9. Discussion question #1, which centers around the conventional roles of men and women and around observing how Constance, Jess, and Cornflower do and do not fit neatly into these conventional roles, helps to address Standard #9 by allowing students to develop an understanding of and respect for diversity in social roles.
10. Research activity #5 on tapestries of the world helps to address Standard #10, which asks students to use their cultural background and perhaps a first language that is not English to develop a deeper understanding of the curriculum.
11. Discussion question #4, which allows students to pool their information knowledge in the form of a book discussion group and compare and contrast the use of the owl in *Poppy* with the use of the owl in *Redwall*, helps meet Standard #11, which asks that students participate as knowledgeable, reflective, creative, and critical members of a literary community.
12. Extension activity #1 allows students to creatively select and prepare a means of sharing their enthusiasm for this book with other potential readers by turning written words into a vivid illustration for a book jacket and using this as a means of advertising the book. It addresses Standard #12, in which students are asked to use spoken, written, and visual language to persuade others.

The Tombs of Atuan

Ursula K. LeGuin

New York: Atheneum, 1972, ISBN 0-689-31684-4

Detailed Synopsis

In the Prologue, the reader meets a little girl playing in the orchard, who finally returns home after her mother calls and learns she is destined to be taken away the following month to begin training as a priestess.

In the first chapter, black-clad women lead a child of 7 to a throne. She kneels in a position for beheading when someone stops the sword. A priestess pours a bowl of liquid on the steps by the child. Two priestesses appear and call out to the Nameless Ones, and the child is led outside in a procession. The procession winds its way to the Hall of the Tombs. The little girl is taken from room to room. Her hair is cut, and she is put in a bed. Someone called Manan comes to check on her, and she tells him that she is no longer named Tenar, but from now on will be Arha, the Eaten One.

As she grows older, the child feels she belongs at the Place of the Tombs. She learns she was chosen for this role because she was born on the same night that the One Priestess

of the Tombs of Atuan died, so she is considered to be the reborn priestess. A female child who was born on the right day, she was located in the countryside and then watched, and when she was 5 years old, she was taken to the tombs to begin her training. She is taught sacred songs, dances, and history and also learns to spin and weave, plant, harvest, and prepare food.

When Arha is 15, the Godking's priestess, Kossil, tells her it is time to go into the Undertomb, which is Arha's private kingdom. After that, Arha learns to walk in darkness in the undertombs and in the labyrinth. One night, Kossil tells her about some men who long ago came to rob the tombs. One was a mighty sorcerer named Erreth-Akbe. He joined with rebel lords but was defeated by the High Priest, who broke in half his witching staff and a large ring that was his amulet of power, and he was slain by a dragon.

Kossil explains that from the High Priest are descended the Godkings of Kaargad, and that Kossil serves the current Godking. She explains that others have come to try to find the broken amulet of Erreth-Akbe and regain power because half of the amulet is believed to be in the Treasury of the Tombs and the other half of the ring was lost and no one knows what became of it.

Kossil and another priestess named Thar describe the magic of the men from the Inner Lands who can perform various tricks and deceptions. These Wizards of the West can raise the winds. Some say they can make light at will, create illusions, and turn themselves into other creatures.

One year in early winter when Arha is still only a teenager, Thar dies. Arha misses her, because Thar has been a stern, but never cruel, teacher. Kossil, the priestess who remains, holds nothing sacred except power, and Arha does not like her. After the Rites of Mourning end, Arha avoids Kossil, and she also begins to be systematic in her exploration of the undertombs, memorizing all the turns and passages.

The only person Arha takes with her when she explores the nearer regions of the labyrinth is Manan, who she knows is faithful to her. She also explores the Hall with its altars, alcoves, chests, and boxes.

One winter night when she is exploring alone, Arha comes upon a stranger with a torch. She shouts, and the torch goes out and the intruder runs. Arha follows the stranger and traps him in the Labyrinth by pulling the door shut behind him. Then Arha leaves. She thinks the stranger may be a wizard from the Inner Lands seeking the amulet of Erreth-Akbe.

Arha goes to the Small House, opens a locked room, pries off a tile, and looks through the peephole into the room where the stranger is just inside the locked door. She studies him and hears him speak in a strange language. In the morning, Arha again looks through the spy hole, but the stranger is gone. She believes that he is now lost in the labyrinth.

Arha tells Kossil about the stranger, and Kossil recommends that they wait six days, by which time the stranger will be dead without food and water, and they can send wardens to drag his body out. Arha says she wants to find the stranger alive and will determine a suitable death for him, but Kossil thinks this is too risky.

Arha spends the next few days feeling restless and looking through various spy holes down into the labyrinth. After three days, she spies the stranger, who by now is looking weak. She calls down to him the directions to follow to make his way to the Painted Room.

The next morning, Arha spies the stranger in the Painted Room and gives him complicated directions to follow to take him to the treasures of the Tombs of Atuan. When Arha and Manan go underground to look for the stranger, they find him near death. Manan carries him back to the Painted Room and chains him there. Arha drips a little water into his mouth and, because it is cold, she leaves her cloak with the man. While he is sleeping, Arha comes back and leaves food and water for him.

Later Arha comes again to talk with the stranger. He calls himself Sparrowhawk and explains that he is from Havnor in the Inner Lands. He claims to be a dragon lord who can speak with dragons. During the next few days, Arha often takes a lantern and comes to talk with him, and he sometime performs illusions.

One night while Arha is talking with Sparrowhawk, Kossil spies down at them through a peephole. Fearing that Kossil will do the stranger harm, Arha sends Manan to move Sparrowhawk to a secret place and to dig a grave and bury an empty casket so that others will believe the stranger is buried there. Arha leads Sparrowhawk to the Great Treasure Room, which is one place where she is sure he will be safe from Kossil.

Above ground, Arha tells Kossil she has buried the stranger alive. Arha and Kossil quarrel. A worried Manan tells Arha that Kossil may try to kill her. Three days later, Arha goes underground and sees Kossil digging where the empty casket is buried. Arha quietly goes on by to the treasure room, where she speaks with Sparrowhawk.

Sparrowhawk explains that the Masters of Darkness are here, but that they are not gods, are not worthy of worship, and have nothing to give. Their only power is to darken and destroy. Sparrowhawk tells Arha that he has found the half ring that was missing, the ring of Erreth-Akbe. It is a large ring, the type to be worn on the arm, and it matches the half-ring that Sparrowhawk used to wear as an amulet and that Arha took from him and now wears. The metal is silver, is pierced with nine holes, and has runes inside.

Sparrowhawk explains that his half of the ring was given to him by an old woman he met on an island and that he didn't know its value until a dragon told him what it was. Then he went to Havnor and volunteered to come to the tombs to try and find the missing half. With both halves of the ring, all the runes will be present, and this should allow a king to rule in peace.

Sparrowhawk tells Arha she must make a choice. She can lock the door, have him killed, and remain here as a priestess. Or she can run away with him and perhaps help restore peace. Sparrowhawk also tells her that his true name is Ged. Using magical powers, Ged mends the broken ring and puts it on Arha's arm. Then they leave the tombs. On their way out, Manan tries to stop them near a dangerous pit, and he falls to his death.

When Ged and Arha reach the exit door, it is weighted down. They suspect that Kossil will be waiting there to kill them. So they leave through a second door in the rocks. As they leave, Arha sees that Ged is using all his strength and power to protect them. Once they are outside, an earthquake causes the stones and tombs to crumble.

Ged calls Arha by her childhood name, Tenar. Ged and Tenar travel through the western mountains on foot. They survive by eating a little bread and cheese and some nuts they find along the way. They travel toward the sea, sometimes under cover of illusions or disguises created by Ged. They pass through towns where they are given food and shelter.

When they finally reach the sea, they find Ged's boat where he has hidden it. Then they sail toward Havnor. On the way, Ged promises Tenar that after she has done her duty and shown the ring, he will take her away from the princes and lords to Ogion, Ged's old master, who lives in a small house on the cliffs of Re Albi in the land of Gont. He promises she will live there amidst silence and kindness.

List of Major Characters: The main character is Tenar, who is taken to the tombs to be a Priestess and is renamed Arha. There are two other priestesses of the tombs named Kossil and Thar; Penthe is another priestess in training; Manan is a servant who looks after Arha; and Sparrowhawk, or Ged, is the stranger who comes to the tombs.

Vocabulary: The following words appear in the book. The numeral following the word gives the page number on which the word appears. Look up each of these words to see how it is used in the book. Then look up each word in a dictionary and write two synonyms after the word.

bellwether (22) _____

haft (52) _____

sparse (54) _____

taciturn (54) _____

scintillations (65) _____

buffeted (69) _____

keened (69) _____

resonant (71) _____

disdained (75) _____

obstinate (78) _____

Comprehension Questions

1. Why are the Wizards of the West thought to be good sailors?
2. How could one take away the power of the sorcerer of the West?
3. What kind of garment does Arha always wear as a Priestess?
4. What sort of picture is painted on the walls of the Painted Room?
5. Where does Arha sit when she questions the stranger in the Painted Room?
6. What are two ways by which Arha thought Kossil might kill Sparrowhawk?
7. What small white creatures live in the labyrinth?
8. Why hadn't Arha learned how to read?
9. What happens to Manan when he comes looking for Arha just before the earthquake?
10. What is the name of Ged's well-traveled boat?

Answers: 1) They put the wind of magic in their sails. 2) Power will be lost if someone takes away the sorcerer's wooden staff. 3) The priestess dresses in rough, homespun, black cloth. 4) The pictures in the Painted Room show men with long wings and great eyes. 5) Arha sits on a folding stool of ivory. 6) The stranger might be killed by blowing poison dust through a spy hole or by sending Duby to kill him. 7) Rare white spiders live in the labyrinth. 8) Reading is considered to be one of the black arts. 9) Manan falls to his death into a pit. 10) Ged's boat is called Lookfar.

Discussion Questions

1. Her mother is so reluctant to let Tenar go to the Tombs of Atuan that she tries to fool the messengers into thinking the child had smallpox, hoping that would make them afraid to come in the house and get her. Why do you think that Tenar's mother does not consider it an honor to be sought after to be a priestess but rather thinks that it was a duty to be avoided?

2. On page 143 of *The Tombs of Atuan,* when Ged and Tenar are hungry and walking through the mountains, Tenar suggests that Ged use magic to prepare them a meal. Ged says he could summon up a supper on golden plates, "But that's illusion, and when you eat illusions you end up hungrier than before. It's about as nourishing as eating your own

words." Hold a discussion on this piece of text with the students. What is the author trying to get across to the reader with this statement?

3. Another young girl who is sent to study to become a priestess in the tombs is a "soft, comfortable looking girl" called Penthe, who often plays and spends time with Arha even though she knows she will be punished for it. Penthe is very different from Arha and has a much different view of the Godkings than do the Priestesses. Have a group of students discuss Penthe and Arha. Which of the girls would they prefer to have for a friend, and why? Cite passages from the book to support opinions.

4. As the story progresses, Kossil becomes an enemy of Arha. Why do you think this enmity develops? Are there things that Arha could have done differently that would have caused Kossil to regard her in a better light? What are these?

5. The people in this book are very aware of their stations in life. One priestess is more important than the others. Some servants, such as Manan, have privileges that other servants do not have. Some of the young girls in training are punished when they break the rules, and others are not. What role in the book did these rigid roles for females and males and for people in certain stations of life play in this book?

6. The Place is not a real geographical place. Yet because of the descriptions given by the author, the reader tends to locate it in the world. Using a map of the world, have students point out spots on Earth where it is possible that *The Tombs of Atuan* might be set. Use descriptions from the book to justify placing it in a certain physical location.

7. Arha was faced with a choice that Ged made clear to her. He advised her that she could remain a priestess and stay in the service of the Nameless Ones or she could leave with him. Ask an interested small group of students to list on the chalkboard the pros and cons that might have gone through Arha's mind as she tried to make this important decision.

8. At the end of the book, Arha is about to face culture shock. She will be in a fairly large city with lots of people. How do you think she will be received and treated? How will she react to the lords and princes that she meets? After she has accomplished her mission in the great port city of Havnor, do you think she will be eager or reluctant to leave? Why? Will she be able to adjust to a new life of solitude with Ged's teacher?

Research Activities

1. Ursula K. LeGuin has written many distinguished books for adults and children. Ask two students to do some research and report to the class orally what they learn about this author and the awards she has won. They should make and post a list in the classroom of other books that LeGuin has written for children.

2. Probably the most famous labyrinth in literature is the one that King Minos of Crete ordered Daedalus to build to hold the bull-man called the Minotaur. Ask a pair of students to research this labyrinth and to write a report to share with the class. They should use books, encyclopedias, and sites on the Internet. One possible site is http://www.minotaur-websites.com/minomyuth.htm. Two other sources of information are *Daedalus & the Minotaur* by Pricella Gallaway (Toronto: Annick Press, 1997) and *Theseus and the Minotaur* by Leonard Everett Fisher (New York: Holiday House, 1992).

3. When Arha is in the Undertombs, she sometimes sees bats. Invite a small group of interested students to research bats. They should use books, magazines, filmstrips, videos, and the Internet to gather sources of information. Ask the group to share what they learn

with the class in an oral and visual presentation. Some sources of information include http://www.torstar.com/rom/batcave and information about cave-dwelling bats at http://home.mira.net/~gah/speleogy/fobc/batpamph.htm. A book with information about bats is *Bats: The Amazing Upside-Downers* by Phyllis J. Perry (New York: Franklin Watts, 1998).

4. Several small creatures that live out their entire lives in caves are white because they have no need for camouflage in the dark, nor do they need protection from the sun. Arha notices small white spiders in the Undertombs. Invite a small group of students who are interested in cave fauna to study the subject and make a written report to share with the class. They should include a bibliography of at least three sources of information. Some possible sources include *Cave Life* by Christiane Gunzi (New York: Dorling Kindersley, 1993), *Caves* by Stephen P. Kramer, (Minneapolis, MN: Carolrhoda Books, 1995), *Caves! Underground Worlds* by Jeanne Bendick (New York: Holt, 1995), http://www. npc.gov/ maca/cavelife.htm, and http://www.saske.sk/cave/sek/sekzool.html.

5. Of interest to some students will be the Christian Catacombs of Rome. In the first century, Rome's Christians did not have their own cemeteries and people were buried in common graveyards. From the second to fifth centuries, Christians buried their dead underground in the Christian Catacombs of Rome. Invite a pair of interested students to research this topic and to report what they learn to the class in an oral report. One source of information is *Subterranean Rome: Catacombs, Baths, Temples* by Portella Ivana Della (Cologne: Konemann, 2000).

6. When Ged and Tenar reach the sea, Ged feasts on raw mussels and Tenar refuses to try one. Depending on which part of the country you are from, mussels may or may not be a familiar dish. There are several families of freshwater mussels, and they are found in North America, South America, Europe, Asia, New Zealand, and Australia. Ask ESL students and others to share with the class descriptions of meals that they have had that include mussels. How big are mussels? What do they taste like? How are they cooked? These students might want to do more research on the topic. One source of information is http://coa.acnatsci.org/conchnet/uniowhat.htm. These students should share what they learn with their classmates in an oral report.

Extension Activities

1. Design a fancy bookmark, print it, and supply a few copies to the school media specialist to hand out in the library. Your bookmark should feature a catchphrase or interesting drawing from *The Tombs of Atuan* and give the title and author of the book so that library patrons will be interested in checking out and reading this book.

2. Suppose that Arha kept a diary. Make diary entries for those few days when she finds and imprisons a stranger underground. What is she feeling and thinking during this period of time? Does she mention Kossil in her diary? Share the diary entries with others for feedback. Do they agree or disagree that these would have been Arha's thoughts and feelings?

3. Write a front-page newspaper story that might appear the day after the earthquake that toppled the tombs of Atuan. Try to give this the tone of a factual story that would be written by an unemotional newspaper reporter. Remember that it will be assumed that Arha was killed in the earthquake, that no one on the outside knows about the stranger in the

tombs, and that Kossil was killed also. The story might speculate about replacements for the lost priestesses.

4. There is a good discussion of The Place where the tombs are located on page 17 of the book. There is also a rough map in the front matter of the book. Invite a pair of interested students to use these two sources to make a large map to post in the classroom showing the location of the temples, The Big House, the Small House, and so on.

5. The labyrinth is very significant in the Greek myth about Theseus and the Minotaur. A small group of students with a parent volunteer director might enjoy presenting a play on this topic to the class. One good source is "Theseus and the Minotaur" in *Greek Myths: 8 Short Plays for the Classroom* by John Rearick (New York: Scholastic Professional Books, 1997).

6. There is no illustration of the Painted Cave in the Undertombs, but the paintings on the walls are described on page 64. Invite interested students to make an illustration of the Painted Room based on this description. Hang these on a bulletin board.

How does reading *The Tombs of Atuan* and engaging in the various activities suggested above help students meet the 12 NCTE/IRA English Language Arts Standards?

1. *The Tombs of Atuan* meets Standard #1 by serving as an example of outstanding fiction.

2. *The Tombs of Atuan* meets Standard #2 because it is a representative work of the broad genre of fantasy.

3. Discussion questions #1 through #4 help students to comprehend and interpret text, and the vocabulary exercise increases knowledge of word meanings, helping students to meet Standard #3.

4. Extension activity #2, which suggests making entries in the form of Arha's diary of the time she was observing the stranger in the tombs, addresses Standard #4, which asks students to adjust written language and style to communicate effectively for different purposes.

5. Extension activity #3, which suggests that a student write up the earthquake that destroyed the tombs as a front-page factual story for a newspaper, helps meet Standard #5, which requires that students use different writing processes for different audiences and for a variety of purposes.

6. Research activity #2, which suggests that students write a report on King Minos and the Minotaur to share with the class, helps to meet Standard #6 by requiring students to apply their knowledge of language structure and language conventions to create a print text.

7. Extension activity #4, in which students use a map and a description in the book to create a map of The Place, helps to address Standard #7 by requiring students to gather, evaluate, and synthesize data from a variety of sources to communicate their discoveries.

8. Research activity #4 involving cave fauna helps to meet Standard #8 by encouraging students to use a variety of technological and information resources to carry out research and to communicate their knowledge.

9. Discussion question #5 about the conventional roles played by men and women in this book and the differences in stations in life of the priestesses and servants helps to address Standard #9 by allowing students to develop an understanding of and respect for diversity in social roles.

10. Research activity #6 asking students from different parts of the country and ESL students from different parts of the world to discuss the eating of mussels and their preparation in certain dishes helps address Standard #10, which asks students to use their first language that is not English to develop a deeper understanding of the curriculum.

11. Discussion question #3 allows students to pool their information knowledge in the form of a discussion group to compare the roles of Penthe and Arha. It helps meet Standard #11, which asks that students participate as knowledgeable, reflective, creative, and critical members of a literary community.

12. Extension activity #1 allows students to creatively design and prepare a bookmark on *The Tombs of Atuan* as a means of sharing their enthusiasm for this book with other potential readers. It addresses Standard #12, in which students are asked to use spoken, written, and visual language to persuade others.

A Wrinkle in Time

Madeleine L'Engle

New York: Bantam, Doubleday, Dell, 1962, ISBN 0-440-99805-0

Detailed Synopsis

One stormy night, Meg huddles beneath a blanket in her bed in the attic feeling miserable. She is doing badly at school and has been placed in the lowest level of her grade, and she was in a fight on the way home from school She can't sleep and finally gets up and goes to the kitchen. Her little brother, Charles Wallace, is there having some chocolate. Then their mother joins them.

Over sandwiches, Charles Wallace tells the others about Mrs. Whatsit and her two friends that he has met and who live in an old shingled house in the woods. Fortinbras growls and Mrs. Murry goes to investigate. She comes back in with Mrs. Whatsit, who says she has been blown off course. Meg fixes a sandwich for Mrs. Whatsit.

After eating her sandwich and emptying the water out of her boots, the strange Mrs. Whatsit leaves. But before she goes, she tells Mrs. Murry that "there is such a thing as a tesseract."

The next morning, Meg wonders if it was all a bad dream, but her mother assures her that they did have a visit from Mrs. Whatsit last night. Meg goes off to school and promptly gets into difficulties with her teacher and the principal. When she gets home from school, her little brother suggests that they go and see Mrs. Whatsit and find out more about "that tesseract thing" that so upset their mother. On their walk, they meet Calvin O'Keefe, a boy that Meg knows slightly from school. He is two years ahead of her and is on the basketball team.

Calvin explains that he sometimes gets a compulsion to do something, and it is a compulsion that has brought him here in the woods to this spot today. Charles Wallace immediately takes to Calvin and says "he is one of us." Meg is puzzled, but they all go on to see

Mrs. Whatsit. Inside the house, they find Mrs. Who and learn that Mrs. Whatsit is currently busy. She is sewing stolen sheets into ghost costumes. She advises them to go home because it's not yet time for action, but she assures them that she won't go without them. Puzzled, the children all go back to the Murry house.

At home, Mrs. Murry is working in her lab and also cooking a stew. Calvin calls his house to tell his mother he is staying at the Murrys' for supper. Calvin and Meg begin to do their homework. Calvin is surprised by how skilled Meg is at math. When the twins get home, they are pleased that a member of the basketball team is visiting them for supper. Calvin reads a bedtime story to Charles Wallace.

Calvin and Meg go for a walk. Meg tells Calvin about her father. She explains that he was sent away on a classified project. At first he wrote, but then his letters stopped coming. They don't know where he was sent or exactly what sort of scientific activity he is involved in. As they are talking, Charles Wallace comes out and says, "This is it." They learn that it is time for them to go off on an adventure to find their father.

Mrs. Whatsit, Mrs. Who, and Mrs. Which appear. Suddenly there is a terrible frenzy of wind. Meg feels all alone, lost in a void. Then Meg hears the voice of Charles Wallace, and finally Calvin materializes a bit at a time. They are all standing in a sunlit field. Mrs. Who, Mrs. Whatsit, and Mrs. Which are there, too. Calvin wants to know where they are and how they got there. Mrs. Which says they are on Uriel, and Mrs. Whatsit explains that they traveled by "tessering."

Then Mrs. Whatsit begins to change form. She becomes a beautiful creature, something like, but also completely unlike, a horse with a man's torso and a pair of wings. The three children climb on top of the new Mrs. Whatsit. They see wonderful things and are each given a special flower. They fly up into the clouds, and when the air gets too thin to breathe, Mrs. Whatsit tells them to use their flowers for oxygen.

They land with a view of one of Uriel's moons. Turning their backs on the moon, they face into the darkness and wait. Meg can see a dark and dreadful shadow. They travel downwards to where the air is not so thin and where they find Mrs. Who and Mrs. Which. Meg asks if the dark shadow that they saw is what her father is fighting. And Mrs. Which says, yes, that her father is behind the dark thing where they cannot see him. She explains that they must go behind the shadow. They will travel in the fifth dimension.

They whoosh off into a void, stop briefly under terrible pressure on a two-dimensional planet, and then whoosh off again through the fifth dimension to Orion's belt. When Meg says that her mother will worry about them, Mrs. Whatsit explains that if everything goes well, they will be back on Earth again five minutes before they left, and no one will have worried about them at all.

The planet they land on is gray and not very distinguished. They walk to a hill of stone and enter because the Happy Medium finds it easier to work within. Inside, they see a beautiful woman with a crystal ball. The children look in the crystal ball and see an evil shadow over the planet Earth. This makes everyone sad, but Mrs. Whatsit reminds them that many people on Earth and throughout the universe are fighting the forces of Evil. Mrs. Whatsit explains that their father is being held on a planet that has given in and is dominated by the power of Evil.

Then the medium shows them how light fights the darkness. In the crystal ball, they see a star fighting the darkness. And they learn that Mrs. Whatsit was once such a star herself. She gave up her life in the struggle with The Thing of Darkness. They take a quick look in the crystal ball at Calvin's mother and at Mrs. Murry before they kiss the medium goodbye and leave.

They zip off again and land in Camazotz. With its hills and trees, it reminds Meg of Earth. Mrs. Whatsit, Mrs. Who, and Mrs. Which explain they have to leave them. The children are on their own with only their gifts and their faults to help them. They are advised to go into town together and not to become separated.

The three children walk off toward town. They find lookalike houses with children playing in rhythm in front of them. The yards, houses, and flowers are all identical. Only one boy remains outside after the mothers call, and his ball bounces away. Charles Wallace carries the ball to his door and knocks. The little boy takes his ball, but the woman is frightened and slams the door.

Next they see a paper boy delivering papers in a very regular and mechanical way. The paperboy points out to them the way to Central Central Intelligence. The children make their way to the building and go inside. Someone reports that they are there, and they go into a room and meet a strange man with red eyes who says he has been expecting them.

The man begins talking to them, and Charles Wallace hits the man, thinking that perhaps he is a robot. Meg demands to see their father. It appears as if Charles is hypnotized. He turns pale, and the pupils of his eyes shrink. He begins walking toward the red-eyed man. Meg jumps on him and knocks her brother down. When he comes to, somewhat dazed by the fall, he behaves normally again.

The red-eyed man is angry with Meg and asks her to cooperate, but she is defiant. She also says they are hungry and requests food. Synthetic food is brought to them. It is disguised as a turkey dinner. In order to understand the red-eyed man and find their father, Charles Wallace again lets himself fall into a spell by looking into the red eyes. Charles Wallace instantly changes and falls under the influence of the red-eyed man, who seems to speak through him.

Meg and Calvin try to hold onto Charles, but he breaks away from Meg and three men remove Calvin from holding Charles. Charles keeps telling them that these people are their friends. The red-eyed man tells them that he is the Prime Coordinator.

Charles Wallace, walking stiffly, leads them away. Calvin and Meg follow. Calvin tries to communicate with Charles Wallace but fails. Charles Wallace says that if Calvin needs a father, he should turn to IT. Meg asks what IT is, but gets no answer. Charles takes them to an elevator, and they go up. He tells them that on Camazotz the individual has been eliminated and that Camazotz is one mind. It's IT. He threatens that if they don't behave, he will take Meg and Calvin to IT. And he refers to IT as the Happiest Sadist. He takes them down a corridor to a room, and they can see through the transparent wall. Inside is a column, and inside the column is Mr. Murry.

They cannot reach inside the column, and Meg's father does not seem to see or hear her. He has grown a beard and is looking upward as if in thought. Again Calvin speaks and tries to reach Charles Wallace, but he can't quite succeed. Meg asks Calvin to try to communicate with her father.

Meg remembers the glasses that Mrs. Who had given her to use as a last resort. She takes them out of her pocket, and although Charles Wallace tries to snatch them, she succeeds in putting them on and is able to walk through the transparent wall and through the column to her father. He puts his arms around her, but says he cannot see. She gives him the glasses, and then he is able to see Meg and recognizes Charles Wallace. Wearing the glasses, Mr. Murry picks up Meg and they are able to walk through the transparent column.

Mr. Murry tries to talk to Charles Wallace, but he cannot get through to him. Charles Wallace insists that they must go to IT. He leads Mr. Murry, Meg, and Calvin out of the building and down the street to a domed building. They feel a rhythmical pulsing and are sucked inside. The building is empty except for a round dais in the center. On the dais is IT, a disembodied brain.

The visitors stand in front of the brain. Mr. Murry shouts to Calvin not to give in. Charles Wallace's eyes are twirling in his head. Meg turns to her faults of anger, impatience, and stubbornness to save herself from being drawn into IT's power. To prevent herself from being caught up in IT's rhythm, Meg recites the Declaration of Independence, and she has a sudden realization that "like" and "equal" are not the same thing.

Then Meg feels herself being drawn into IT's power. Very faintly she hears her father's voice shouting, "The periodic table." Meg begins to recite the table aloud, but she feels herself being pulled into IT's power. She hears Calvin shout, "Tesser," and she is wrenched away on a painful, terrifying flight. When Meg wakes on Ixchel, she can hear her father and Calvin talking but is unable to speak or move herself. She feels as if she is frozen. Finally, although she cannot move, she manages to say a few words.

Hateful words and questions come tumbling out of Meg. Her father massages her hands and fingers, and she begins to have feeling in her limbs again. Three tall figures approach. These are creatures that walk upright. They have four arms and many tentacles in place of fingers. They have indentations in place of features. One of the creatures touches Meg, and she feels warmth. It picks her up. Calvin is the one among them best able to communicate with these creatures.

One of the Beasts explains that Meg needs special care because she is under the influence of the Black Thing, but Mr. Murry and Calvin simply need food and rest. They are taken away, and when Meg awakens she is warm and able to move again. A Beast talks to her and promises that they will help their three visitors. The creature says Meg should call her Aunt Beast, and they must eat and rest.

When they wake, Meg asks Aunt Beast if those on Ixchel are fighting the Black Thing and learns that they are. They rejoin Mr. Murry and Calvin. Meg gets angry and accusatory again, but she tries to describe for the Beasts Mrs. Who, Mrs. Whatsit, and Mrs. Which. And then, suddenly, Mrs. Who, Mrs. Whatsit, and Mrs. Which appear among them. Meg begs them to go and rescue Charles Wallace, but they explain that is not their way. Father asks to be taught more about how to tesser so that he can go back. They say he will only become lost. Calvin offers to go, but they say he will simply be drawn into IT's power.

Then Meg speaks up and says she realizes that she has to be the one to go and rescue Charles Wallace. Her father and Calvin do not want Meg to go, and Meg doesn't want to go either, but there is simply no other choice. Mrs. Who, Mrs. Which, and Mrs. Whatsit give her special gifts to help her, and then Mrs. Which takes her back to Camazotz.

Left alone once more in Camazotz, Meg sets off through the dark streets. She reaches the building where IT is and is sucked inside. Charles Wallace crouches near the brain. Meg does not know what to do. How can she fight? What is it that she has that IT does not have? Suddenly it comes to her. She has love. She speaks her love for Charles Wallace, and slowly he slips out of the spell and comes running to her.

They are quickly whisked back to planet Earth. Cal and Mr. Murry are already there. Mrs. Murry and the twins come rushing to meet them, and Mrs. Who, Mrs. Which, and Mrs. Whatsit are with them briefly. There is great joy that all have been rescued.

List of Major Characters: Margaret Murry (Meg), the oldest child in the Murry family; Charles Wallace, her youngest brother; Sandy and Dennys, her twin younger brothers;

Mrs. Murry, her mother; Mr. Murry, her father; Calvin O'Keefe, a friend; three strangers, Mrs. Whatsit, Mrs. Who, and Mrs. Which; a red-eyed man on Camazotz called the Prime Coordinator; the brain called IT on Camazotz; and Aunt Beast from the planet Ixchel.

Vocabulary: Look up these words on the page number indicated in parentheses to see how the word was used in this book. Then write an original sentence using the word and indicating that you understand its meaning.

prodigious (8) _____

supine (17) _____

tractable (23) _____

belligerent (23) _____

inadvertently (26) _____

dilapidated (30) _____

diverting (118) _____

pinioned (126) _____

connotations (127) _____

annihilate (130) _____

sinister (132) _____

intoned (133) _____

Comprehension Questions

1. When the story opens, it is stormy and three of the characters gather in the kitchen to eat and drink. What special kind of sandwich does Charles Wallace make for his mother?
2. What enabled Mrs. Whatsit to identify the house as Charles Wallace's house?
3. Why had Mrs. Whatsit taken Mrs. Buncombe's sheets?
4. In what two science fields does Mrs. Murry hold degrees?
5. What "typical props" greeted visitors who knocked on the door of Mrs. Whatsit's house?
6. Mrs. Whatsit explains that they don't travel at the speed of light or the speed of anything. How do they travel?
7. Mrs. Whatsit gives each of the three children a flower before taking off into the clouds. For what purpose are these flowers used?
8. Exactly how old (in Earth time) is Mrs. Whatsit?
9. What gift did Mrs. Who give to Meg to use on Camazotz as a last resort?
10. Synthetic meals on Camazotz were disguised to look and taste like Earth food. What kind of meal was the first one given to the children by the red-eyed man?

Answers: 1) Charles Wallace makes his mother a liverwurst and cream cheese sandwich. 2) Mrs. Whatsit identifies Charles Wallace's house by the smell. 3) Mrs. Whatsit took the sheets because she needed them. 4) Mrs. Murry has degrees in biology and bacteriology. 5) Visitors to Mrs. Whatsit's house were greeted by creaking rusty door hinges, the caw of a black crow, the rat-a-tat of a woodpecker, and a scuttling rat. 6) They "tesser" or "wrinkle." 7) The flowers that the children carry supply them with oxygen. 8) Mrs. Whatsit is 2,379,152,497 years, 8 months, and 3 days old. 9) Mrs. Who gives Meg glasses to use as a last resort. 10) It is disguised as a turkey dinner with potatoes, dressing, peas, sweet potatoes, and gravy.

Discussion Questions

1. If someone invited you to go to a newly discovered galaxy, would you go? Why, or why not? What are the factors that would lead you to want to go? What factors might hold you back?

2. Mrs. Which says, "The only way to cope with something deadly serious is to try to treat it a little lightly." Discuss this statement. Do you agree with it?

3. On page 93 of *A Wrinkle in Time,* Mrs. Whatsit says that she will give each of the three children a talisman to help them on their dangerous mission. ESL students and students with knowledge of various cultures and backgrounds may be familiar with different sorts of talismans that are used as "good luck" charms. Encourage a group of children to discuss their knowledge of talismans from different cultures. They may wish to read a section of a story in which a talisman is mentioned.

4. Charles explains, while in a trancelike state, that no one is allowed to suffer on Camazotz. If someone gets ill, they are annihilated. They do not call this murder. Discuss this approach to health care by a state. Is it murder?

5. There are some similarities between *A Wrinkle in Time* and *The Giver* in that "the state" makes important decisions for the benefit of the citizens. Bring together students who have read both books and discuss how life in the world of *The Giver* and life on Camazotz are the same and different. Individualism suffers in both places. If you had to live in one of these two worlds, which would you choose, and why?

6. While under his trancelike spell, Charles insists that the reason things are so good on Camazotz is that everyone is alike. He maintains that differences are the source of problems. There appear to be strong guidelines for the behavior of men and women. All the mothers, for example, dress alike and come to the door at exactly the same time to call their children to come in. Only men seem to be coming home from work. Do you think that differences are a source of problems, a source of strength, or both? Discuss the effects of stereotypical sex roles in a society.

7. Meg's father had several nicknames for her, and when he uses these after his long absence, their use brings tears to Meg's eyes. He calls her Megaparsec and Megatron. Look up the meanings of these words. Discuss why they appear to be especially appropriate nicknames for Meg. Are there relatives or friends you know who have particularly appropriate nicknames? What are these, and why are they appropriate?

8. Sometimes Mrs. Who interrupts the action of the story with a long quotation. She does this in Chapter 12 on page 189. Look up the quotation that begins with "The foolishness of God . . ." Discuss the meaning and importance to the story of this quotation.

Research Activities

1. At one point, the three children find themselves in Orion's Belt. Invite two interested students to write a report about the star constellation Orion, using at least three sources of

information and presenting what they learn to the class. Possible sources of information include *Janice Pratt Van Cleave's Constellations for Every Kid: Easy Activities that Make Learning Science Fun* by Janice Pratt Van Cleave (New York: John Wiley, 1997), *Orion, the Hunter* by Necia H. Apfel (New York: Clarion Books, 1995), and E.M. Hans's *Constellations* (Austin, TX: Raintree Steck-Vaughn, 2001). Also see http://www.astro.wisc.edu/~dolan/constellations/constellations/Orion.html and http://www.spacekids.com/skywatch/eyes_kies_000124.html for additional information.

2. Mrs. Whatsit explains that many people on Earth have been fighting the battle against Evil. She names Copernicus as one of the fighters from the planet Earth. Invite a pair of students to learn more about Copernicus and make an oral report from their findings to the class. During the report, students might want to play a part of the audiotape *Galileo and the Stargazers* by Jim Weiss (Charlottesville, VA: Greathall Productions, 1999, 1 sound cassette, 60 minutes). Possible sources of information include http://www-gap.dcs.st-nd.ac.uk/~history/Mathematicians/Copernicus.html and http://www.blupete.com/Literature/Biographies/Science/Copernicus.htm. Additional information is available in *Copernicus: Founder of Modern Astronomy* by Catherine M. Andronik (Beverley Heights, NJ: Enslow Publishers, 2002) and in Stuart R. Kallen's *Exploring the Origins of the Universe* (New York: Twenty First Century Books, 1997).

3. IT turns out to be a disembodied brain. A small group of interested students may want to present information on the brain to the class. They might plan their presentation and write it in the form of a moderator holding a television panel discussion show. For a piece of this presentation, they might want to show part of the videocassette *All about the Brain* (Wynnewood, PA: Schlessinger Media, 2001). Members of the panel can be "experts" on some aspect of the brain. Notes to assist them in making their contribution to the discussion should be written on note cards to which they can refer. Sources of information include http://www.med.harvard.edu/AANLIB/homre.html and http:// www.vh.org/Providers/Textbooks/BrainAnatomy/BrainAnatomy.html. Useful books include *When the Brain Dies First* by Margaret O. Hyde (New York: Franklin Watts, 2000) and *Brain and Nerves* by Steve Parker (Brookfield, CT: Copper Beech Books, 1998).

4. Ask a group of interested students to make up a chart for Meg, Charles Wallace, and Calvin. List the strengths and weaknesses of each of these three characters on their charts. Then poll the students in the class. Keep track of whether you are asking questions of boys or girls. Find out which is the favorite character of the boys who were polled and which is the favorite character of the girls who were polled. Also ask, "If you were going on a dangerous space adventure, which of these three characters would you choose to go with you?" Enter the data on a bar graph and report your findings to the class. Were their significant differences in the responses of girls compared with the responses of boys?

5. At one point in the story, Calvin asks who have been Earth's fighters against the Powers of Darkness. One of those who is named is Bach. A small group of students may wish to make a class presentation on Bach. They might consult with the school music educator for advice on a short selection of some of his music to play for the class. And they should share in an oral report highlights of his life and musical achievements. Possible sources of information include *Introducing Bach* by Roland Wernon (Philadelphia: Chelsea House Publishers, 2001), *Johann Sebastian Bach* by Mike Venezia (New York:

Children's Press, 1998), and *Bach: Meet the Musicians* (New York: LLC, 2000, 1 video-cassette, 52 minutes) with Dennis Kobray as Johann Sebastian Bach. Information is available at http://www.classical.net/music/comp.lst/bachjs.html as well as at http://www.jsbach.org/biography.html.

6. On page 82 of the book, Michelangelo is named as a fighter against the Powers of Darkness. A small group of students may wish to make a class presentation on Michelangelo. They might consult with the school art educator for help in obtaining a few prints of some of his work to show to the class. And they should share in an oral report highlights of his life and artistic achievements. Possible sources of information include http:www.ibiblio.org/wm/paint/auth/michelangelo and http:www.michelangelo.com/buon/bio-index2.html. Additional information can be found in *Michaelangelo* by Diane Stanley (New York: Morrow Junior Books, 2000) and in *Michelangelo* by Gabriella DiCagno (New York: Peter Bedrick Books, 1996).

Extension Activities

1. At one point in the book, Mrs. Whatsit is vividly described as being dressed as an old tramp. At another point she is described after she changes into a creature that is horselike with a human torso and wings. Invite interested students to use one of these images in designing a poster to encourage others to read *A Wrinkle in Time*. With permission, hang it in the school library media center.

2. Toward the end of the book, Mrs. Whatsit compares human life to a sonnet. It has a strict form, but within that form, there is freedom. Suggest that interested students read some of the sonnets of William Shakespeare and John Donne, and that they then try to write an original sonnet in this strict poetic form (English or Italian sonnet) on a topic that they choose. Post their completed works on a classroom bulletin board.

3. Most students will have seen rules of conduct that are often posted near public swimming pools. These might include: 1) No diving except from the diving board, 2) No running near the pool, and 3) No food or beverages allowed in the pool area. Ask students on their own to make up ten rules of conduct for children living in Camazotz. Discuss, compare, and post the rules that the students come up with.

4. Mrs. Whatsit, Mrs. Who, and Mrs. Which have distinctive ways of talking. Write a page of dialogue to come just before the last page of the book, where these three make a farewell speech to Calvin and the Murrys assembled in the garden before they rush off on their next mission. Be sure that each has dialogue representative of her usual speech patterns.

5. *The Tempest* by William Shakespeare is quoted more than once in the book. A small group of students, with help from a parent volunteer, may want to read this play and prepare a short scene to present to the class. Very simple props and costumes will enhance the production.

6. What do you suppose Charles Wallace Murry will do in the course of his life? Have a few interested students read the format for the obituaries that appear in your area newspaper. Then have them make up a life of Charles Wallace Murry and highlight the major events by writing it in an obituary style. When and where did he die? How old was he? Had he married and had children? What career(s) did he pursue? What was his cause of death? These might be shared in a class bulletin board display.

How does reading *A Wrinkle in Time* and engaging in the various activities suggested above help students meet the 12 NCTE/IRA English Language Arts Standards?

1. *A Wrinkle in Time* meets Standard #1 by serving as an example of outstanding fiction.
2. *A Wrinkle in Time* meets Standard #2 because it is a representative work of the broad genre of fantasy.
3. Discussion questions #2, #3, #4, #6, and #8 help students to comprehend and interpret text, and the vocabulary exercise increases knowledge of word meanings, helping students to meet Standard #3.
4. Extension activity #3, which suggests writing out the rules of conduct for children living on the planet Camazotz in the form of ten posted swimming pool rules, addresses Standard #4, which asks students to adjust written language and style to communicate effectively for different purposes.
5. Research activity #3, which suggests that a group of students use note cards to prepare for a television panel discussion on the brain, helps to meet Standard #5, which requires that students use different writing processes for different audiences and for a variety of purposes.
6. Extension activity #4, which suggests that students write a page of dialogue for the last chapter featuring the speech patterns of Mrs. Who, Mrs. Which, and Mrs. Whatsit, helps to meet Standard #6 by requiring students to apply their knowledge of language structure and language conventions to create a print text.
7. Research activity #4, in which students conduct a poll and prepare bar graphs to present to the class, helps address Standard #7, which asks students to gather, evaluate, and synthesize data that they communicate.
8. Research activity #2 involving the contributions of Copernicus to the study of astronomy helps to meet Standard #8 by encouraging students to use a variety of technological and information resources to carry out research and to communicate their knowledge.
9. Discussion question #6 about the conventional roles played by men and women in this book helps to address Standard #9 by allowing students to develop an understanding of and respect for diversity in social roles.
10. Discussion question #3 asking ESL students and others interested in different cultures to discuss the use of talismans, or good luck charms, in literature helps address Standard #10, which asks students to use their first language that is not English to develop a deeper understanding of the curriculum.
11. Discussion question #5 allows students to pool their information knowledge in the form of a book discussion group and compare and contrast the role of the individual versus the state in *A Wrinkle in Time* and in *The Giver*. It helps meet Standard #11, which asks that students participate as knowledgeable, reflective, creative, and critical members of a literary community.
12. Extension activity #1 allows students to creatively prepare a poster as a means of sharing their enthusiasm for this book with other potential readers. It addresses Standard #12, in which students are asked to use spoken, written, and visual language to persuade others.

Ella Enchanted

Gail Carson Levine

New York: HarperCollins, 1997, ISBN 0-06-027510-3

Detailed Synopsis

This fantasy is a version of the old Cinderella story. When Ella is born, the fairy, Lucinda, who likes to come to birthday and wedding celebrations, gives her the gift of obedience. Right after bestowing the gift, Lucinda says, "Now stop crying, child," and Ella stops. From then on, Ella has to obey any direct order she is given.

Ella's mother, Lady Eleanor, tries without success to remove the enchantment. Ella learns not to tell anyone about her curse of obedience, because if she does so, they may control her. Her kind mother seldom commands her, and Ella's father is almost always away on business as a merchant.

When Ella is almost 15, she and her mother catch cold. Mandy, their cook, makes a curing soup. Ella obediently eats hers and feels fine the next day. Ella's mother picks out the unicorn hairs from her soup before drinking it, and she is very ill the next day.

Lady Eleanor dies. Ella cries so hard at the funeral that she is sent away from the guests by her father. After weeping for a time beneath a tree, Ella meets Prince Charmont and talks with him. Ella and her father ride home from the funeral in a carriage to entertain the funeral guests. Among these are Dame Olga and her two daughters, Hattie and Olive. Ella politely shows the girls around the house and watches as they eat lots of food, but she doesn't like them. That night while cleaning up, Ella learns from the cook, Mandy, that Mandy is really Ella's fairy godmother.

Mandy explains that she doesn't do big magic, only little magic. She also tells Ella that Ella has a drop of fairy blood in her and that like all fairies, Ella will have very small feet. Ella always seems to be especially clumsy around her father, who finally decides to send her away to a finishing school for young ladies. It is the same school that Dame Olga's daughters will attend.

On the day she is to leave for school, Ella goes to the royal menagerie outside the huge palace. There she meets Prince Charmont again. They eat apples and visit the exotic birds that Ella likes. She is able to mimic the languages that the parrots speak. Then they go to visit the ogres. When the ogre commands, "Come to me and bring the child," Ella starts to obey, but the prince commands her to stop, and he rescues the toddler gnome who is in harm's way.

Ella and the prince take the little gnome to his grandmother and others who are searching for him. The little gnome goes willingly with Ella largely because she parrots some Gnomic words she has learned from the birds, and this makes the child feel safe and comfortable. When the gnome's mother comes to thank them, she tells Ella that when she looks into the future she sees that Ella will go on a quest. She warns Ella to be on guard against three figures that are close to her but are not her friends.

Ella leaves for finishing school in a coach with Dame Olga's daughters, Hattie and Olive. During the coach ride, Hattie orders Ella to give her the precious necklace Ella is wearing that had belonged to her mother. Ella is forced to obey and Hattie realizes how convenient Ella's obedience will be to her. Olive orders Ella to give her money, and she does. After the two sisters fall asleep, Ella begins to read the magic book that Mandy gave her as a farewell gift.

The pages of the book keep changing. Sometimes they contain stories. Sometimes there are scenes of home. Ella sees Mandy, the cook, and Prince Charmont in the book. The rest of the journey is miserable for Ella, who is commanded to do everything Hattie wishes, including giving up her food. On the last day, the carriage is chased by ogres, but the girls escape.

At the finishing school, the girls are met by the headmistress, Madame Edith. A sewing class is in session, and Ella quickly makes one friend, Areida, who begins to teach her the Ayorthorian language Because Ella gets so little sewing done, she is sent to her room without supper as a punishment.

That night, Areida comes to Ella's room ahead of the other girls and brings her a roll to eat. When the others go to sleep, Ella opens her magical book again. She finds there a letter from Mandy. The letter tells her that Simon, the parrot man, has given her a bird that Mandy will keep for her, and that Prince Charmont brought Ella a centaur colt, named Apple, which he is keeping for her.

Although she does not like it, Ella is obedient and begins to fit into the routine of the finishing school, learning manners and how to sing, dance, and sew. Ella enjoys practicing languages and even begins to learn some Ogrese. Only Areida is a comfort to her. When Hattie orders Ella to end her friendship with Areida, Ella is desperate.

That night, Ella reads more letters in her magic book and decides to run away from the finishing school and to join her father in time to attend a giant's wedding, where she hopes to see the fairy Lucinda and beg her to remove the curse of obedience.

Running away from the finishing school on her quest to find Lucinda and get rid of her curse, Ella meets friendly elves. They send her on her journey with food and a pony to ride. But Ella runs into a group of eight ogres. They eat her horse and are about to eat her, too. Ella mimics the soothing, persuasive voices of the ogres and lulls them to sleep. Then Prince Charmont, who is on border patrol, arrives with some knights.

Ella uses her facility with languages to imitate and charm the ogres into falling asleep again so that Prince Charmont and the knights can take them captive. Then Prince Charmont sends Ella on her way with Sir Stephan as her escort. These two finally meet a giant, who takes them to the wedding of Uaaxee's daughter. There Ella manages to see Lucinda and asks to have "more mettle" instead of being so obedient. But Lucinda insists obedience is a marvelous gift and a happy blessing.

Ella sees her father and learns he has lost most of his money. She rides in a carriage with him and discovers that he wants to marry her off to someone rich. When they get home, he orders Mandy to serve magic mushrooms that are a love potion. He invites to dinner the old Earl of Wolleck, and Ella does fall in love with him, but her father rejects him as a suitor because he isn't rich enough.

Ella's father decides to marry Dame Olga, who doesn't know he has lost his fortune. They are married in a week, and at the wedding, Lucinda gives the couple the gift of eternal love. After the wedding, Ella and Prince Charmont race about upstairs looking for a secret passage. They don't find the passage but do find a pair of glass slippers that fit Ella. The two have a wonderful time dancing to the music and sliding down the banister.

When Prince Charmont comes back the next day to see Ella, Dame Olga and Hattie banish Ella to her room and order her not to come see the Prince. By reading in her magic book, Ella learns that Prince Charmont thinks Ella is angry with him and avoiding him. Ella writes a letter to him and directs it to the royal family in Ayortha since the Prince is going there on a yearlong visit.

Because of Lucinda's enchantment, Ella's father loves his wife, but he can't stand to be around her, so he leaves as soon as possible after the wedding. Then Dame Olga moves Ella from her nice room to a tiny room in the servant's wing. Dame Olga and her daughters begin to treat Ella as a servant. Ella sends a letter to her father urging him to return home and rescue her from this ill treatment.

Ten days later, a letter arrives from Prince Charmont, by way of Mandy, followed by other letters, but Ella's father does not write. In one of his letters, Charmont finally professes his love for Ella, and rather than agree to become his wife and become a dangerous burden because of her curse of obedience, which could allow some evil person to command her to do the prince harm, Ella sends Prince Charmont a letter, pretending it is from Hattie. In the letter, she describes how Ella has eloped with a rich man.

When Mandy learns what Ella has written to protect the prince from having an enchanted wife, she summons Lucinda. She challenges Lucinda to try out her own gifts and to learn how it feels to be turned into a squirrel for three months or to have to be obedient for three months. Mandy's hope is that Lucinda will become enlightened and then lift the curse. Finally a letter comes from Ella's father. He says he will not return, but he will try to find Ella a rich husband.

Months later, when Prince Charmont comes home, three royal balls are scheduled to welcome him back, and it is rumored he will soon pick a wife. Lucinda returns from her experiences of being a squirrel and being an obedient human. She is much wiser but refuses to do big magic again and won't remove the curse of obedience from Ella.

Ella decides to go to the balls wearing her mother's old gown and masked so she won't be recognized. Lucinda is summoned to help and creates a magnificent coach with horses and footman, all made from a pumpkin, mice, and lizards. Ella is warned to leave the ball by midnight.

Ella attends all three balls and the prince is much taken with her. At the third ball, Hattie tears away Ella's mask, and the prince recognizes her. Ella flees. She and Mandy are going to run away, but the prince and his followers come to the house. The prince asks Ella to marry him. In order to protect him, Ella wages an internal battle not to be obedient, refuses to marry the prince, and in this way breaks the enchantment.

The prince learns that Ella loves him and only wrote the letter about elopement in an effort to protect him. Once she is free of the spell and the possible harm she might bring on the prince, Ella agrees to marry Prince Charmont. Ella and the prince marry a month later. With Mandy acting as their cook and godmother to their children, Prince Charmont and Ella live happily every after.

List of Major Characters: Ella, the major character, is a teenage girl. Her mother, Lady Eleanor, dies, and her father, Sir Peter, remarries Dame Olga. Dame Olga has two daughters, Hattie and Olive. Mandy is a cook in Sir Peter's house and is also a fairy godmother. Lucinda is a fairy who gives to Ella the gift (or curse) of obedience. Prince Charmont eventually marries Ella. Areida is a friend Ella meets at finishing school.

Vocabulary: A list of words follows. A page number in parentheses indicates on which page the word appears in the story. Read the sentence to see how the word was used in the story. Look up each word in a dictionary and study its definitions. Then write an original sentence using the word to demonstrate that you understand its meaning.

interrogated (3) _____

conniver (31) _____

voluminous (33) _____

menagerie (40) _____

impertinence (65) _____

posturing (31) _____

vouchsafed (86) _____

topiary (88) _____

diverted (119) _____

gullible (136) _____

irrefutable (137) _____

elude (198) _____

Comprehension Questions

1. What trophy does Ella take with her when she runs away from the finishing school?
2. What does Ella notice that is special about the elf trader's teeth?
3. Of the pieces of beautiful pottery that the elves show Ella, which one is her favorite?
4. How does Prince Charmont prevent himself from being charmed by the lulling voices of the ogres?
5. How does Ella describe the voice of the singing mistress?

6. Why does Ella have trouble eating at the giant's wedding party?
7. What do the giants pantomime at the wedding ceremony?
8. Just before his wedding to Dame Olga, why does Sir Peter keep everyone away from the manor?
9. To get even with her stepmother for having worked her so hard before a banquet, what does Ella do to the trout that is served to Dame Olga?
10. Although she leaves the first two balls before the stroke of midnight, why does Ella want to stay later at the third ball?

Answers: 1) Ella takes Hattie's wig with her when she runs away from finishing school. 2) Ella notices that the elf's teeth are pale green. 3) Ella's favorite piece of elfin pottery is a stirrup cup of a wolf's head. 4) Prince Charmont protects himself from the seductive voices of the ogres by putting wax in his ears. 5) She says the singing mistress has a voice as thin as a string. 6) The silverware is too big. 7) They pantomime their entire lives together until death. 8) Sir Peter doesn't want anyone to notice that all the furnishings in the manor are being sold off to pay his debts. 9) She sprinkles ground passiflora on the trout with the parsley, causing Dame Olga to fall asleep before the meal ends. 10) Ella wants to stay late to hear the prince sing.

Discussion Questions

1. On page 50, Hattie comments, "I would never embrace a cook." What does this comment tell the reader about the very different ways in which Hattie and Ella view and treat the people around them?
2. Ella and a little gnome almost come to harm when Ella is commanded by an ogre to come to him and bring the child. Have students discuss whether such dangerous creatures should be kept in the menagerie. Since ogres are capable of charming people, their presence constitutes a danger. Invite a pair of interested students to draw up a serious petition to King Jerrold, using formal language and using the best arguments presented during the discussion to request that the ogres be removed from the menagerie.
3. Which of Dame Olga's daughters, Hattie or Olive, do you think is the most difficult for Ella to endure? Why?
4. Ella's father has made and lost a lot of money in business. From what you learn of him in the story, would you think he will be a success or a failure as a businessman in the future? Why?
5. Why do you think that Dame Olga and Ella's father do not take part in Ella's royal wedding?
6. Some of the creatures in the story speak in strange languages, and what they say is represented with letters such as, "Vib ol pess waddo." Do you think this adds to the story or detracts from it? Why?
7. Lucinda always believes that the gifts she gives people are wonderful. When she is forced to try them out, she learns more about them firsthand. Do you think by the end of the story that she has reformed or not? What details from the story support your position?
8. After marrying, Ella refuses to take the title of princess. Instead she takes the titles of Court Linguist and Cook's Helper. Do you think this made her popular or unpopular with her subjects? Why?

Research Activities

1. Among the many variants that exist of the Cinderella story, there are several Native American versions. Two that are well known are Algonquin. These are *The Rough-Face Girl* by Rafe Martin (New York: G. P. Putnam's Sons, 1992) and *Little Firefly* by Terri Cohlene (Mahwah, N.J.: Watermill Press, 1990). Invite a pair of students to find these variant versions of the Cinderella tale, read them, and share with the class orally the main ways in which they are like or different from the typical Cinderella story. In what ways do these stories reflect Native American beliefs?

2. There are many excellent sites on the Internet for recipes. Have an interested group of students research the Web for some simple recipes, and choose and type them into a Fantasy Meal Menu to share with the class. There should be a main dish, salad, side dishes, beverage, and dessert. One receipe for Fairy Godmother Rice is at http://sidedish.all-recipes.com/AZ/FiryGdmthrRic.asp. The recipes included may also be old favorites that have been given a fantasy-appropriate name by the menu committee. As a special event, and with parental help, one or more items from the Fantasy Meal Menu could be prepared for the class.

3. Ella attends the wedding of a giant in this story. There are many different kinds of giants, but among the most famous is the Cyclops of ancient Greece. Invite a pair of interested students to find out what they can about the Cyclops and make an oral report on what they learn. Among the possible sources of information is *Giants! Stories from around the World* by Paul Robert Walker (San Diego, CA: Harcourt Brace, 1996). An Internet site for the version of the Cyclops story by Euripides is http://classics.met.edu/Euripides/cyclops.html.

4. Several times in this book, Ella rides in a carriage. Even today, elaborate carriages are used for special state occasions such as the coronations of kings and queens. Invite a pair of interested students to research royal carriages, to find photos of them in books and magazines or on the Internet, and to bring these to class to share. The following sites are among those that show pictures of famous royal carriages: http://www.royalinsight.gov.uk/19904/gallery_online/gallery_online_coach-parade.html (for a picture of the carriage used by Queen Elizabeth of England), http://www.nicholasandalexandra.com/carriage.html (for a picture of the carriage used by Nicholas and Alexandra of Russia), and http://www.khm.at/system2E.html?staticE/page331.htm (for a picture of the carriage used by Empress Caroline Augusta of Hungary).

5. A group of students might want to research the names of modern queens and kings. In carrying out this research, they may use encyclopedias, magazines, books, and the Internet. Place a map of the world on a bulletin board. Use pins and yarn to go from a country of the world to three-by-five cards around the edge of the map. On each three-by-five card, have students list the name of the country and the name of the present king and/or queen. How many current monarchs can the class find?

Extension Activities

1. Ella reclaims her mother's necklace from Hattie and wears it on her wedding day. This scene is not shown in the book. Have a pair of students write this scene with dialogue. Make Hattie syrupy-sweet and eager to please Ella, knowing that she will soon marry the prince. When the scene is complete, have the two students read the dialogue to the class.

2. Invite a pair of interested students to write a new short chapter for the book. In this chapter, have Princess Ella summon Areida to visit her in the palace. How would they act toward one another, and what would they have to say to each other after their long separation?

3. Except for the cover picture, this book is without illustrations. Have interested class members make bookmarks to encourage others to read this book. On each bookmark, include a drawing of a scene from the book. Duplicate one or more bookmark designs, and, with permission, place these in the library to advertise this book.

4. In the book *Poppy,* Poppy is very obedient, always doing exactly what her father or her boyfriend want her to do. Ella is also obedient because of her enchantment. Invite students who have read both of these books to discuss the trait of obedience. Do they regard it as a blessing or a curse? Why?

5. The Cinderella or rags-to-riches story is common in many cultures. Interested ESL students in the class and others should search to see what some of these many Cinderella stories are like. These students should bring in a variety of versions, share the stories, and compare and contrast the various versions. Possibilities include *Tattercoats, Cap o' Rushes, The Princess and the Golden Shoes,* and many other versions that are Korean, German, French, Italian, Norwegian, Chinese, Irish, Serbian, Russian, Slavic, and so on. In what ways do elements in each story reflect aspects of its native country?

6. Visit the Internet, where there is a reader's theater edition of *The Hidden One,* a Native American Cinderella legend retold by Aaron Shepard. Have a group of interested students present this story to the class as reader's theater. It can be found at http:// www.aaronshep. com/rt/RTE12.html.

How does reading *Ella Enchanted* and engaging in the various activities suggested above help students meet the 12 NCTE/ IRA English Language Arts Standards?

1. *Ella Enchanted* meets Standard #1 by serving as an example of outstanding fiction.
2. *Ella Enchanted* meets Standard #2 because it is a representative work of the broad genre of fantasy and of the sub-group of fairy tales as fantasy.
3. Discussion questions #7 and #8 help students to comprehend and interpret text, and the vocabulary exercise increases knowledge of word meanings, helping students to meet Standard #3.
4. Extension activity #1, which suggests writing a dialogue in which Hattie is extremely sweet to Ella knowing she will soon be a powerful princess of the land, addresses Standard #4, which asks students to adjust written language and style to communicate effectively for different purposes.
5. Discussion question #2, which involves drawing up a petition outlining the dangers of ogres and requesting their removal from the royal menagerie, helps meet Standard #5, which requires that students use different writing processes for different audiences and for a variety of purposes.
6. Extension activity #2, which suggests that students write a new chapter in which Ella and her friend, Areida, meet again after a long absence, helps to meet Standard #6 by requiring students to apply their knowledge of language structure and language conventions to create a print text.

7. Research activity #3, which involves giants and the Cyclops, helps to address Standard #7 by requiring students to gather, evaluate, and synthesize data from a variety of sources.

8. Research activity #5 involving finding information about current queens and kings active in the twenty-first century helps to meet Standard #8 by encouraging students to use a variety of technological and information resources to carry out research and to communicate their knowledge.

9. Discussion question #1 about the conventional roles of servants as seen by Hattie and by Ella helps to address Standard #9 by allowing students to develop an understanding of and respect for diversity in social roles.

10. Extension activity #5 asking ESL and other students to find rags-to-riches Cinderella stories from their own cultures and to compare and contrast them helps address Standard #10, which asks students to use their first language that is not English to develop a deeper understanding of the curriculum.

11. Extension activity #4 allows students to pool their information about the types of obedience shown by the main characters in *Poppy* and in *Ella Enchanted* in the form of a book discussion group. It helps meet Standard #11, which asks that students participate as knowledgeable, reflective, creative, and critical members of a literary community.

12. Extension activity #3 allows students to creatively select and prepare a series of bookmark illustrations as a means of sharing their enthusiasm for this book with other potential readers. It addresses Standard #12, in which students are asked to use spoken, written, and visual language to persuade others.

The Lion, the Witch and the Wardrobe

C.S. Lewis

New York: HarperCollins Publisher, 1994, ISBN 0-06-023481-4

Detailed Synopsis

This is Book Two of the seven books of *The Chronicles of Narnia.* It tells the story of what happens to Peter, Susan, Edmund, and Lucy when they are sent away from London during World War II because of the air raids. The children go to the country to stay in the house of an old Professor. The Professor has a housekeeper called Mrs. Macready. Mrs. Macready sometimes shows the house to visitors, and she asks the children to keep out from under foot when she is busy in this way.

One morning when the children awaken, it is raining, so they go off exploring through the big house. They come to a room that has no furniture except for a big wardrobe. The other children leave the room, but Lucy steps inside the wardrobe to feel the soft fur coats that are stored there. And a moment later, she finds herself in a wood where snowflakes are falling.

Lucy comes upon a faun. He is like a man from the waist up, but he has a goat's legs and feet. The faun carries an umbrella in one arm and several parcels in the other. The faun introduces himself as Mr. Tumnus and explains that they are in Narnia. He admits he's never met a real girl before.

Mr. Tumnus invites Lucy to tea in his cave. He tells her stories and plays music on a strange little flute. Then he begins to cry and says he is in the service of the White Witch. Mr. Tumnus explains that the White Witch is the cause of it always being winter in Narnia. He confesses to trying to kidnap Lucy to take her to the Witch, but he repents and leads Lucy back to the lamppost where he first saw her. From there, she finds her way back to the wardrobe and rejoins the other children.

The children don't believe Lucy when she tells of her adventures. When they all go back to the wardrobe and look at it, it appears to be quite ordinary. The others tease Lucy, but she insists she is telling the truth. Several days later when it's raining again, the children play hide and go seek. Lucy ducks into the wardrobe and Edmund follows her.

To his surprise, Edmund finds himself in a snowy wood. There is no sign of Lucy. He hears sleigh bells and sees a sledge (sleigh) with reindeer being driven by a fat dwarf. On the sledge is a great lady. The sledge stops and Edmund meets the Queen or White Witch. The Queen invites Edmund to join her on the sledge and offers him something hot to drink. She also gives him Turkish delights.

Edmund loves the candy and wishes he could have more. The Queen tells him that he will have more Turkish delights if he brings the other three children to her house to visit. She shows him the way to the lamppost, and then she leaves. Shortly after, Lucy appears, having finished her tea with Mr. Tumnus, and she and Edmund go back into the wardrobe. Lucy is glad that this time Edmund will be able to back up her story about visiting Narnia.

When they reunite with the other children, Edmund looks very superior and denies that there is a country to be found by entering through the wardrobe. Lucy runs off to cry. Peter and Susan decide to share with the Professor the fact that there is something wrong with Lucy. They tell him the whole story.

The Professor asks if Lucy's story might be true. He suggests that they assume that Lucy is telling the truth and that the other world may have a separate time of its own, so that however long you stay there, it doesn't take up any of our time. His final surprising suggestion is that instead of worrying about Lucy, "We might all try minding our own business."

For a time, no one speaks any more about the wardrobe. But one day some visitors come to look at the Professor's famous house, and Mrs. Macready gives them a tour. While trying to keep out of the way of the visitors, all four of the children climb into the wardrobe.

Finding themselves in the woods, Peter promptly apologizes to Lucy for not having believed her. Before they go off exploring, they put on coats from the wardrobe. Lucy leads them to the house of Mr. Tumnus, where they find that everything is in disarray. Things have been smashed and there is a note saying that Mr. Tumnus is awaiting trial. Of course Lucy wants to help him.

A robin appears and leads them through the forest. When the robin disappears, a beaver comes along and takes its place, leading the children deeper into the woods. To prove he is a friend, the beaver holds up the white handkerchief that Lucy had loaned Mr. Tumnus when he was crying. The beaver tells them Aslan is on the move. Mr. Beaver leads them to a dam and then into his beehive-shaped house. Soon they are enjoying a dinner of fish, potatoes, marmalade, rolls, and tea.

Then Mr. Beaver lights his pipe and tells the children that Mr. Tumnus was taken off by the police to the White Witch's house. He also tells them about Aslan, a great lion who is king of the whole wood and King of Beasts. It has been arranged that the children and the beavers are to meet Aslan the next day at the Stone Table.

The children also hear about the prophecy concerning the four thrones at Cair Paravel, the castle on the seacoast. The prophecy says that when two Sons of Adam and two Daughters of Eve sit on the thrones, the White Witch's life and power will end. Everyone suddenly notices that sometime during the conversation, Edmund has disappeared. They call and search but do not find him. Mr. Beaver is certain that Edmund has gone to betray them to the White Witch.

It turns out that Mr. Beaver is right. Edmund slips away and goes off to find the Queen. The moonlight helps him follow the course of the river to the White Witch. In the courtyard, Edmund sees a crouching lion. With relief, Edmund realizes that it is a statue, and he bravely scribbles on it. Then Edmund meets a wolf, Maugrin, who leads him to the White Witch. On hearing what he has to say, the Queen orders her sledge, without its bells, to be brought to them.

Back at the beaver house, everyone packs a load of food, and then they leave in single file. Mr. Beaver leads them to a cave where they stop to rest. In the morning, they are awakened by the sound of Father Christmas and his sledge. Father Christmas has gifts for everyone.

Edmund is expecting the White Witch to be nice to him for coming to her with information about the others, and he asks for Turkish delights. Instead, the dwarf brings him water and dry bread. The White Witch sets off in her sledge after sending two wolves on ahead of her to kill whatever they find in the beaver's house. After that, they are to go to the Stone Table.

The White Witch and Edmund ride a long way and come upon a party of small animals enjoying their gifts from Father Christmas. The angry White Witch turns them to stone. Edmund feels sorry for them and realizes what a dreadful mistake he has made in trusting the Witch. The sledge becomes stuck in the melting snow, and they see that the frozen streams are also quickly melting. Spring is finally coming. Since they can ride no further, they get out and walk. Edmund's hands are tied behind him.

The children and the beavers also find themselves walking through the countryside in springtime. In a few hours, the season has changed from winter to spring. They leave the stream, which is turning into a flood, and climb a hill to the Stone Table. There they meet Aslan and his many followers. They explain to the lion what has happened to Edmund.

A wolf comes and chases Susan into a tree. Peter rushes at the wolf with his sword that was a gift from Father Christmas. Peter kills the wolf, and the centaurs, unicorns, deer, and eagles chase the second wolf, hoping it will lead them to the White Witch. Aslan takes Peter's sword and knights him, calling him Sir Peter Wolf's-Bane.

The second wolf returns to the White Witch to tell her what happened at the Stone Table. She sends the wolf to gather her people—giants, werewolves, ghouls, Minotaurs, hags, and specters. Edmund is tied to a tree, and the Witch sharpens her knife. Before she can kill Edmund, Aslan's creatures arrive and rescue him. They fail to capture the White Witch and her dwarf, because the Witch has disguised them as a stump and a boulder. Rejoined with the others, Edmund has a long talk with Aslan and is forgiven by all.

The Witch's dwarf arrives, asking that his Queen be given safe conduct to come and speak. Aslan grants this if she will agree to leave her wand at the great oak. The Witch comes and speaks of Deep Magic. She insists that every traitor belongs to her and that she has the right to kill Edmund. Then Aslan talks privately with the Witch, and she renounces her claim to Edmund's life.

The Witch leaves, and Aslan tells the others they must leave, too. Aslan outlines two battle plans, one for attacking the Witch and her people in the wood and another for fighting them in the castle. Aslan discusses with Peter what he must do and explains he cannot promise to be at the battle.

That night in camp, Susan and Lucy have a feeling that something is wrong, and they cannot sleep. They look for Aslan and see him slipping away. They follow him and are discovered, but Aslan allows them to come with him to the Stone Table. The girls hide in the bushes while Aslan goes on alone. Aslan is sacrificing himself to save Edmund. Four Hags bind the lion, then they shave off his mane and muzzle him. The crowd drags Aslan to the table, where the Witch kills him.

The Witch and her people race down the hill to war. Susan and Lucy creep out of hiding to go cry and kiss the dead Aslan. The girls remove the muzzle, and mice bite through the cords that bind him. Morning comes, and the great table cracks into two pieces. Aslan appears, standing whole again. He explains that "when a willing victim who has committed no treachery is killed in a traitor's stead, the Table will crack and Death itself will start working backwards."

Aslan, with the girls riding on his back, races to the Witch's castle. Aslan jumps over the walls into the courtyard and breathes life into the statues. Then, as all the creatures come alive again, Aslan runs inside the castle and repeats the process. The giant, Mr. Rumblebuffin, breaks the gates and lets them all out. They set off to meet Peter and his troops, who are already engaged in battle.

Peter's troops are weary and outnumbered but fighting bravely when Aslan and the others appear. The battle ends quickly after Edmund breaks the Witch's wand and Aslan kills the Witch. Edmund is wounded, but to save him Lucy uses her gift from Father Christmas and pours a drop of the liquid into her brother's mouth. Then she helps the others who are wounded. Aslan breathes life into those who were turned to stone, and Aslan makes Edmund a knight.

That night, they have a fine high tea, and the next day they travel to the castle, Cair Paravel. There they are crowned King Peter, Queen Susan, King Edmund, and Queen Lucy. The children sit on their thrones and during the great feasting and celebration, Aslan quietly slips away. The four children reign wisely for a long time.

One day when they are out hunting the White Stag, it leads them to the long-forgotten lamppost. They follow it back to the wardrobe and tumble back into the house they had left. They tell the Professor of their adventures. He suggests that they shouldn't talk about it, but promises that they will get back to Narnia again some day.

List of Major Characters: The four children who travel to Narnia, Lucy, Susan, Peter and Edmund; the Professor and his housekeeper, Mrs. Macready; Mr. Tumnus and Mr. and Mrs. Beaver, creatures who live in Narnia; the White Witch, who has Narnia in her power; Aslan, who is king of the woods; and Father Christmas, who arrives with gifts.

Vocabulary: The following words appear in the story on the page shown in parentheses after the words. Look up each of the words. Write its definition. Come up with a mental picture, and draw it to help you to remember the word.

cloven (2)   jollification (16)

hoax (25)   courtiers (39)

stratagem (78)   pavilion (125)

scepter (141)   forfeit (142)

prodigious (168)   ransacking (171)

saccharine (173)   centaurs (174)

Comprehension Questions

1. What does Mr. Tumnus serve to Lucy at tea when they first meet?
2. What awful things does Mr. Tumnus expect would happen to him if the White Witch learns he has betrayed her?
3. What is Mrs. Beaver doing when the children arrive at her house?
4. What does Edmund do to the stone lion in the courtyard of the White Witch?
5. What two gifts does Father Christmas give Peter?
6. What does Father Christmas say when Lucy insists that she could be brave enough to fight?
7. What does the Stone Table look like?
8. What animal helps Aslan get the freed statues organized for battle?
9. What do Lucy and the faun do after he is released from being a stone statue?
10. How do the four children feel when they go hunting the White Stag and find the lamppost?

Answers: 1) He serves an egg, sardines on toast, honey, buttered toast, and cake. 2) She would cut off his tail, saw off his horns, pluck out his beard, change his cloven hoofs to solid hoofs, and might turn him into a stone statue. 3) Mrs. Beaver is working at her sewing machine. 4) Edmund scribbles a moustache and spectacles on the lion statue with a lead pencil. 5) Father Christmas gives Peter a shield and a sword. 6) Father Christmas says, "Battles are ugly when women fight." 7) The table is a slab of stone cut all over with strange lines and figures. 8) A big sheepdog helps Aslan organize the freed statues for battle. 9) Lucy and the faun hold hands and dance. 10) They feel uneasy and generally apprehensive when they see the lamppost.

Discussion Questions

1. Father Christmas gives Peter a sword and shield that he needs to protect his sister against a wolf. He gives Lucy a cordial that helps to save the wounded in battle and also gives her a dagger. And he gives Susan a quiver of arrows and a horn. Edmund does not get to meet Father Christmas. If he had been there, what do you think his gift would have been? Why?

2. Although he receives information from several sources suggesting that the Queen is evil, Edmund continues to put his trust in her for a long time. Why do you think he is so ready to trust the Queen? To which of Edmund's character traits is she appealing? Invite a pair of students to pose these questions to their classmates and to communicate the results of their survey to the class.

3. After having served as kings and queens for quite some time, suddenly the children abandon Narnia and return to the Professor's house. What do you suppose happened in Narnia when Edmund, Susan, Peter, and Lucy did not return from their hunting trip?

4. There is a giant in *The Lion, the Witch and the Wardrobe* called Giant Rumblebuffin. He knocks down the gates and towers at the Queen's house and releases the one-time statues back into the world to fight in the battle. There is also a giant in *The Lost Years of Merlin.* This giant, named Shim, helps Rhia and Emrys and rescues them when the revolving castle comes tumbling down. Invite students who have read both books to discuss the roles of the two giants. How are they alike, and how are they different?

5. Father Christmas tells Lucy that "battles are ugly when women fight." Aren't all battles ugly? What makes it uglier when women are involved? Would the White Witch fight differently if she were not a woman? Does this statement reflect the view of the author toward traditional roles of men and women?

6. The Professor plays a very small role in this story, but twice the children go to him for advice and direction. Although he is always saying, "Bless me, what *do* they teach them at these schools?" he seems to respect the good judgment of the children. Discuss whether you think that the Professor did or did not understand their problems and whether the advice he gave was good advice or poor advice.

7. Lucy is the first child to wander into Narnia, and when she returns and tells her adventures, the others don't believe her. The second child that the author sent into Narnia is Edmund. Why do you think that the author chose to send these children first and second rather than Peter and Susan? What might have been very different if the order in which they visited were changed?

8. The sacrifice of Aslan on the Stone Table is a particularly terrifying scene. Yet when the children come out of hiding and go to the lion, they try to remove the muzzle, help untie the cords, wipe away the blood, and kiss Aslan. The children are not frightened. Discuss the emotions they must have felt and discuss why fear was not among them.

Research Activities

1. Father Christmas is presented in this story as a symbol of Christmas. He travels in a sleigh and gives out packages. There may be ESL students and students from many

different backgrounds and cultures in the class. Invite those who are interested to discuss how Christmas is traditionally celebrated in different countries of the world. What are other names for Father Christmas? Set aside a class period when students can share a discussion of stories and traditions, and show pictures to the class.

2. Invite a pair of students to research the habitats of beavers, their food, their lodges, and their dams. They should share this written report, containing at least three sources of information, with their classmates. Among sources of information are *Beaver* by Glen Rounds (New York: Holiday House, 1999) and *Building Beavers* by Kathleen Martin-Jones (Minneapolis, MN: Lerner Publications Co., 2000). Check with the media specialist at your school to see if a video on beavers might be available to show; if so, arrange for a presentation at a convenient time. Two useful Internet sites for additional information are http://www.alienexplorer.com/ecology/m41.html and http://fund.org/library/documentViewer.asp?ID=81&table=documents.

3. Several of the sledges described in this book are pulled by reindeer. Invite a pair of students to make an oral presentation on reindeer for the class. Among sources of information are *Reindeer* by Mary Ann McDonald (Chanhassen, MN: Child's World, 1999) and *Horns and Antlers* by Allan Fowler (New York: Children's Press, 1998). On the Internet, http://www.nps.gov/bela/html/reinmoss.htm provides information as does http://www.ultimateungulate.com/caribou.html.

4. For reasons of safety, Peter, Susan, Lucy, and Edmund are sent to live in the country at the Professor's house because during World War II, London suffered bombing almost every night from the Germans with whom they were at war. Invite a small group of interested children to learn more about the evacuation of children from London and the blitz of the city. Have them write a report to share with the class and include a bibliography of at least three sources of information. Possible resources include http://www.what-if-you.comww2memorial/wwii_chapter_7.htm and http://www.newsday.com/news/education/sbp/ny-sbp//30.htmlstory?coll=ny-sbp-headlines. Two useful books on this topic are *The Battle of Britain* by Earle Rice (San Diego, CA: Lucent Books, 1996) and *Battle of Britain* by Wallace B. Black and Jean F. Blashfield (New York: Crestwood House, 1991).

5. When spring comes to Narnia at last, many beautiful wildflowers are seen by the children. Invite a member of the community with knowledge about wildflowers to visit the class and show pictures or slides and discuss some of the native wildflowers of your area as well as the wildflowers mentioned in the book. These include celandines, snowdrops, crocuses, primroses, and bluebells.

6. The White Witch calls many creatures to come and help her fight in the war against Aslan. Hags, ogres, incubuses, wraiths, efreets, sprites, werewolves, specters, and minotaurs are summoned. Ask a pair of students to research the Minotaur famous in Greek legends and make an oral report to the class on what they learn about this creature. One source of information is http://www.tatooine.fortunecity.com/vonnegut/422/two.htm.

Extension Activities

1. Make a mural of several scenes from the story. For one part of the mural, reread page 73 and draw a picture of the inside of Mr. and Mrs. Beaver's house including as many of the details as possible. Use the mural to stir up interest and to encourage students to read *The Lion, the Witch and the Wardrobe.* Hang the mural in the library media center.

2. Edmund loves Turkish delights. Perhaps a pair of students could work with a parent at home who volunteers to supervise the process to make Turkish delights and then bring a candy treat to share with classmates. (Always be sure to check on allergies before giving food of any kind to students.) Making this particular candy is fairly complex. One recipe for Turkish delights can be found on the Internet at http://thefoody.com/sweets/turkishdelight.html.

3. The language used from page 184 to page 187 is different from the rest of the language in the book because the author explains that the children start talking in a different style when they become kings and queens. Invite interested students to rewrite these pages, providing the same basic information but writing with dialogue that is typical of how the children speak throughout most of the book.

4. Some classes enjoy cooking at school. There are beaver-related recipes that require little time found at http://www.moonchildren.com/beavers/recipes.htm. These are all on a beaver theme and include Sweet, Tasty Bark, which is made from white chocolate and toasted almonds; Twigs and Sticks, made with butterscotch chips, chocolate, and pretzels; and an ambitious edible beaver lodge made from ground beef, beans, and tortilla chips. For such cooking activities involving the class, volunteer parents to help are essential.

5. Encourage interested members of the class to write a poem in any form as a response to this book. One example, called "Nightmare," can be found at http://www.storiesfromtheweb.org/happening/world/poetryparty/meanfishsmile/nightmare/intro.htm. Post the poems written by students on a classroom bulletin board.

6. Invite interested students to add one chapter to the book made up of four letters home to their parents in London from the children in the Professor's house telling how they pass their time in the country. The letters should reflect what you have learned about the character and personality of Lucy, Susan, Edmund, and Peter.

How does reading *The Lion, the Witch and the Wardrobe* and engaging in the various activities suggested above help students meet the 12 NCTE/IRA English Language Arts Standards?

1. *The Lion, the Witch and the Wardrobe* meets Standard #1 by serving as an example of outstanding fiction.

2. *The Lion, the Witch and the Wardrobe* meets Standard #2 because it is a representative work of the broad genre of fantasy.

3. Discussion questions #1, #2, #3, #5, #6, #7, and #8 help students to comprehend and interpret text, and the vocabulary exercise increases knowledge of word meanings, helping students to meet Standard #3.

4. Extension activity #3, which suggests rewriting a section of the book in the usual language style of the children rather than in the formal language of kings and queens, addresses Standard #4, which asks students to adjust written language and style to communicate effectively for different purposes.

5. Extension activity #5, which suggests that students write a response to this story in the form of an original poem, helps meet Standard #5, which requires that students use different writing processes for different audiences and for a variety of purposes.

6. Extension activity #6, which suggests that students add a new chapter to the book in the form of four letters written home by the children in the country to their parents in London, helps to meet Standard #6 by requiring students to apply their knowledge of language structure and language conventions to create a print text.

7. Discussion question #2, which asks students to survey class members about Edmund's beliefs and behaviors, helps to address Standard #7 through gathering, evaluating, and synthesizing data and communicating discoveries.

8. Research activity #2 involving beavers and their habitat helps to meet Standard #8 by encouraging students to use a variety of technology and information resources to carry out research and to communicate their knowledge.

9. Discussion question #5 about whether or not war is uglier when women are involved in battle helps to address Standard #9 by allowing students to develop an understanding of and respect for diversity in social roles.

10. Research activity #1 asking ESL students and members of the class from different ethnic and cultural backgrounds to compare and contrast the use of figures such as Father Christmas helps address Standard #10, which asks students to use their first language that is not English to develop a deeper understanding of the curriculum.

11. Discussion question #4 allows students to pool their information knowledge in the form of a book discussion group and compare and contrast the giant Rumblebuffin in this story with the giant Shim, who appears in *The Lost Years of Merlin*. It helps meet Standard #11, which asks that students participate as knowledgeable, reflective, creative, and critical members of a literary community.

12. Extension activity #1, creating a library mural, allows students to creatively select and prepare a means of sharing their enthusiasm for this book with other potential readers. It addresses Sta1ndard #12, in which students are asked to use spoken, written, and visual language to persuade others.

The Giver

Lois Lowry

Boston: Houghton Mifflin Co., 1993, ISBN 0-395-64566-2

Detailed Synopsis

When the book opens, it is late in the year and 11-year-old Jonas is eager and apprehensive like all of the Elevens who live in his community who are awaiting the special ceremony that will soon be held. At dinner, the family has a time of sharing feelings. Lily explains how angry she became that day at a visiting child who didn't follow playground rules. Father talks of his worry at work over a newchild who may have to be released because he isn't thriving. Mother describes a repeat offender who appeared before her at the Department of Justice. And Jonas discusses his apprehension at facing the Ceremony of Twelves.

Jonas's father describes his own Ceremony of Twelve. He explains that he had been fairly certain what his assignment would be in the community, because he had an aptitude for being with children and was drawn to volunteering his free time at the Nurturing Center. As expected, he was assigned to be a Nurturer. But Jonas realizes that he feels no such certainty for his future.

When the ceremony finally takes place, Jonas rejoices at what appear to be the excellent assignments given to his close friends but becomes alarmed when he is passed over. Finally Jonas is brought on stage and learns he has been selected to be the next Receiver of Memories. This is a great honor, but it also means that Jonas will suffer pain.

The very next day, Jonas reports to the old Receiver and begins his training. He lays down on the bed, and the old man, who now calls himself The Giver, transmits to Jonas a memory of sledding down a hill through the snow. The Giver explains to Jonas that this is a memory from long ago, before the community gave up snow and hills and opted for Sameness.

Jonas begins to have moments when he sees the color red, in an apple and in Fiona's hair. When he asks about it, The Giver explains that a long time ago people made the choice for colors to disappear. Gradually, Jonas learns, through memories, the names of colors and begins to see them all. And slowly, The Giver adds doses of pain to his lessons. Jonas has memories of warfare, birthday parties, love, and grandparents.

At home, the newborn that his father had worried about, Gabriel, starts spending evenings with them. His father has secured permission to give the newborn this extra care in hopes that he will thrive and won't have to be released. Gabriel grows, but he does not sleep well at night. Jonas offers to let Gabriel sleep in his room. And to quiet him at night, Jonas gives Gabriel gentle memories.

One day when Jonas sees his friends playing, he realizes they are playing at war. He knows from his memory training just how painful war is, and he tries to get them to stop. After this, his friends become uneasy around him.

Jonas continues his lessons for almost a year. One night at home, Father explains that twins have been born. He must choose one to be nurtured and one to be released Elsewhere. When Jonas tells The Giver that he wishes he could see the releasing ceremony, he is reminded that as Receiver, he has access to everything. The ceremony has been recorded, and when Jonas wants to see it, it is played for him. As Jonas watches, he is horrified to see his father inject the smaller twin, killing it.

Jonas is so upset that he cannot return home that night. He questions this life the community has chosen without colors, without weather, without hills, without grandparents, without love, and without memories. Jonas wants to change things. He hatches a plan with The Giver. The boy will leave and go Elsewhere.

The well-thought-out scheme does not get put into effect, because Jonas discovers his father is about to "release" little Gabriel in the morning. Without the planned preparations, Jonas must leave on his father's bicycle that very night with little Gabe. By luck and skill and by traveling only at night, Jonas succeeds in getting away.

It is cold and snowy and Jonas and Gabriel are hungry and weak at the close of the story. But Jonas manages to make it to the top of a hill, and he and the child slide toward the lights of a town, a place where families keep memories, where they celebrate love, and where they are waiting for him and the baby.

List of Major Characters: The main character is Jonas, a boy just turning 12; his mother, father, and 6-year-old sister, Lily; his friends, Fiona and Asher; the old Receiver of Memories, who becomes The Giver when Jonas is named to succeed him; and a newborn, Gabriel, who comes from the Nurturing Center to spend time with Jonas's family.

Vocabulary: Use the numeral following the word, which indicates the page number on which it appears, to look up and see how each of these words is used in the story. After each word, write a synonym, and then draw a simple sketch or symbol that will help you to remember the meaning of the word.

distraught (4)   apprehensive (14)

chastise (20)   petulantly (22)

buoyancy (48)   meticulously (48)

vibrance (99)   carnage (119)

excruciating (140)   luminous (141)

solace (161)   languid (166)

Comprehension Questions

1. Although mirrors are not forbidden, they are rare where Jonas lives. Why?
2. In Jonas's world, what sort of jacket do children receive when they are 7?
3. At 9, children receive bicycles. What is the bicycle a symbol of?
4. To be matched as a spouse in this society, what four factors have to correspond? Do men and women hold "conventional" roles in this society?
5. In this society, how often are elections held for the Chief Elder or leaders of the community?
6. What assignment does Jonas's best friend, Asher, receive at the Ceremony of Twelves?
7. What are the five qualities that the Receiver of Memories must have?
8. What does The Giver choose for the first memories transmitted to Jonas?
9. Rosemary had been trained as the Receiver of Memories for five weeks before she asked to be released. When she was released, what happened to her memories?
10. According to The Giver, what is the worst part of holding the memories?

Answers: 1) These are no colors to be seen and there is no real need of mirrors. 2) The jackets are front-buttoned. 3) The bicycle is a symbol of moving into the community.

4) Spouses must be matched for disposition, energy level, intelligence, and interests. 5) Elections are held every ten years. 6) Asher is assigned to be Assistant Director of Recreation. 7) The Receiver must have the qualities of intelligence, integrity, courage, wisdom, and the capacity to see beyond. 8) Snow is the first memory transmitted. 9) Rosemary's memories came back to the people after she was released. 10) The worst part of holding memories is the loneliness of it, because memories need to be shared.

Discussion Questions

1. What is the first thing that Lily and Jonas notice about the tiny newborn that their father brought home?
2. Why doesn't Lily's mother want Lily to be assigned to be a Birthmother when it comes time for her assignment? Do you think this is a prejudice simply held by Lily's mother, or do you think it is a prevalent opinion in this society?
3. As Jonas and Gabriel try to escape, why does Jonas try to hang on to his memories of cold?
4. When did you become suspicious that "being released" meant being killed? What clues did the author give that led you to this suspicion?
5. If you had a chance to choose having weather that was always the same or having a world with seasons of the year, which would you choose, and why?
6. Almost a year's worth of memories would be released back into the society after Jonas and Gabriel made their escape. How do you think the community reacted? Do you think that for the third time they would choose a new Receiver of Memories, or do you think the community will keep its memories this time? What makes you think as you do?
7. *The Giver* is very different from high fantasy novels such as *The Hobbit* and *The Dark Is Rising*. With others who have read all three of these books, discuss *The Giver* as an example of fantasy literature. In what ways is it similar to high fantasy, and in what ways is it different? What other book(s) have you read that seem similar to *The Giver?*
8. The Giver offers a lot of reasons why he cannot make the escape with Jonas. What do you think is the best or real reason that The Giver is going to stay behind while Jonas goes Elsewhere?

Research Activities

1. One set of difficult decisions is made for all individuals in *The Giver.* When a child is 12 years old, he or she is assigned to training for a particular job in society. Most students will want to take an active role in their own career exploration. Are there various service agencies or outreach programs in your community that help youth to investigate potential careers? If so, ask representatives to come to class at an appropriate time and describe various careers and the training that is involved. Are the careers explored equally open to men and women?
2. There are various opportunities online for people to explore career interests and opportunities. If your school district has a vocational technical center, someone there may suggest some possible sites appropriate for elementary and middle school students. One site is http://www.ncsu.edu/careerkey/. This is a free public service to help people make sound career decisions. It was developed by Lawrence K. Jones, Ph.D. When you have identified some appropriate sites, suggest that a few interested students visit these career sites and share back with the class what they learned through this preliminary career exploration.

3. Memories are stored in the brain, and the brain is very complex. Invite a pair of interested students to learn more about the human brain and how it functions. Using a model or charts plus information from their research, invite these students to share what they have learned with the class. Possible sources of information are *The World of the Brain* by Alvin and Virginia Silverstein (New York: W. Morrow, 1986) and *The Human Body* by Laurie Beckelman (Pleasantville, NY: Reader's Digest Children's Publications, 1999). An Internet source for some additional information on memory is http://www.epub. org/br/cm/n01/memo/mechanisms.htm.

4. Lois Lowry, the author of *The Giver*, has written more than 20 books for young adults. Invite a pair of students to research Lois Lowry's books. What awards has she won? Which of her titles are in your school library? With this information, ask these students to make and, with permission, place in the library an inviting and thought-provoking poster encouraging students to read more of Lois Lowry's books. Ask these same students to follow up with the librarian to see if there was an increase in the circulation of Lois Lowry's books.

5. The Horn Book Award, which is a greatly coveted recognition of fine writing for children, was won by Lois Lowry. Ask a pair of students to research this award. When was it first given? What is the title of the last book to receive it? What are the criteria set forth for winning this award? Ask these students to report what they learn to the class.

6. There is a number of famous books written about a supposedly Utopian society. One of these is *Utopia* by Thomas More. Ask a pair of students to research this topic. When and why did More write *Utopia?* What reaction did it provoke? Have these students prepare a written report on this topic that has a bibliography including a list of at least three sources of information.

Extension Activities

1. In 1949, George Orwell wrote a book called *1984*. In it, he made predictions of what the world would be like in 1984. He described a society where members were held in subjugation by a standard of laws centered around efficiency, manipulation, and physical and mental control. Aspects of this book will remind readers of what society is like in *The Giver* and in *A Wrinkle in Time*. Invite a group of interested students to read and discuss these three books. In what ways are the societies shown in *1984*, *The Giver*, and *A Wrinkle in Time* alike and different?

2. At the beginning of Chapter 13, Jonas and The Giver have a conversation. It is about daring to let people make choices. Ask two students to practice this scene, and then present it to the class as a reader's theater. With this as an introduction, encourage a class discussion about allowing choice in a society.

3. Readers often disagree about how to interpret the ending of *The Giver.* Invite readers to add a few more pages to the ending of the book making clear what they think happens next. Those who are willing to do so should share these with the class and take part in a class discussion. Does there seem to be one clear understanding of the ending of the book, or are there several interpretations?

4. Write a new chapter to come just before Chapter 21. In this new chapter, have Jonas share his plan of escape with someone. He might share his plan with Asher or with Fiona.

Knowing what you know about the characters, how would they respond? What would happen? Does Jonas convince them of the wisdom of his plan, or does he fail? Try to keep the same tone and approach that has been used throughout the book by Lois Lowry.

5. Suppose that the citizens who live in Jonas's world have a weekly newspaper called *The Same Old Thing*. How might an article about the fact that Jonas and Gabriel have disappeared be written up in that newspaper? Remember that to appear at all, such an article would have to be reassuring and not lead others to try to escape. How would the same information be written in a report to the Chief Elder pointing out that a new Receiver of Memories is needed right away?

6. If there are ESL students enrolled, ask a resource person who is fluent in their language(s) to suggest works of literature from their native culture in which there is some sort of "utopia" or "well-regulated" society where in exchange for a life of "sameness" people have given up the right to make personal choices and mistakes. If there is a well-known story or legend of this type, share it with the ESL students, and have them in turn share it with the class to shed additional light on *The Giver.*

How does reading *The Giver* and engaging in the various activities suggested above help students meet the 12 NCTE/IRA English Language Arts Standards?

1. *The Giver* meets Standard #1 by serving as an example of outstanding fiction.

2. *The Giver* meets Standard #2 because it is a representative work of the broad genre of fantasy.

3. Discussion questions #1, #3, and #8 help students to comprehend and interpret text, and the vocabulary exercise increases knowledge of word meanings, helping students to meet Standard #3.

4. Extension activity #4, which suggests writing a chapter to appear just before Chapter 21, in which Jonas tries to convince others of the wisdom of his plan to escape, addresses Standard #4, which asks students to adjust written language and style to communicate effectively for different purposes.

5. Extension activity #5, which suggests that students write up the disappearance of Jonas and Gabriel in the form of an article for *The Same Old Thing* and as a report to the Chief Elder, helps meet Standard #5, which requires that students use different writing processes for different audiences and for a variety of purposes.

6. Extension activity #4, which suggests that a student write a new chapter to be added to the book, helps to meet Standard #6 by requiring students to apply their knowledge of language structure and language conventions to create a print text.

7. Research activity #1, which centers around careers and equal opportunities in the work force, helps to address Standard #7 by requiring students to gather, evaluate, and synthesize data from a variety of sources.

8. Research activity #3 involving the structure of the brain and the storage of memories helps to meet Standard #8 by encouraging students to use a variety of technological and information resources to carry out research and to communicate their knowledge.

9. Discussion question #2 about the fact that Lily's mother looks down on an assignment as Birthmother helps to address Standard #9 by allowing students to develop an understanding of and respect for diversity in social roles.

10. Use extension activity #6 as a means for ESL students and regular students in the classroom to compare *The Giver* with a folk tale or story about a Utopia. This will help address Standard #10, which asks students to use their first language that is not English to develop a deeper understanding of the curriculum.

11. Extension activity #7 allows students to pool their information knowledge in the form of a book discussion group and compare and contrast the society portrayed in *The Giver* with the societies shown in *A Wrinkle in Time* and in *1984*. It helps meet Standard #11, which asks that students participate as knowledgeable, reflective, creative, and critical members of a literary community.

12. Research activity #4 allows students to creatively select and prepare a means of sharing their enthusiasm for this book with other potential readers. It addresses Standard #12, in which students are asked to use spoken, written, and visual language to persuade others.

Dragonflight

Anne McCaffrey

New York: Ballantine Books, 1968, ISBN 0-345-33546-5

Detailed Synopsis

Dragonflight is Volume 1 of a series of books called *The Dragonriders of Pern*. The book combines traditional fantasy with science fiction. In the Introduction, the reader learns that Rukbat, in the Sagittarian sector, is a G-type star with five planets plus one stray that it has attracted. Men settled on its third planet and named it Pern. Every 200 Terran years, the stray planet comes close and its indigenous life forms seek to come to the more temperate and hospitable planet.

To protect against the Threads that drop onto Pern from the wandering planet, the Pernese developed winged, tailed, and fiery-breathed dragons with dragonmen trained to use the animals with the ability to teleport.

When the story begins, Lessa awakes in the straw where she sleeps with the other kitchen drudges within the walls of Ruatha Hold. She is cold, and she senses danger. She get up and goes to the tower, searching for the source of her unease. She is just in time to see the dawn appearance of the Red Star. Lessa looks at the valley and tries to remember what it was like before Fax came and conquered Ruatha. She goes back inside, stopping to caress the watch-wher, a creature with a scaly head and clipped wings. It is the only creature in Pern that knows who Lessa really is, and the only one she trusts.

F'lar, a dragonman, riding on his dragon, Mnementh, appears in the skies above the chief Hold of Fax, the Lord of the High Reaches. F'lar disapproves of the disrepair he sees on his arrival. When he and the other dragonmen land, they are cooly greeted by Fax, a man who own seven Holds through inheritance or conquest.

F'lar explains that the dragonmen ride in a Search because the Weyr needs a new dragon Queen. F'lar seeks the hospitality of the Hold for himself; for his half-brother, F'nor; and for the other dragonriders. F'lar inquires if they still mount tower guards and is assured that they do, even in these peaceful times.

They go to the women's quarters. F'lar greets Lady Gemma and is welcomed by her. She is pregnant with Fax's child. Among the other women, F'lar does not see one who is spirited enough to be considered for a dragon Queen. F'lar sees to his men and dragons and then wanders through the crafthold. He checks out the drudges in the Great Hall but finds no women among them that he thinks would make a Weyrwoman. He tells his dragonmen to look about carefully and to return by sundown with names of any likely candidates.

F'lar is aware that Fax is barely being courteous to them and that respect for dragon-men has declined. They visit the craftsmen's hall and find it filled with looms and tapestries. F'lar talks with a former dragonman, Lytol, who says they will find no worthy women here, and he also secretly begs the dragonmen to kill Fax for the safety of the land. He says that Fax scoffs at tales of the history of the Threads and has banned dragon lore from the ballads. Fax is obviously upset at their coming to the Hold.

Lessa hears the news that Fax and several dragonmen have come to Ruatha. She hopes that somehow she will be able to humiliate Fax and reclaim her birthright as a member of royal blood and rule Ruatha herself. She goes to the kitchen and is put to work scrubbing utensils. She uses her special powers to try to ruin the meal that is being prepared for the guests.

F'lar wonders what is going on because he senses a power at work. The Great Hall and rooms are untidy. The food that is served is burned and of poor quality. In the midst of dinner, Lady Gemma goes into labor. F'lar speaks out and says that Fax must renounce Ruatha. He realizes some power must have made him speak this challenge, but at that moment Lady Gemma groans and leaves to give birth. Fax says he will renounce Ruatha for his child if it is male. Lady Gemma is taken to a room, and Lessa is sent to bring the birthing-woman to Gemma.

Lady Gemma dies in childbirth, and Lessa races to tell Fax that his baby son lives and will be the new Lord of Ruatha. Fax knocks Lessa down and begins a fight with F'lar in which Fax is killed. F'lar takes the injured Lessa to his chamber and examines her, finding that beneath the dirt and disguise is a young woman who might possibly be considered for a Weyrwoman.

When she wakes, Lessa says she is of Ruathan blood and wants to reclaim the Hold as her own. Lessa tries to run away but is caught by Mnementh, the dragon. F'lar wants her to willingly become a Weyrwoman and does his best to persuade her. He knows she is aware of the danger of the Red Star.

F'lar leaves some men to guard Ruatha, sends to the High Peaks to get Lytol to come and be Warder for the new baby who will eventually rule Ruatha, and prepares to take Lessa to the Weyr.

As soon as they arrive at Benden Weyr, F'nor and F'lar tend to feeding their dragons while Lessa has a bath. The other dragonriders fly in with the candidates from their search for a Weyrwoman. F'lar comes back and orders food for himself and Lessa. He explains that baby dragons will soon hatch from their eggs. They go inside the mountain where, on the floor of the cavern, there are ten mottled eggs and one golden one.

As the dragons hatch, they each go to a young boy and pair off. Twelve young women are brought to the hatching ground. Finally the golden egg hatches, and a clumsy female dragon staggers out. Two of the young women are accidentally killed, but Lessa grabs the dragon's head and scratches the spot on the soft eye ridge. She finds she can communicate with Ramoth, the newborn queen dragon, and so becomes Lessa of Pern, Weyrwoman to Ramoth the Golden.

Manora, a woman who lives in the Lower Caverns, is responsible as head woman for domestic management of the Weyr. She comes to see Lessa and explains they have not received enough supplies to see them through the cold. The other Weyrs are neglecting to send tithes to support the dragonmen. They no longer believe in Threads and think that dragons are unnecessary to them.

Lessa tells the head dragonman, R'gul, that supplies are short and they must raid or barter for what they need. But R'gul insists that nothing can be done at this time when they are busy caring for and training young dragons. Lessa convinces a young dragonrider named K'net to do a little pilfering of food.

F'nor explains to Lessa that F'lar's father was killed when F'lar was only 19. The older men of the dragonweyr did not want to be led by one so young, so they saw to it that R'gul's dragon rather than F'lar's dragon mated with the queen dragon, thus making R'gul head dragonman. And since it has been an interval of 400 years since the Red Star passed close enough to excrete Threads, R'gul doesn't sense any danger ahead of them.

It is time for Ramoth to fly and mate, but Mnementh and F'lar are away trying to intercept K'net before the other lords get angry enough over his raiding to march on the Weyr. R'gul plans to take advantage of their absence, but F'lar returns just in time. Ramoth flies and mates with Mnementh.

F'lar worries that it is time that the Red Star will gleam through the Eye Rock and herald the coming of the Threads. Then a new worry appears. A large body of armed men from many of the Holds approaches. F'lar, as the new Weyrleader, takes control of the situation. He sends some of his men to the unprotected Holds to take prisoners, he has dragons fly right over the armed men to terrify them, and he talks with their leaders, reminding them that the Threads will soon come and that dragons and dragonmen will be needed. F'lar orders the men to go home, destroy greenery near their holds so as not to attract Threads, send their tithes to the Weyr, and post guards.

F'lar decides to teach Lessa to fly *between*. They practice, and Lessa learns that she can travel not only between places but between times as well. She goes back to Ruatha three years ago and then returns to the present. F'lar convinces Lessa to trust him at least until spring and help him to get ready for the Threads that are coming.

They discuss and try to get at the meaning of a plate that was nailed to one of the chests in which records are stored. By studying history and concentrating on the new young dragons and riders, F'lar hopes to be ready before the Thread attacks become more frequent. Ramoth begins to lay her first clutch of 41 eggs. Among them is a golden queen egg.

When the eggs hatch, the Impressions are made quickly with no accidents. The young queen bonds with Kylara, which means she will become a new Weyrwoman. F'nor comes in from patrol in Tulek. He is covered in black dust. This is an indication that Threads are falling. F'lar and Lessa study maps, and Lessa reveals that she can speak with all the dragons.

This will be valuable in keeping in contact and directing an attack. Since Threads are already falling into cold air and freezing into dust, F'lar sends dragons to go *between* so they will be present when the Threads begin to fall.

Everyone rushes into action. Because the Star is just beginning to pass by, after this attack, there will be a few days before the next one. F'lar and his dragonwing go *between* to Nerat and arrive in time to attack the falling threads. The riders feed their dragons firestone, and inside the dragons, their stomach acids churn. When the dragons belch forth gas, they ignite the threads in the sky and soil. When Threads land on them, they burn the riders and dragons. Then the dragonmen briefly go *between* for a few seconds of intense cold to ease the pain before coming back to fight again.

Lessa sends K'net's wing to attack the threads at Keroon. The women at Benden make a salve to be ready to use to treat the injured dragons and dragonmen. The first Thread attack ends, and the dragons and riders turn home. F'lar tries to decide how to attack the few Threads that have managed to reach the surface of the planet. He plans to send F'nor back ten Turns to the Southern Continent, allowing the new Queen, Pridith, to mature and raise several clutches of dragons. This plan works, but F'nor comes back ill from his time travel.

A Council of Lords and Craftmasters is held. They discuss ways to destroy the Threads that reach the ground. They try to recall words from ancient ballads and scenes from tapestries to give them clues on how to make flamethrowers to kill the Threads. F'nor and Lessa go to hunt a suitable place in the Southern Continent to establish a Weyr. They find one and report back.

F'lar wonders why five Weyrs fell empty. It occurs to Lessa that the inhabitants may have gone ahead in time to come to rescue them. Lytol brings an old tapestry that shows a flamethrower, and craftsmen begin to try to recreate these. After they are finished, Lessa insists on taking the old tapestry back to Ruatha. When she does not return to the Weyr after her trip, F'lar fears that she has gone back 400 Turns to show the people of the Weyrs how to travel forward in time to help them in this attack of the Threads. As her reference point, she uses the Hall door from the old tapestry.

Lessa arrives in the past and convinces the people to go *between* 400 Turns to help. They use the Red Star dwindling in the evening sky as their reference point. They successfully return to Ruatha Valley with 1,800 dragons. They also bring old flamethrowers with them.

With these greatly increased numbers and their equipment, they are sure they can mount a successful attack on the Threads. And since so many queens are present, the queens will fly in a dragonwing, too. Lessa will be part of the Queen's dragonwing. For the time being, Pern is safe.

List of Major Characters: F'lar is a dragonrider; Mnementh is F'lar's dragon; Fax is Lord of the High Reaches before he is killed by F'lar; Gemma is Fax's lady; F'nor is a dragonrider and half-brother to F'lar; and Lessa is Weyrwoman to Ramoth, the dragon at Benden Weyr.

Vocabulary: The numerals in parentheses indicate the page numbers on which the following vocabulary words appear in the book. Look up the meaning for each word in a dictionary; and then use it in an original sentence that demonstrates you understand its meaning.

perihelion (xi) _____

prescient (2) _____

laconically (14) _____

garrulity (18) _____

usurper (26) _____

portent (29) _____

imperatively (45) _____

contrition (48) _____

injudicious (57) _____

machinations (60) _____

bemusement (72) _____

iridescently (76) _____

Comprehension Questions

1. At the time the story begins, who is the only friend that Lessa has in Ruatha?
2. What is the name given to the special form of travel taken when a dragonman wants his dragon to cover great distances quickly?
3. When he is at home in Benden, a dragonweyr, where does F'lar bathe?
4. What secret ability involving dragons does Lessa have?
5. Which dragonflier has the main job of instructing the new Weyrwoman in her duties?
6. On what basis is the Weyrleader selected?
7. Why are Threads not so dangerous when it is unusually cold?
8. Why are the craftsmen so eager to look closely at the old tapestry of Ruatha?
9. What is the name of the cinnamon-flavored hot drink that everyone in the book keeps sipping?
10. Since traditionally, Queens fly into battle with Threads, why isn't this the case at Benden Weyr?

Answers: 1) A watch-wher is Lessa's only friend. 2) When dragons cover great distances quickly, it is called going *between*. 3) F'lar has a bathroom with water provided by a natural warm spring where he bathes. 4) Lessa can hear and talk to any dragon in the Weyr. 5) R'gul has the major duty of instructing the Weyrwoman. 6) The Weyrleader traditionally is the rider of the Queen dragon's mate. 7) Threads turn brittle and blow away as dust when it is cold. 8) The tapestry shows an old flamethrower, which they want to recreate. 9) The hot drink is called klah. 10) Benden Weyr has only one queen.

Discussion Questions

1. During the first Impression, two of the young women who are brought in to be considered for Weyrwomen are killed by the young dragon. Why does no one seem to care about this?

2. Were you surprised at how easily Lessa was convinced by F'lar to leave her claim to rule Ruatha and go with him to try to become a Weyrwoman? Why, or why not?

3. Gather together in a discussion group those students who have read both *Dragonflight* by Anne McCaffrey and *Redwall* by Brian Jacques. Have them discuss the function of the large tapestries that play a major role in each book.

4. Lessa is frustrated when, at first, she is not allowed to ride a dragon. But when other Weyrwomen and queen dragons arrive, she is delighted at the prospect of being able to fly into battle as part of the queens' wing under the direction of the senior Weyrwoman, Mardra. F'lar, on the other hand, has more conventional ideas about appropriate roles for men and women, and he appears shocked that women will fight against the Threads. How do you feel about Weyrwomen flying into battle?

5. There are at least three levels of difficulty of flying a dragon *between*. Easiest is to go *between* and experience the cold for simply a few seconds, which dragonriders do when they are burned by Threads. Harder is to cover considerable distance by going *between*. And hardest of all is going *between* when the dragon and rider travel in both space and time. With any time travel, there is the problem that an action taken when one travels back in time can alter the future. Discuss how time travel works in the book.

6. F'lar makes a point of holding a Council in which he listens to and honors the Craftsmen as much as he does the Lords of the various Holds throughout Pern. Why do you think he does this?

7. Lessa is a complex character. She has many traits that are admirable and many traits that are not admirable. Have an interested group discuss Lessa and make a chart on which the participants list her traits. How do all of these combine to make her such a good choice for Weyrwoman?

8. F'lar has learned the importance of history and of keeping good records. Do you think he will take any special steps to record in detail and preserve the history of this latest fight against the Threads? Regardless, do you think that in another 200 or 400 Turns, the people living then will have forgotten about flamethrowers again and will not believe in Threads?

Research Activities

1. Threads and spores are often associated with mushrooms. Invite a pair of interested students to research mushrooms. Where and how do they grow? What kinds are there? How are they raised commercially? Are there special magazines with information about mushrooms? Have these students prepare an oral report, with pictures, to show the class what they have learned. Sources of useful information include: http://www.allaboutmushrooms.com, which provides a good introduction to the world of mushrooms and includes many pictures. A history of humans and their interactions with mushrooms is at http://www.deoxy.org/mushman. htm, and information about wild mushrooms is at http://ohioline.osu.edu/hyg-fact/3000/ 3303.html. Additional information can be found in *Good Mushrooms and Bad Toadstools* by Allan Fowler (New York: Children's Press, 1998) and in *Katya's Book of Mushrooms* by Katya Arnold (New York: Henry Holt, 1997).

2. Dragons have a long history in myths and legends throughout the world. Invite ESL students and other interested students from a variety of backgrounds to research dragons in literature throughout history and to share a representative dragon tale from another

country. One useful book about Chinese dragons is *A Time of Golden Dragons* by Song Nan Zhang and Hoo Yu Zha (Toronto: Tundra Books, 2000). An Internet site of interest discussing the history of dragons around the world is http://www.draconian.com/history/history.htm.

3. The closest thing we have to living dragons is the Komodo dragon. Invite a pair of interested students to write a paper on this topic, including a bibliography of at least three sources of information. One useful source is a *Scientific American* article, "The Komodo Dragon," which is at http://www.sciam.com/1999/0399issue/0299ciofi.html. Another source at http://www.heptune.com/komodo.html discusses "Komodo Dragons and Their Islands." Two useful books are *Komodo Dragons* by Geoff Miller (Danbury, CT: Grolier Educational, 1999) and *Komodo Dragon* by Kathy Darling (New York: Lothrop, Lee & Shepard Books, 1997).

4. The dragons in this book eliminate Threads by burning them with phosphine gas, created by the dragons eating firestone. Invite a pair of interested students to learn more about phosphine gas, which is hydrogen phosphide or phosphorous hydride, and make an oral report to the class on what they learn. Phosphine gas is used as a grain fumigant and is an industrial gas used in silicon chip manufacture. Sources of information include http://www.voltaix.com/nsds/newph3.htm, and more information appears at http://www.cdc.gov/neosh/00-126.html about preventing poisoning and explosions during fumigation processes.

5. Perihelion is mentioned on page xi in the Introduction to the book. Ask a pair of students to find out what "perihelion" means and give an oral report to the class in which they explain what perihelion is and tell when Earth's next perihelion will occur. A useful page with dates covering 1992 to 2005 can be found at http://ac.usno.navy.mil/data/docs/EarthSeasons.html.

6. The other planets going around the sun have more elliptical orbits than does Earth. Invite a pair of interested students to research this topic and present a report to the class in which they use charts to share the information they have found. One good source is http://science.msfc.nasa.gov/headlines/y2001/ast04jan_1.htm. Additional information is at http://www.bbc.co.ui/science/space/solarsystem/index.shtml. Other information can be found in *The Solar System* by Tim Furniss (Austin, TX: Raintree Steck-Vaughn, 2001) and in *The Sun: The Center of the Solar System* by Michael D. Cole (Berkeley Heights, NJ: Enslow Publishers, 2001).

Extension Activities

1. Encourage interested students to make posters advertising *Dragonflight* and, with permission, post them in the library to encourage others to read books in the series. Dragons would be good to incorporate in the poster design. A useful book is *Kids Draw Knights, Queens, and Dragons* by Christopher Hart (New York: Watson Guptill, 2001).

2. An entertaining play with a reading by a full cast is available on four sound cassettes from Random House Listening Library (New York: Random House, 2002). It is called *Searching for Dragons*, and the author is Patricia C. Wrede. A class might enjoy listening to one of the cassettes as a group, with the other tapes available for individuals to use at a listening center as time permits. Your media specialist might be of help in locating this resource.

3. Throughout the book, verses are quoted at the beginning of each chapter and many important ballads recounting the history of the planet Pern are discussed. Invite students

to adopt the tone and style of the verses in this book and compose a ballad about the Queens' wing of dragonriders and their battle against the Threads to save Pern. Post these on a classroom bulletin board.

4. F'lar is often exasperated by Lessa, who does not easily follow directions. Perhaps he could ask Lessa to write Ten Commandments for Weyrwomen, which could be used in the Southern Continent as the new Weyr there gets established. These could be formal or humorous in tone. Post the results.

5. A few interested students might want to add a new chapter to the book in which F'lar and Lessa both return after engaging the Threads in battle and share with each other the stories of their adventures.

6. There are people who believe that bodies can be placed in some type of artificial hibernation. The hope is that they could be reawakened in a future time when with additional knowledge and skill in medicine, a life-threatening illness, defect, or injury of the present day might be corrected or cured in the future. Others dispute this. Research into HIT (hibernation inducement trigger) is ongoing as scientists study hibernation and its relevance to humans. Ask a pair of interested students to try to find out more information on this and to try to evaluate their sources of information. They should give an oral report to the class on what they learn. One source of information is *Life in the Cold: Ecological, Physiological, and Molecular Mechanisms* by Carey, Florant, Wunder, and Horwitz, eds. (Boulder, CO: Westview Press, 1993).

How does reading *Dragonflight* and engaging in the various activities suggested above help students meet the 12 NCTE/IRA English Language Arts Standards?

1. *Dragonflight* meets Standard #1 by serving as an example of outstanding fiction.

2. *Dragonflight* meets Standard #2 because it is a representative work of the broad genre of fantasy.

3. Discussion questions #1, #2, #4, #5, #6, #7, and #8 help students to comprehend and interpret text, and the vocabulary exercise increases knowledge of word meanings, helping students to meet Standard #3.

4. Extension activity #3, which suggests writing out a series of new verses in the tone and style used in the book, addresses Standard #4, which asks students to adjust written language and style to communicate effectively for different purposes.

5. Extension activity #4, which suggests that a student write Ten Commandments for Weyrwomen, helps meet Standard #5, which requires that students use different writing processes for different audiences and for a variety of purposes.

6. Extension activity #5, which suggests that students write a new chapter to be added to the book, helps to meet Standard #6 by requiring students to apply their knowledge of language structure and language conventions to create a print text.

7. Extension activity #6, which requires students to evaluate and synthesize data from a variety of sources on the topic of the hibernation inducement trigger and to communicate their discoveries, helps to address Standard #7.

8. Research activity #1 involving commercial and wild mushrooms helps to meet Standard #8 by encouraging students to use a variety of technology and information resources to carry out research and to communicate their knowledge.

9. Discussion question #4 about the queens' wing going into battle against the Threads and about F'lar's more conventional notion of the roles that should be played by men and women helps to address Standard #9 by allowing students to develop an understanding of and respect for diversity in social roles.

10. Research question #2 asking ESL students and those interested in different cultural backgrounds to share stories of the use of dragons in traditional ethnic literature helps address Standard #10, which asks students to use their first language that is not English to develop a deeper understanding of the curriculum.

11. Discussion question #3, which allows students to pool their information knowledge in the form of a book discussion group and compare and contrast the use of the tapestry in *Red Wall* with the use of the tapestry in *Dragonflight* as a story element and plot device, helps meet Standard #11, which asks that students participate as knowledgeable, reflective, creative, and critical members of a literary community.

12. Extension activity #1 allows students to creatively select and prepare a means of sharing their enthusiasm for this book with other potential readers. It addresses Standard #12, in which students are asked to use spoken, written, and visual language to persuade others.

The Moorchild

Eloise McGraw

New York: Margaret K. McElderry Books, 1996, ISBN 0-689-80654-X

Detailed Synopsis

Old Bess, the Wise Woman of the village, suspects that the new baby at her daughter's house is a changeling, or strange child left by fairies in place of their real baby. Little Saaski is unusual looking. She has pale hair, dark skin, and long hands and feet, and the color of her eyes keeps changing. She does not resemble her mother, Anwara, or her blacksmith father, big Yanno, who both have blue eyes.

Old Bess, who lives alone and is skilled in using herbs to cure anything, keeps her suspicions about the baby to herself. But the infant cries much of the time and only seems comforted by a spoonful of honey. Old Bess suspects that sometime between the baby's birth and christening, Anwara's child was taken, and a changeling, who fears and hates iron, salt, and holy water, has been left in her place.

Old Bess finally tells her daughter, Anwara, and her son-in-law, Yanno, what she fears. Anwara will not listen to her, but Yanno asks how they might get rid of the changeling and get their own baby back. The cure for their problem appears to be too harsh on the infant changeling, so the couple refuses to pay any attention to Old Bess.

In fact, Saaski, or Moql as she had been called, howls because she misses her homeland and the fairy Folk. She had once lived a carefree life with time for pranks and idling. But one day, after the Moorfolk younglings were turned loose in the daytime and told to hide if any humans came along, Moql carelessly wandered into a flock of sheep and was spied by the shepherd. Although she tried to "wink out" or turn invisible, she failed and the human grabbed her. He said he would let her go if she showed him where to find gold. While he was gathering up gold coins, Moql managed to escape, but she was brought by her teacher, Pittittiskin, back to the Mound to see the Prince.

In front of the Prince, Moql fails to "wink out" or change her shape. Then Talabar, Moql's mother, is sent for. She comes and admits to having coaxed a fisherman named Fergil to live with her a while. The prince realizes that Moql is half-human and will never be wholly successful as Moorfolk, so he decides she'll be swapped for a human child who will come and make a good servant for them.

Moql goes to bed, but when she wakes, she finds she has been changed. She is starting life over as a baby with Anwara and Yanno, but she hasn't completely forgotten the Folk or the Mound. Slowly, as she grows up, her memories of her earlier life fade, but she attracts attention from the villagers because of her dark skin, pale hair, and variable colored eyes.

Saaski is an active child, often out at night and blamed for any strange happenings in the village. At 6, she is sent out with the other children to gather wood. They tease her and call her a changeling. Old Bess hides and watches. There is a moment when Old Bess thinks of throwing Saaski into the pond as she bends over to see her own reflection, but Old Bess cannot bring herself to do so.

Saaski grows up with the other village children, but she is regarded as strange and never is included in their games. One spring when she is 11, the tinker, Bruman, comes to the village and stays up on the moor with his cart; three goats; his dog, Warrior; and an orphan boy named Tam.

Saaski is having a bad day. First she burns the bread, and then the calf seems to have taken all the cow's milk. She takes the cow up the winding hillside to pasture. While she is there, she comes upon a shepherd and his dog. He calls her a pixie, and says he's sure he's seen her before. But she insists she is the local blacksmith's child, and she runs away from him.

Then she bumps into the goatherd, Tam, and his three sheep. The boy explains that he's an orphan who lives with the tinker, Bruman. Tam explains that he takes care of himself and the animals most of the time because Bruman is drunk. Saaski immediately likes the boy. She goes home but promises to come again to hear Tam play his pipe and to watch him juggle.

When Saaski returns to the village, she sees the shepherd and his dog there. He is telling stories about her, saying he knows she is a pixie. Anwara and Yanno order Saaski to stay away from the moor.

Saaski sees a rune on the barn wall and finds that someone has milked the cow before she arrived. She talks to Old Bess about the sign, which only Saaski can see. Old Bess washes the sign away and asks Yanno to put a horseshoe over the barn door to keep away unwanted sprites.

Now that she is forbidden to go to the moor, Saaski is restless and filled with excessive energy. One day she climbs up into the rafters of her house to a strange hiding place and finds Yanno's father's bagpipes, which have been stored there. She begins to play them and refuses to put them away.

From then on, Saaski plays bagpipe tunes all the time. One day, Fergil, the fisherman, comes to the village for hooks, and he hears Saaski playing a tune that is strangely familiar to him. He stares at the child and makes everyone uneasy. Yanno allows Saaski to take the cow to the Highlands and play her pipes. While there, she gathers herbs for Old Bess. She looks at the illustrated books of Old Bess and asks to learn to read. Old Bess teaches her and also tells her stories about how Bess was found and raised by gypsies.

Saaski goes back to the moor, unable to keep away from it. She finds Tam there, and they play their instruments together. One day while they're eating lunch, Saaski sees a little man come up and steal part of Tam's lunch. He is invisible to Tam, but Saaski can see him plainly. He is one of the Moorfolk.

On another day, Saaski sees the bees swarming and helps Yanno get a new skip ready for them. Then she goes to the moor, plays her pipes, and takes a nap. While she sleeps, Moorfolk come. She chases them away and talks with Bruman, the tinker, who can also see them. Saaski returns to the village and learns that she's missed seeing the gypsies, who have been visiting the town for the day. When Saaski tries to join the children in play, they are especially mean to her. One gypsy woman is kind to her and offers to read Saaski's hand in exchange for a lump of beeswax, but then the gypsy says she cannot read her palm.

Eleven days after the gypsies leave, children in the village of Torskaal start to fall ill with the rosy pox. Although Old Bess tries to explain that the pox probably came from a fevered gypsy boy that she had cared for, many villagers blame the illness on Saaski. They think that because the children were mean to her, she has called a curse down on them. When a cow gets tangled in its chain and dies, Saaski is blamed for this, too. Just before Midsummer's Eve, a group of villagers comes to Yanno and insist that Saaski must be sent away for the good of the village.

Saaski hates Midsummer's Eve, celebrated on Saint John's Day, for several reasons. One is that the bonfire is built of rowan wood, something she particularly dislikes. She also hates the garlands of St. John's wort, which are hung everywhere for this celebration. Still suspecting Saaski, the villagers are also cold-shouldering Anwara and Yanno.

Up on the moor, Saaski manages to catch by the wrist one of the Moorfolk. He is called Tinkwa. She offers to let him play her pipes if he will do her a favor. In talking with him, Saaski is reminded of the time she was Moql and lived in the Mound.

Saaski runs back to Old Bess to tell her she has realized that she is a changeling. Then she goes to tell Anwara and Yanno the news that she is Moorfolk. But on the way, the villagers attack her in the street and drive her up on top of the smithy's thatch roof. To hide from them, she manages some change of shape and color, but not enough to completely disappear. Yanno comes and drives the mob away, but the villagers insist that Yanno has only until tomorrow night to get rid of Saaski.

Yanno and Anwara take the child inside, and Saaski explains that she will leave during the night and not come back. She slips away and goes to the house of Fergil, the fisherman. He can remember little of his time with the Folk in the Mound and cannot help her much even though he is her father. Saaski leaves her pipes there with him and gives him instructions on what he must do when someone comes for them.

She takes the chanter with her, and the next morning she climbs the hills to see Tam. Saaski explains that she is going into the Mound to steal back and return Anwara's child. She plays the chanter and Tinkwa comes. She offers to give him the pipes and chanter if he will lead her and Tam to the door of the Mound and be her guide in finding the stolen child.

That night, Saaski, Tam, and Tinkwa meet and slip through the door into the Mound. Unknown to them, Bruman, the tinker, also slips inside. Tinkwa runs off and Saaski is on her own to find her way to the Nursery and then to the Spinning House, where they find the human child, Lekka. Saaski orders the child to come with them. They finally get through the Turning Door and back onto the moor.

On his way out, Tam sees Bruman and realizes that he is eating and drinking and planning to stay in the Mound. Tinkwa says that the Prince will throw him out one day, but it may be in a year or 100 years. As soon as they are outside, Lekka changes from a girl to a baby again. Tam takes Saaski and Lekka in the tinker's cart to the house of Old Bess and hands the baby over to her. Then he and Saaski drive out of town to begin new lives together.

The baby, named Leoran, thrives with Anwara and Yanno, and most of the villagers quickly forget about the changeling who once lived with them. Now and then something reminds Yanno or Anwara of Saaski, and once Anwara thought she heard the sound of two shepherd's pipes playing beautifully in the hills near the village, although she wasn't too sure about that.

List of Major Characters: Saaski (Moql), the changeling; Old Bess, mother to Anwara; Anwara and Yanno, parents of the child who is taken by the fairies; Tam, an orphan gypsy boy who temporarily lives in the hills with Bruman, the tinker; Leoran, the child stolen by the Moorfolk and returned to Anwara and Yanno; and Tinkwa, one of the Moorfolk.

Vocabulary: Look up each of the words listed below, which appears in the book on the page indicated in parentheses. Rewrite the sentence in which the word appears, using a synonym or phrase in place of the vocabulary word.

placid (7) _____

jaunty (25) _____

plaguing (32) _____

enigmatically (59) _____

blithely (62) _____

prodigious (80) _____

reciprocate (93) _____

plagued (102) _____

erratically (103) _____

dawdled (120) _____

disconsolately (150) _____

gulled (194) _____

Comprehension Questions

1. What are four ways Old Bess suggests for getting rid of a changeling?
2. On what three occasions does the old Prince still go out on the moor?
3. Who had drawn the pictures of the plants in the books in Old Bess's cottage?
4. When Saaski delivers Fergil's fishhooks, how is she received?
5. For what use does Old Bess keep spiderwebs in a box above her hearth?
6. When iron and salt burn raw spots on Saaski's arms, how does Anwara treat these?
7. What reward does Tinkwa receive for helping Saaski?
8. How do the villagers intend to get rid of Saaski on Midsummer's Eve?
9. In the Mound, why does Tam see truth with one eye and glamourie with the other?
10. What does the word "Lekka" mean in Folkish?

Answers: 1) You can get rid of a changeling by making it tell its age, by throwing it in a well or into a fire, or by beating it. 2) The Prince goes out on May Day, for Harvest Dancing, and on Midsummer's Eve. 3) Brother Oswic, a wandering monk, drew the plant pictures. 4) Fergil's dog barks at her and she leaves the fishhooks in a mug, where she finds the coppers she is owed. 5) Old Bess uses spiderwebs to stop bleeding. 6) Anwara rubs plantain leaves on the spots. 7) Tinkwa gets the chanter and bagpipes. 8) They plan to throw Saaski into the bonfire. 9) Saaski is only able to touch one of Tam's eyelids with the Nursery ointment. 10) In the Folk language, "Lekka" means stolen.

Discussion Questions

1. At one point early in the story, Old Bess has the opportunity to drown Saaski when she is trying to look at her reflection in the pool. Old Bess is unable to do this. What do you think restrains Old Bess from getting rid of the changeling?

2. The tinker, Bruman, manages to sneak into the Mound. Using what you have learned about this character, discuss the following questions. How long do you think the Prince will allow him to stay? When Bruman finds himself back in the real world on the moor, what will he do? Do you think he will ever see Tam again?

3. Discuss the conventional roles of men, women, and children in the village of Torskaal. How did Old Bess and Saaski fail to live up to these conventional roles? In what ways did they meet the expectations of others? If the village had not suffered an outbreak of rosy pox, do you think that Saaski might have grown up and been accepted in the village as Old Bess was? Why, or why not?

4. Form a discussion group of students who have read both *The Moorchild* by Eloise McGraw and *Into the Land of the Unicorns* by Bruce Coville. Cara finds herself in another world and Saaski finds herself in another world. Both girls meet a tinker along the way who plays a major part in their story. How are the adventures of these two girls similar, and how are they different?

5. Tam proves to be a very special friend to Saaski. Although he cannot see the Moorfolk when they come to take his sandwich, he believes her when she says she can see them. When she must barter away her bagpipes, he says he will buy more for her some day and in the meantime will make her a flute. What are other examples of Tam's devotion to Saaski?

6. The gypsy woman is very protective of Saaski. She steps in to help her when the village children and the gypsy children are hurting her, and she at first offers to read her fortune in her hand, then she says she can't read it. She gives a hint of a bow and makes a gesture in the air. Why do you suppose the gypsy doesn't read Saaski's fortune? What does she think about the child?

7. Where do you think that Tam and Saaski will go when they leave the village in the cart? What will they do? Will they ever be able to "fit in" somewhere else?

8. If you were Anwara or Yanno, do you think you would be able to be friendly and on ordinary terms with the villagers as you raise up your new daughter, Leoran, or would you always hold against them the way they threatened and treated Saaski?

Research Activities

1. Invite a pair of students to research bagpipes and report to the class what they learn in an oral report. At http://www.hotpipes.com/whazzit.html they will find pictures with labeled

parts of bagpipes. If a computer is available in the classroom, students could play bag-pipe tunes for their classmates at http://www.bagpipesatbest.com/. Information on the history of bagpipes can be found at http://www.tartans.com/bagpipes.html, and additional information is available in *The Book of Bagpipes* by Hugh Cheape (New York: McGraw-Hill, 2000).

2. Invite a small group of students interested in bees and beekeeping to prepare a panel discussion for the class, writing their information on note cards to consult during their presentation. Various panel members should explain the differences between modern beekeeping and skep beekeeping, which was used by Yanno in *The Moorchild*. An article called "The Mediaeval Custom of Skep Beekeeping" by Mike Reddy can be found at http://www.comp.glam.ac.uk/pages/staff/mreddy/skepFAQ/skepFAQv2.htm, and information about "Queen Cell Starting Methods" can be found at http://website.lineone.net/~dave.cushman/cellstarting.html. An interesting article called "Beekeeping in the North Yorkshire Moors" appears in the 1997 autumn-winter issue of the North Yorkshire Moors Association and can be found at http://www.north-yorkshire-moors.org.uk/ issue50.htm. Two books that may be of interest are Bobbie Kalman's *Hooray for Beekeeping* (New York: Crabtree Pub., 1998) and *The Fascinating World of Bees* by Angels Julivert (New York: Barron's, 1991).

3. It was made very clear to Saaski and Tam that they must eat nothing while they visit the Mound or they might not be able to leave. The same idea of being forbidden to eat in another world plays an important role in the Greek tale of Persephone. Invite a pair of students to research the legend of Persephone and present what they learn in an oral report to the class. At http://www.mythicimages.com/printpersephone.htm they will learn about Persephone, Queen of the Dead. Other information appears at http://www.loggia.com/muytjh/persephone.html. Two books that provide useful data are Laura Geringer's *The Pomegranate Seeds: A Classic Greek Myth* (Boston: Houghton Mifflin, 1995) and *Bright-Eyed Athena: Stories from Ancient Greece* by Richard Woff (Los Angeles: J. Paul Getty Museum, 1999).

4. Old Bess washes away the strange signs that appear in the barn that she cannot see but that Saaski can see. Ask a small group of interested students to research and report to the class about the hex signs placed by Pennsylvania Dutch (Amish) farmers on their barns. One source of information is *Hex Signs: Pennsylvania Dutch Barn Symbols and Their Meaning* by Don Yoder and Thomas E. Graves (Mechanicsburg, PA: Stackpole Books, 2000). Ask your media specialist if there are arts and crafts books or videos that might show these signs. Information from World Book Online is available at http://www.discoveryschool.com/students/homeworkhelp/worldbook/atozhistory/p/421460.html. Many of these colorful signs with descriptions are shown at http://freepages.genealogy.rootsweb.com/~aferm/pennsylvania/hex.htm.

Extension Activities

1. Form a discussion group of students who have read both *The Moorchild* by Eloise McGraw and *Into the Land of the Unicorns* by Bruce Coville. Cara finds herself in another world and Saaski finds herself in another world. Both girls have an uneasy relationship with their fathers. Do you think either girl will spend time with her father in the future? Why, or why not?

2. Suppose that Lekka or Leoran has some residual memories of her life in the Mound with the Moorfolk. Write a section of her memories with Leoran talking to Old Bess as part of Chapter 24 of the book. Read aloud and share this new section with the class.

3. Suppose the village of Torskaal had a newspaper, the *Torskaal Weekly*. Write up an article for the paper that discusses the crowd at the smithy's the night before Midsummer's Eve, Saaski's strange appearance on the roof, and the disappearance of the child the next day. This should be written in the form of a factual newspaper account and might even have quotes from some of the villagers.

4. Midsummer's Eve is celebrated in a variety of ways. If there are ESL students in the class or students interested in a variety of backgrounds and cultures, invite them to find out if Midsummer Night's Eve is celebrated in some special way in other countries and to report orally to the class on what they learn. Possible sources of information include *Gatherings & Celebrations: History, Folklore, Rituals and Recipes for the Occasions that Bring People Together* by Burton Wolf (New York: Doubleday, 1996). On the Internet at http://www.world-party.com/wp_cms/website/index.cfm?page_ed=251, there is a brief description of celebrations in Sweden, Latvia, Estonia, Finland, Portugal, and Spain. At http://www.cornishlight.freeserve.co.uk/kilhill.htm there is an explanation of the celebration in Cornwall.

5. It is left uncertain as to whether or not Bruman will live out his life in the Mound or will be turned out by the Prince and live among humans again as the fisherman, Fergil, does. It is also uncertain as to how much he will age while he stays in the Mound and whether or not Tam and Saaski will come back for him. Take a poll among classmates who have read the story. Ask both boys and girls if Bruman is likely to spend one year, 100 years, 200 years, or his whole life in the Mound. For those who think he will be turned out at some time by the Prince, ask if Tam and Saaski will or will not come back and care for Bruman. Indicate the results of your survey, comparing the opinions of boys and the opinions of girls. Is there any difference? Show the results of your survey in a bar graph.

6. Invite interested students to pick an exciting scene from *The Moorchild* and use it as the basis for a poster advertising the book and encouraging others to read it. With permission, hang the poster in the school library media center.

How does reading *The Moorchild* and engaging in the various activities suggested above help students meet the 12 NCTE/IRA English Language Arts Standards?

1. *The Moorchild* meets Standard #1 by serving as an example of outstanding fiction.

2. *The Moorchild* meets Standard #2 because it is a representative work of the broad genre of fantasy.

3. Discussion questions #1, #2, #3, #4, and #6 help students to comprehend and interpret text, and the vocabulary exercise increases knowledge of word meanings, helping students to meet Standard #3.

4. Research activity #2, which suggests writing out information for panel discussion participants on three-by-five note cards, addresses Standard #4, which asks students to adjust written language and style to communicate effectively for different purposes.

5. Extension activity #3, which suggests that students write up the events leading to Midsummer Night's Eve as a newspaper article to appear in the *Torskaal Weekly,* helps meet

Standard #5, which requires that students use different writing processes for different audiences and for a variety of purposes.

6. Extension activity #2, which suggests that students write a new section for Chapter 24 on Lekka's memories from life in the Mound, helps to meet Standard #6 by requiring students to apply their knowledge of language structure and language conventions to create a print text.

7. Extension activity #5, which involves taking a poll of boys and of girls who have read the book and presenting the results of the survey in a bar graph, helps to meet Standard #7 by requiring students to evaluate and synthesize data from a variety of sources and to communicate their discoveries.

8. Research activity #4 involving the arts and crafts of the Pennsylvania Dutch helps to meet Standard #8 by encouraging students to use a variety of technological and information resources to carry out research and to communicate their knowledge.

9. Discussion question #3 about the conventional roles played by men, women, and children in this book and about how Old Bess and Saaski do and do not meet these expectations helps to address Standard #9 by allowing students to develop an understanding of and respect for diversity in social roles.

10. Extension activity #4 asking ESL and other students to research and report on the way Midsummer Night's Eve is celebrated in different cultures helps address Standard #10, which asks students to use their first language that is not English to develop a deeper understanding of the curriculum.

11. Extension activity #1 and discussion question #4 allows students to pool their information in the form of a book discussion group and to compare and contrast *Into the Land of the Unicorns* with *The Moorchild*. It helps meet Standard #11, which asks that students participate as knowledgeable, reflective, creative, and critical members of a literary community.

12. Extension activity #6 allows students to creatively select a scene and share their enthusiasm for *The Moorchild* in the form of a poster to encourage others to read this fantasy. It addresses Standard #12, in which students are asked to use spoken, written, and visual language to persuade others.

The Blue Sword

Robin McKinley

New York: Greenwillow Books, 1982, ISBN 0-688-00938-7

Detailed Synopsis

Three months after a young woman with the unlikely nickname of Harry Crewe comes to live at The Residency in Istan with Sir Charles and Lady Amelia, she finds herself drawn to the bleak landscape at the edge of the desert of Daria, which has been conquered by the Homelanders. This last outpost of the Homelander empire is where her brother, Richard, is stationed, and where he arranges for her to come and live after their father's death. Though she comes from a relatively impoverished background, Harry tries to fit into the routine of the great house and its many servants.

Harry is taller than most women and enjoyed being a tomboy as a young girl. She loves riding horses, and this enthusiasm has helped her make some friends. She rides with Cassie and Elizabeth Peterson. She also attends the balls and parties given in the area escorted by her brother, who depends on his fellow soldiers at Fort General Leonard Ernest Mandy to be her dance partners.

One morning, Sir Charles and his secretary, Philip Mortimer, come to breakfast with the news that a war may be brewing. Colonel Dedham and Richard join Lady Amelia and Harry and explain that King Corlath of the Hill people is coming. The colonel believes some curious thing has happened, or some sign has been given, that brings the king here. The colonel is the only one of the group who still believes in the magic of the Hill people, which was well known during Damar's golden age.

Not knowing what to expect from the native chieftain, everyone nervously awaits Corlath's arrival. Harry goes riding off on her horse, but after an hour, she, Cassie, and Beth return, hoping to catch a glimpse of King Corlath. On their arrival, they see seven beautiful Hill horses and watch as an angry-looking King Corlath takes his leave. He and his men see the girls, and then they ride away. Harry is struck by the strange look in the Hill king's eyes.

After the departure of King Corlath, the people at the Residency have a quiet lunch. Reflecting back on their meeting of that morning, they do not think that Corlath will come back, but they also do not believe that he will ally against them with the Northerners since he wanted arms and men to help close the mountain passes to keep an invading army of the Northerners out. The Homelanders would only agree to help Corlath if he would put himself and his people under their administration, which he refuses to do.

Corlath has "kelar," or the Gift, and this gives him strange powers, thoughts, and visions. He finds himself thinking about Harry as he and his men plan what they should do next. Corlath knows that Thurra leads the bands of the Northlands and will soon attack. Corlath announces that he is going back to the Residency to get Harry.

Corlath uses his "kelar" to help him sneak into the Residency unobserved and kidnap Harry, and he breathes a few words over her to be sure she sleeps. He and his riders go across the sands with Harry draped over a horse like a bundle.

When Harry awakes, she finds herself under a tent roof, wrapped in a hooded cloak. Corlath brings her food and drink. They break camp, and this time when they ride away, Harry sits upright on Fireheart, Corlath's red bay. They ride back to Corlath's camp. Harry goes inside his colorful tent that has tapestries on the wall and soft rugs on the floor. She takes a bath and dresses in Hill robes.

She sits down to dinner in the tent with Corlath and eighteen of his Riders. At the end of the dinner, a leather bag is passed around. It contains Meeldtar or Water of Sight. When Harry sips it, she has a vision of a battle and describes what she sees to the others, unknowingly using the Old Tongue or language of the Gods.

The next day, the camp tents are taken down, and Corlath and his group ride off again. This time Harry rides Red Wind. When a bonfire is built, Harry sees the image of the Lady Aerin and her blue sword in the flames. Harry begins to learn some words of the Hill tongue with the help of Mathin, one of King Corlath's Riders.

Corlath gets a new horse for Harry, a golden stallion named Sungold. And he also gives her a sword. Corlath calls Harry by the name of Harimad-sol, and he announces that Harimad-sol will ride in the laprun trials. Mathin takes Harry to a valley and begins to train her for these trials. Harry gets good enough at riding and using a weapon to unseat Mathin from his horse. She enters the laprun trials as Daughter of the Riders and wins first place. Then she is taken into the city, where Harry stays in one wing of King Corlath's castle.

At the banquet after the trials, the Water of Seeing is passed around in a leather sack. Harry drinks and envisions herself riding to the eastern gate of the General Mundy outpost. Then a sword with a blue stone in its hilt is brought to the table. It is Gonturan, kept as a treasure in Corlath's family. It was the Lady Aerin's sword. It is presented to Harry, and she is made a Rider.

For several days following the trials, Harry sleeps. Then she spends time riding Sungold on a practice field, using the sword Gonturan. The Riders finally assemble and head west, away from the city. Their spies have told them that the Northerners are on the move. An army of many thousands is only a short distance away.

Other Hill people join King Corlath's army as it moves along. Finally, they head toward the home of Luthe, who is known for his wisdom and visions and who lives near the Lake of

Dreams. Corlath plans to meet the Northern army at a gap that leads from the mountains to the plains and the desert of Damar. King Corlath does not expect his forces to win, but he hopes to weaken the Northerners so that pockets of Hill folk may survive in the hills and under the kelar of the city.

When Harry points out that a narrow pass, northwest of the Homelander's station, might allow the Northerners to come up behind Corlath's army, and says that Colonel Dedham should be informed of this and his aid enlisted, Corlath grows angry. Harry becomes sullen that her advice is ignored. They continue on their way to visit Luthe.

At breakfast, Luthe explains to Harry that she is a bridge between two worlds. Harry goes to see the Lake of Dreams. After three days at Luthe's, Corlath leads his group back down the mountain, and they head for Bledfi Gap. Harry again confronts Corlath about defending the northwest pass. Again, he is angered by her mentioning it.

That night, Harry slips away and, without realizing it, leaves her sash behind her. Terin and Senay follow her. The three spend the next two days making their way to Colonel Jack Dedham's fort. Harry is stopped at the gate to the fort, but then is recognized by an old friend, Tom Lloyd. She jumps her horse over the gate and talks to Colonel Dedham.

The colonel and a few of his men leave with Harry to go and try to guard the pass. They pick up more help at Senay's hometown. Then Kentarre and her archers join Harry. They finally arrive at Ritger's Gap, the Madamer Gate, and rest before the next day's battle.

When the battle begins, it is discovered that some of the enemies are not all human. They are led by Thurra. In the very first skirmish, one half of Harry's forces are killed. There is a retreat, and in the pause that follows, Richard, Harry's brother, comes riding up to join them.

As the Northerners prepare to attack again, Harry climbs a hill, points her blue sword at the sky, and begins under the spell of kelar to speak in the Old Tongue. Blue light flashes about, and suddenly the whole mountain goes crashing down the valley and crushes Thurra's army.

Richard, Senay, Colonel Dedham, and Terim go up the hill to look for Harry. They find the landscape has changed. Harry is crumpled near the edge of a glade. The sword, Gonturan, looks dull. Uncertain of their reception because they have acted without his approval, they all return to Corlath's camp. Corlath greets them wearing Harry's sash and asks her to marry him. She happily agrees.

They visit the tent of the injured, and Harry uses kelar to cure Mathin and other soldiers of their injuries. Corlath and Harry marry, and soon after, Richard marries Kentarre. Colonel Dedham is made a member of the king's Riders. Harry bears a son, Tor Mathin, and then a daughter. She names the red-haired daughter Aerin Amelia and wants to invite Sir Charles and Lady Amelia to the naming to be held in the city. A small group goes to invite Sir Charles and Lady Amelia, who are happy to come to the naming. By working together, they establish diplomatic relations between the Homeland and Damar, and some Damarians begin to visit Istan and cities to the south.

King Corlath and Harry live in peace and often take their children to visit Luthe in his valley.

List of Major Characters: Harry Crewe (Angharad) is the central character. She is carried off to live with the Hill people by King Corlath. Mathin is one of the Riders of King Corlath, who befriends and teaches Harry. Narknon is a hunting cat who is close to Harry.

Sungold is Harry's horse. Richard, Harry's brother, is stationed at the Outlander Fort; Colonel Dedham commands the Fort. Luthe is a mountain oracle.

Vocabulary: The following words appear in the book on the pages indicated within the parentheses. Look up the definition for each word, and then write an original sentence using it and showing that you clearly understand its meaning.

unprecedented (15) _____

decipher (20) _____

surreptitiously (74) _____

quelling (82) _____

irascibly (87) _____

repudiate (93) _____

abashed (120) _____

prodigiously (123) _____

sentience (149) _____

deigning (155) _____

Comprehension Questions

1. At their first meeting, Colonel Dedham says something to King Corlath just before the king leaves. In what language did Colonel Dedham speak?
2. How is Corlath's tent in the desert distinguished from the other tents?
3. What sorts of animals did the Hill hunters kill and bring back to camp?
4. What animal in King Corlath's desert camp quickly befriends Harry and likes to eat her breakfast porridge?
5. What is Harry's given name?
6. What is the tradition that is followed if your sash is cut in two pieces at the field trials by the king?
7. During the time when Corlath's army marches out to meet the Northerners, why is Mathin's stew pot a favorite at each night's camp?
8. Harry's two worlds are the worlds of the Outlander and the Hillfolk. What are Luthe's two worlds?
9. When overcome by strong emotions, what happens to Corlath's eyes?
10. What is different about Mathin's wounds after Harry uses kelar to cure him?

Answers: 1) Colonel Dedham speaks in the Old Tongue. 2) Corlath's tent is white with black stripes, and a black-and-white banner flies from it. 3) Desert hares, orobogs, and horned dundi are hunted in the desert. 4) Narknon, the cat, befriends Harry. 5) Harry's given name is Angharad. 6) If your sash is cut by the king, you mend it and wear it proudly. 7) Mathin's stew pot is popular because Narknon hunts and brings in meat. 8) Luthe's two worlds are the past and the present. 9) When overcome by strong emotions, Corlath's eyes turn yellow. 10) Mathin recovers from his wounds but has a severe burn on his arm where Harry touched him.

Discussion Questions

1. Invite a group of interested students who have read both *The Blue Sword* by Robin McKinley and *The High King* by Lloyd Alexander to discuss similarities and differences in the two stories, especially as they relate to the use of the enchanted swords. Harry uses the blue sword, Gonturan, to bring the mountain down on Thurra and his army. Taran dislodges a stone at the peak of Mount Dragon and crushes his enemies as he finds Dyrnwyn, the black sword.

2. Colonel Dedham has had a long career as a military man. He thinks he has given up his military pension and career when he leaves the fort and goes with Harry to fight the Northerners. But later, when he reunites with Sir Charles, he learns that he is honorably listed as "missing in action." Ask students to discuss whether in the future they think Colonel Dedham will remain as a Rider with King Corlath or will rejoin Sir Charles and get involved in military diplomacy.

3. Invite a group of interested students to discuss why a threat from one direction (the Northerners) can cause other divided people (the filanon) to come together again as Hill people. Do you think that once the threat is gone, the Hill people will remain unified under King Corlath? Why, or why not?

4. Discuss what clues the author has placed in the story about the young Harry and the way Harry feels about this desert area, which cause the reader not to be shocked on finding out that Harry's great grandmother was one of the Hillfolk.

5. One does not learn a great deal about the "Northerners" in this book. The reader is told that some of them are "not quite people" or are "demonkind" and that when their remains are sent to science labs for study, the scientists don't know exactly what they are. The "horses" that they ride are not really horses, either. Why do you think the author did this? What is the effect of having Corlath and Harry fighting against an army of demons?

6. Two animals play major roles in this story. One was essential to the story. Harry could not have become a Rider or taken part in the battle without her horse, Sungold, but she could have done so without the cat, Narknon. What special role does Narknon play in this story?

7. There were no women in Corlath's camp when the story begins. But after Harry becomes a Rider, two other women, Senay and Kentarre, prove to be major warriors. Do you think that soon after the marriage of Corlath and Harry, other women will be admitted to the small circle known as the king's Riders? Why, or why not?

8. Sir Charles undergoes major changes during the course of this story. Describe Sir Charles as he acts during the first chapters of the book and as he behaves in the final chapters of the book. What brings about this change?

Research Activities

1. Harry uses kelar to bring the mountain down on Thurra's army. But some of the people in Istan say that the slight trembling they felt must be due to the fact "that the mountains

were not so old as they thought, and were still shifting and straining against their place upon the earth." Apparently, some thought this was an earthquake. Invite a pair of students to do some research about earthquakes. Which major quakes have been felt in the continent of North America? Against what scale is an earthquake measured? Have students present a written paper citing at least three sources of information and share what they learn with the class. Possible sources of information include two Internet sites, http://www.nysm.nysed.gov/geodame.html and http://quake.wr.usgs.gov/prepare/alaska; as well as *Earthquakes* by Mark Maslin (Austin, TX: Raintree Steck-Vaughn, 2000) and *The San Francisco Earthquake of 1986* by Lisa A. Chippendale (Philadelphia: Chelsea House Publishers, 2001).

2. Some of the people of Istan felt a slight tremble when Harry used kelar to bring the mountain down on Thurra, and they thought it was due to volcanic activity. Invite a small group of interested students to prepare a presentation to the class on volcanoes. They should try to include a video taken of an active volcano and to show pictures of volcanic areas in addition to making an oral presentation in which they share what they have learned from books, magazines, and the Internet. Some possible sources of information are: http://www.pbs.org/wnet/savageearth/volcanoes/html/sidebar1.html, which discusses the volcanoes of North America; *Mount St. Helen Volcano: Violent Eruption* by Carmen Bredeson (Berkeley Heights, NJ: Enslow Publishers, 2001); *Volcano!* by Ellen J. Prager (Washington, DC: National Geographic Society, 2001); and *Eruption! The Story of Volcanoes* by Anita Ganeri (New York: Dorling Kindersley Pub., 2001).

3. At the wedding of King Corlath and Harry, the bride and groom threw kaftpa or small cakes to the audience. People from different countries and different cultures have special traditions that are used at weddings. If the class has ESL students or students from a variety of backgrounds, this would be a good chance for them to describe some of their traditional wedding ceremonies for the class. If possible, they should bring in books, photos, and the like.

4. The reader is told that the fictional outpost of civilization in this book is mainly important because of the Aeel Mines that were discovered in the Ramid Mountains. Although the mines are mentioned several times, it is not made clear what is mined there. Ask a pair of students to conduct a class survey of those who have read the book to determine what they think is mined there: coal, copper, gold, silver, diamonds, or something else. What leads them to their opinion? Is there a consensus? Have these students report what they learn from their survey in an oral report to the class enhanced by a bar graph showing the survey results.

5. Near Istan, a local tassel-headed grain called korf is grown in carefully irrigated fields. In North America, several types of wheat and corn are grown commercially. Invite a pair of interested students to find out more about wheat farming and raising corn in North America. Where are these crops raised? How valuable are these crops? When does the harvest take place? Invite these students to make an oral presentation to the class using a map of North America and pointing out where the major corn- and wheat-raising regions are.

6. The battles fought by King Corlath and Harry at special, narrow mountain passes are reminiscent of the Khyber Pass through the Hindu Kush mountain range connecting the northern frontier of Pakistan with Afghanistan. The long history of this pass includes its

use by Alexander the Great in 326 B.C. and the famous battle of 1842 involving British and Indian troops. Invite a pair of interested students to learn what they can about the Khyber Pass, write a paper including a bibliography showing at least three sources of information, and share it with the class. One source of information is http://www.afghan-network.net/culture/khyber.html. Another source is *Karachi to Khyber Pass* with Mark Tulley, a videotape that was a BBC production (Bethesda, MD: Atlas Videos, 1994).

Extension Activities

1. The mythical kingdom of Damar is populated with desert animals. Invite a small group of students to prepare a class bulletin board on real desert animals. They should collect pictures that, with permission, they cut from magazines, or draw illustrations for their bulletin board display. They should also include information about a variety of desert animals of the world, which might include the aardvark, aardwolf, bat-eared fox, camel, guanaco, kangaroo, kangaroo rat, llama, pangolin, pocket gopher, and vicuña. Possible books of interest include *Watching Desert Wildlife* by Caroline Arnold (Minneapolis, MN: Carolrhoda Books, 1994), *Desert* by April Pulley Sayre (New York: Twenty-First Century Books, 1994), and *Life in the Deserts* by Lucy Baker (Chicago: World Book, 2001).

2. If some students in the class have chosen to read *The Blue Sword* but others have not, allow time for a pair of students to present a book talk in which they try to persuade others to read it by pointing out what is interesting and exciting about it. The two students should make a mural showing exciting scenes from the book. After the class presentation, the mural might be placed in the school library together with the title and author of the book.

3. There must have been a considerable uproar at The Residency when people awoke to find that Harry had been kidnapped. Invite a student to write this chapter using what is recalled of the incident and recounted to Harry by Colonel Dedham when she returns to the fort for his help. Have the students read this "missing" chapter to the class.

4. Assume that the *General Mundy News* is a paper printed and shared with the community of Istan. Invite class members to serve as reporters for the *News* and to contribute articles for an issue of the paper. The following are possible topics: the strange disappearance of Harry Crewe; the recent visit to The Residency of King Corlath, the impending departure of some wives and children due to the kidnapping of Harry, reports of volcanic activity or earthquakes; reports of a possible Northern invasion, activity at the mines, and training of the troops for battle. Publish for the class this special edition.

5. Ask a student to write a formal invitation to be carried to Sir Charles and Lady Amelia requesting them to come as guests to Corlath's City for the ceremonial naming of Harry and Corlath's baby girl.

6. Although it takes place in a mythical kingdom, the book contains information that would allow a small group of interested students to make a large map of the area and post it in the classroom. The map should show the port of Stzara, the city of Istan, the Fort, The Homeland, the northeast frontier of Damar, Bledfi and Ritger's gap where the battles with the Northerners took place, the valley of Luthe, Senay's hometown, Corlath's City, and the land of the filanon.

How does reading *The Blue Sword* and engaging in the various activities suggested above help students meet the 12 NCTE/IRA English Language Arts Standards?

1. *The Blue Sword* meets Standard #1 by serving as an example of outstanding fiction.
2. *The Blue Sword* meets Standard #2 because it is a representative work of the broad genre of fantasy.
3. Discussion questions #1, #2, #4, #6, and #8 help students to comprehend and interpret text, and the vocabulary exercise increases knowledge of word meanings, helping students to meet Standard #3.
4. Extension activity #5, which suggests writing a formal invitation to Sir Charles and Lady Amelia asking them to attend the naming of King Corlath and Harry's baby girl, addresses Standard #4, which asks students to adjust written language and style to communicate effectively for different purposes.
5. Extension activity #4, which suggests that students write articles on different topics for the *General Mundy News* about recent events in Istan, helps meet Standard #5, which requires that students use different writing processes for different audiences and for a variety of purposes.
6. Extension activity #3, which suggests that students write a new chapter to be added to the book telling what happened the morning after Harry was kidnapped, helps to meet Standard #6 by requiring students to apply their knowledge of language structure and language conventions to create a print text.
7. Research activity #4, which requires gathering opinions on the profitable Aeel mines, helps to address Standard #7 by having students conduct research, generate ideas, synthesize data, and communicate their discoveries to an audience.
8. Research activity #2 involving a class presentation on the topic of volcanoes helps to meet Standard #8 by encouraging students to use a variety of technological and information resources to carry out research and to communicate their knowledge.
9. Discussion question #7, which centers around the conventional roles of men and women and how the roles of women are extended by the recognition of Harry and her special gifts, helps to address Standard #9 by allowing students to develop an understanding of and respect for diversity in social roles.
10. Research activity #3 asking ESL students and students from a variety of backgrounds and cultures to discuss some of their wedding traditions and compare them with the activities surrounding the wedding of King Corlath and Harry in this story helps address Standard #10, which asks students to use their first language that is not English to develop a deeper understanding of the curriculum.
11. Discussion question #1 allows students to pool their information knowledge in the form of a book discussion group and compare and contrast the enchanted swords of *The High King* and *The Blue Sword*. It helps meet Standard #11, which asks that students participate as knowledgeable, reflective, creative, and critical members of a literary community.
12. Extension activity #2 allows students to creatively select and prepare a book talk and a mural as a means of sharing their enthusiasm for this book with other potential readers. It addresses Standard #12, in which students are asked to use spoken, written, and visual language to persuade others.

The Amber Spyglass

Philip Pullman

New York: Alfred A. Knopf, 1999, ISBN 0-679-87926-9

Detailed Synopsis

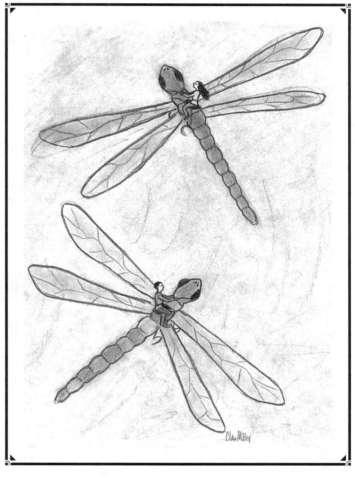

The Amber Spyglass is Book 3 of *The Dark Materials Trilogy*. Book 1 is *The Golden Compass* and Book 2 is *The Subtle Knife*.

As the story resumes in Book 3, Mrs. Coulter is living in a cave near a small village, close to a stream. She has let it be known that she is a holy woman engaged in meditation and prayer. She speaks to no one except her one visitor, a village girl named Ama who brings her food. On this morning when Ama visits, Ama's father comes with her and waits a short distance off.

It seems that although the villagers are glad to have a holy woman nearby, there are rumors that she has with her a companion who may be dangerous. Ama asks who is with her, and Mrs. Coulter explains that her companion is her daughter who is under a spell that makes her sleep, and that they are hiding from the enchanter while Mrs. Coulter tries to cure the girl.

Mrs. Coulter take Ama back in the cave to see her daughter. They find Lyra asleep. Mrs. Coulter says Ama may tell her father what she sees, but Lyra's presence must be kept secret from others, for the enchanter is still seeking to destroy her. Satisfied with this explanation, Ama and her father leave while Mrs. Coulter stirs a concoction of dried leaves. Mrs. Coulter takes a beaker of the liquid into the cave. Lyra begins to stir. Mrs. Coulter helps the girl to sip the liquid, and Lyra falls asleep again.

In Chapter 2, the scene shifts back to a time just after Lyra has been taken by Mrs. Coulter and Will has come from the mountains after the death of his father. Two shapes that call themselves angels are with Will. They want to take him to Lord Asriel, but Will refuses to go until he has found Lyra. The two figures agree to help him search for her.

The angels go to look for Lyra while Will sleeps. One returns and wakes him, explaining that some distance away they found a spot where Lyra must have camped. They also found a dead man there. From the description, Will thinks the dead man is Sir Charles Latrom. The other angel is still seeking Lyra and will come back when he has found out where she is.

Will goes to look at the dead bodies of several witches who had escorted him and Lyra last night to a meeting with his father. He learns that the two angels helping him are named Balthamos and Baruch. In daylight, they are invisible.

Will decides to go back into the mountains to the lake. He notices that his injured hand, which his father treated, is healing. After several hours he reaches the lake and then goes to look at the campsite. In the tents, he picks up some matches and dried meat and views the body of Sir Charles, a powerful and dishonest man, who has been poisoned. Sir Charles had stolen Lyra's alethiometer, a magical object that will answer questions if you know how to use it.

Will checks the tent and decides what to take with him. He chooses many useful items and packs them all in a rucksack. Will sits down to eat and look at the alethiometer, which is composed of 36 little pictures painted on ivory. He does not know how to read it, nor does the angel. Will takes out the subtle knife, which will cut anything, and cuts a small window in front of him. Looking through the window, he sees a landscape of his world. He makes several small cuts and looks into different worlds, trying to figure out exactly how to use the subtle knife.

In the distance, he sees a group of travelers approaching, so Will picks up his things and leaves. He finds a trace of where the other angel went as well as a window to another world. Seen through this window, the landscape is flatter than the mountains of the Cittagazze world. The angel moves through the window, and Will follows. The angel explains to Will that this is Lyra's world.

Since it is cold in Lyra's world, Will suggests that they step back into the Cittagazze world where he can light a fire in the woods, and then leave in the morning. He also asks if the angel can take another shape because he knows that in the girl's world, people have daemons, or familiar spirits in animal form. Will suggests the angel take the form of an animal and pretend to be his daemon. The angel agrees to become a black bird.

The next day, Will walks south but sees no sign of human habitation. He makes camp and has a simple meal. Baruch, the angel, comes back and explains that Lyra is in a Himalayan valley 4,000 or 5,000 miles away, high up near a glacier, and is being kept asleep and held captive by a woman in a cave.

Suddenly something appears above them. Baruch murmurs, "The Chariot." Before Will is able to do anything, something comes hurtling down. It is another, larger angel. They struggle as the other angel calls loudly for the Lord Regent. As the Lord Regent bears down on them, Will uses the subtle knife to cut into another world, which he and Baruch and Balthamos enter and close behind them.

Balthamos explains that Metatron is hunting them. The two angels explain that The Authority or the Almighty was never the creator but was an angel formed of Dust. Other angels were formed, and the Authority told them that he had created them. Then an angel formed who was wiser than the Authority, and she knew the truth, so he banished her.

Balthamos and Baruch serve her, but the Authority still reigns in the Kingdom of Heaven, and Metatron is his Regent.

The Authority lives in a citadel known as the Clouded Mountain. Balthamos and Baruch visited the Clouded Mountain and learned a secret that they want to share with Lord Asriel, who is Lyra's father. The angels confer and decide that Baruch will go ahead to deliver the information while Balthamos stays with Will and tries to find Lyra.

Chapter 3 opens on Serafina Pekkala, the clan queen of the witches of Lake Enara. She flies north to the kingdom of the bear-king, Iorek Brynison. Serafina approaches the bear-king, lays her weapons down, and asks to speak with him. Serafina tells him that in another world, Lee Scoresby died fighting a force of Muscovites. She tells Iorek that Lee Scoresby was looking for the man known as Stanislaus Grumman, that the barrier between the worlds had been breached by Lord Asriel, and that the melting of the ice was one of the consequences.

The bear-king asks about Lyra, and Serafina says she left the child with her sisters. The bear-king says he will go to look at Lee Scoresby and then will go south. While the bear-king goes on his errands, Serafina leaves to go find the gyptians to enlist their help, because she feels they and Lord Faa will be needed.

Iorek Brynison makes his way to the scene of the earlier battle, where he finds the body of Lee Scoresby, a Texan aeronaut, esteemed by the bear-king. Iorek accepts the man's final gift to him by eating his body.

Chapter 4 takes the reader back to Ama, the herdsman's daughter who continues to worry about the sleeping girl in the cave. Ama goes to Pagdzin tulku, a great healer who lives in a monastary. He grants her wish for a remedy. Happily, Ama takes the medicine to the cave. Mrs. Coulter is gone, so Ama goes back to steal a look at Lyra. When Mrs. Coulter returns, Ama hides. From her hiding place, she watches as Mrs. Coulter forces Lyra to drink something that puts her to sleep again. Mrs. Coulter also cuts a lock of the girl's hair and puts it in a gold locket. After Mrs. Coulter and her daemon, a golden monkey, are asleep, Ama, now suspicious of Mrs. Coulter, quietly leaves the cave.

Chapter 5 takes the reader to a mountainous area where tools of war are being manufactured. A sentry watching on the ramparts hears a knock at the door. Three men are half-carrying Baruch, who says he has an urgent message for Lord Asriel. Lord Asriel is with his spy captain, Lord Roke, a tiny creature only as big as a human hand. The spy captain shares some information about Lord Asriel's daughter, Lyra, and then leaves as a messenger brings Lord Asriel word about the wounded angel.

The badly injured angel is brought in and says he has three things to tell Lord Asriel. He says they learned that the Authority has retired to a chamber deep within the Clouded Mountain. Ruling the day-to-day affairs is a prideful and ambitious angel called Metatron. The new plan of the Authority and his Regent, Metatron, is to intervene more actively in human affairs. They intend to move the Authority from the Clouded Mountain and turn it into an engine of war, and their first campaign will be to destroy Lord Asriel's Republic.

The angel, Baruch, goes on to tell Lord Asriel about a knife that can cut openings between worlds. Baruch explains that his companion angel is with the boy who holds the subtle knife, but the boy will not come to Lord Asriel because he is a friend of Lord Asriel's daughter, Lyra, and he is trying to find her.

The dying angel explains to Lord Asriel that the boy with the subtle knife is the son of the shaman, Stanislaus Grumman. Baruch also tells Lord Asriel that Lyra is somewhere in the Himalayas, but before he can pinpoint an exact spot on the map, the angel simply fades away. Lord Asriel calls his men and goes into action.

Chapter 6 begins with the Consistorial Court of Discipline in its eighth day of hearings with Fra Pavel on the stand. Pavel recalls as best he can that the witch said Lyra would have power to make a fateful choice on which the future of all the worlds depended. He also tells of the boy with the special knife. Fra Pavel does not know the exact location of Lyra. He says another branch of the Magisterium, the Society of the Work of the Holy Spirit, may be closer to knowing exactly where Lyra is.

Fra Pavel is excused and the twelve members of the Court meet to discuss what they should do next. With the blessings of the group, one of the court members, Father Gomez, is given the assignment of finding and killing Lyra before she has a chance to be tempted like Eve and fall. The Court, however, is unaware that a tiny Gallivespian spy is up in the ceiling of the room and hears everything they are planning.

The President of the Court questions a prisoner to try to learn more about the source of the colossal energy that Lord Asriel released on Svalbard. Then the president sends Father Gomez on his mission to kill Lyra. He suggests that rather than search for the girl, he should search for the woman who will try to tempt the girl.

Meanwhile, Dr. Mary Malone, an Oxford researcher who is considered to be the one who will tempt Lyra, is in a farmer's cottage. She walks away uncertain as to what to do. She has recently left her own world, and she is looking for Will and Lyra in this world. She sits down and uses the Chinese method of the *Book of Changes* to help her. She decides she is being encouraged to climb upward. She climbs and finds a window cut long ago to another world that has not been closed. She steps through it.

In the morning, Dr. Malone begins walking in this new world. She visits a stand of trees and finds that the trees drop giant seedpods that exude a kind of oil. She sees strange, wheeled animals coming toward her, and at first she hides out of sight. When Mary finally announces herself to the animals, one offers her a ride. She calls the creatures mulefa.

Chapter 8 returns to Will's adventures. Balthamos, the angel, mourns the death of Baruch. Balthamos flies high to get the lay of the land and then leads Will toward a village where a priest invites Will inside his house. Will learns that a boatload of armed bears is heading south. Although pressed to stay, Will heads for the river. A battle is going on there. Will challenges the bear-king to combat with the understanding that after the fighting stops, the bears will get the fuel they need and then will leave.

Will asks for one piece of the bear's armor to make the fight more even. The bear gives him his helmet. With his subtle knife, Will quickly cuts the helmet to bits. Seeing this, the bear gives up, and the battle between bears and townspeople is averted. The bear-king agrees to take Will with him on the next leg of their journey to reach Lyra.

The bear-king explains that the bears are moving because ice is melting and currents are changing and they can no longer live where they once did. They are headed for the same mountains as those where Lyra is being held captive. They travel by ship a long ways. The bear-king reminds them that though they must live differently for a time, when the Arctic freezes again, they will be alive to go back and reclaim it, whereas if they had stayed, they would have starved.

Unable to go any farther, Will and the bears disembark, and Will studies a map that the captain of the ship gave him. The bears scatter, and Iorek and Will go in search of Lyra. Iorek kills animals to provide meat for them. Will exchanges coins for bread and extra clothing in a village. Balthamos accompanies them. They find they are about a three days' walk from where they think Lyra is.

Lord Asriel and his forces in gyropters are also going toward Lyra, hoping to save her. They are at the opening between the worlds, the breach in the sky above Svalbard, and have a long way yet to travel. Through spies, Lord Asriel knows that the two arms of the church, the Consistorial Court and the Society of the Work of the Holy Spirit, are now working together and know exactly where Lyra is. They are sending a flight of zeppelins with a crew hoping to kill Lyra. There are also spies aboard the zeppelins, Chevalier Tialys and Lady Salmakia, who hope to protect Lyra until King Ogunwe's forces can come to the rescue.

Father Gomez is also tracking Lyra, but no one knows exactly where he is. In chapter 10, Father Gomez questions people and tries to learn Lyra's location. He is told that the girl went south.

Mary Malone is still in the company of the wheeled creatures. The mulefa take her to a village where, in a friendly way, Mary and the mulefa explore one another. Mary begins to learn their language and to write it in a notebook. Mary uses I ching to reassure herself that she is doing the right thing at the right time. Mary sees how the mulefa work. Two mulefa, working together, use their trunks in the way Mary uses her pair of hands. She sees the mulefa kill and skin some of the grqzers for meat, lay their fishnets, and care for the groves of seedpod trees.

One afternoon, the mulefa are attacked by 40 gigantic birds. The mulefa run away, calling "Tualapi." They watch helplessly while the birds devour their food, knock seedpods into the water, and destroy the village. When the mulefa return, Mary swims out into the water and rescues five of the seedpods. The mulefa explain that the wheel-pod trees are dying, and the pods are very precious to them.

Chapter 11 returns to Ama, the village girl, outside the cave where Lyra is sleeping. She and her daemon climb up high and see the bear-king and Will approaching. Will's daemon, in the form of a bird, and Ama's daemon in the form of a butterfly fly together and get to understand each other. Will explains he is looking for a girl, and Ama tells him she knows where the girl is.

Will and Ama leave Iorek in the stream above and climb down to the cave where Lyra is sleeping. Will sets a time to meet Ama, who will bring medicine to awaken Lyra. Will walks to the cave and demands to see Lyra. Mrs. Coulter takes him to her. After seeing her, Will leaves, saying that now he knows Lyra is alive and being protected, he is going to go to Lord Asriel, as he has been ordered.

As he plans what to do next, Will realizes that Mrs. Coulter has cast some sort of spell on him, and he wants to see her again. In the distance, he hears the sound of eight zeppelins approaching. On one of the zeppelins, the two spies are reporting and getting their orders. They are to defend the girl and cooperate with Will. If he takes the girl to another world, they are to go with Will and the girl.

Each of the groups prepares to land and be the first to get to Lyra. Will meets Ama, and the two enter the cave through a hole Will has cut in a corresponding world. Before they are able to take Lyra and escape into the other world with her, Will loses his concentration while cutting a hole, and the subtle knife breaks. Will orders Ama to awaken Lyra, and he prepares to fight those who approach from outside the cave. Both the zeppelin and the gyropters land some troops. Tialys and Salmakia arrive. Mrs. Coulter is frozen in place by Tialys, but her daemon, a golden monkey, has caught Salmakia in its paws. Mrs. Coulter drops her gun, and Will picks it up.

The two tiny spies, along with Will and Lyra, sneak out of the cave and up the path to the window that Will had cut previously. They fight their way through, and then the four of them tumble into another world. Will tells Lyra that he has the alethiometer, which Lyra consults. Lyra explains that she must visit the land of the dead to see Roger. She consults the alethiometer to find out how to get there.

The two spies agree to work with Lyra and Will. They sleep peacefully and then reenter the world they left. Many have been killed in battle. They hike a long way in search of Iorek. When they find him, he takes them to his cave and agrees to mend the subtle knife. They build a perfect fire for the task, and Iorek sets to work. Will, Lyra, and Iorek forge the knife although Iorek continues to worry whether or not he should do this.

Iorek gets angry when Will won't tell him precisely what he is going to do with the knife, but Will explains that he is not entirely certain. Iorek tells Lyra that he is not sure she should journey to the land of the dead, but that if she is to go, Will is the best person for her to have as a companion. Will cuts a window into another world, and he, Lyra, and the two spies step into it.

In the next scene, Mrs. Coulter is with Lord Asriel in the tower. They are joined by King Ogunwe, Lord Roke, and an angel called Xaphania. It is suggested that Mrs. Coulter can't be trusted and should be sent away, but she insists that she no longer holds allegiance to the Authority and that now her concern is for her daughter's life. She immediately begins to pick up as much information as she can and learns that their aim is to create the Republic of Heaven, not to support the Kingdom of Heaven. They seek a world of equals where there are no kings, bishops, or priests.

They go to the armory for a look at the "intention craft." Lord Asriel takes off in it. A raiding party comes and is quickly destroyed by the intention craft. The craft can be flown only by a human with a daemon. Mrs. Coulter asks to be shown how it works. Once she is inside and knows how to control it, she pushes Lord Asriel out and takes off, but the tiny Lord Roke slips inside and flies away with her. Lord Asriel is pleased. He thinks she will go to the Consistorial Court, spy for them, and lead them to Lyra.

Mary Malone continues to live among the mulefa. Mary learns that the mulefa have something called scraf. Since Mary doesn't have any scientific equipment with her, she makes a mirror knowing scraf has something to do with reflected light. She applies many coats of lacquer to a smoothed piece of wood and polishes it. Then she removes the wood backing, breaks the lacquer in half, applies oil to it, and by looking through two sheets can see Dust, or scraf, or Shadows.

Mary is surprised when her mulefa friend, Atal, says that now she can finally see Mary must come with her. The mulefa gather, and an old one speaks. He hopes Mary can save their trees and find a way to keep the birds, called tualapi, that are growing more numerous each year from destroying them.

In their new world, Lyra reads the alethiometer hoping to learn how to get rid of the spies. It tells her not to get rid of them, because her life depends on them. They cut through to another world to gather food before hunting for the land of the dead. They find themselves on a farm where people have been killed and more soldiers are approaching. Will cuts through to another world, and the dead people are in it. They are all walking down a road, and the colors of everything outside are fading.

They continue down the road until they reach the town of the dead. A man stops Will and Lyra and says since they aren't dead, they can't enter but must go to a holding area where they find other people waiting for death. They learn everyone has a death, who escorts them to the land of the dead when it is time. Lyra finds her death and persuades him to take her and Will to the land of the dead even though they are still alive. He says they will have to find their own way back.

Meanwhile, Mary Malone decides that she will make a rope long enough to allow her to climb the seedpod trees and look in the tops of them to see what might be happening to cause them to die. The mulefa turn her lacquer pieces into a sort of spyglass. She takes the spyglass with her high into the tree. She sees that the scraf is not entering the blossoms of the tree but is blowing by. Mary wants to make more observations, and the mulefa agree to make her a platform. They set to work on this, unaware that in another world, Father Gomez has accidentally come upon the same window through which Mary entered the mulefa's land. He climbs through to their world.

When Lyra and Will awake, Death leads them and the two spies down a path to the water. An old rowboat comes up, and Will and Lyra climb in with the spies on their shoulders. The boatman refuses to take their daemons. They cross the water to an island. A harpy flies down and attacks, but Will cuts a way into the door with the subtle knife. Will puts a bandage and ointment on Lyra's cuts, and they continue onward.

The dead talk to Will and Lyra in whispers, but there are so many of them that Lyra fears they will never find Roger and Will's father. Word spreads among the ghosts and Roger begins to move toward Lyra. Finally Lyra finds Roger, and they talk. Will tries to cut into another world, but wherever he cuts, he is still underground. Lyra begins to tell the ghosts a story.

Lyra's plan is to lead all the ghosts back into the world. The harpies will be nourished with true stories and will lead ghosts back into the world through the opening that Will cuts. They make a treaty. The dead will drift apart and become a part of everything when they return to the world. Most of the dead plan to follow her. Some stay behind, fearing Lyra will be leading them to Hell. The harpies begin to lead them to a part of the land of the dead that is close to the upper world.

Far away, Mrs. Coulter flies the intention craft to Geneva to land near the Consistorial Court of Discipline. She talks to the Lord President, and then is taken to a guest room and locked in. Only then does she find that the tiny Lord Roke is with her. During the night, Brother Louis creeps in and steals her locket that has Lyra's lock of hair in it.

When Brother Louis leaves, Lord Roke follows him and learns of the President's plan. They will use Lyra's hair and set off a bomb that will hone in on Lyra's cut hair and destroy her. Dr. Cooper leaves with the hair in an envelope. Lord Roke knocks out Dr. Cooper and takes the envelope containing the hair back to Mrs. Coulter. Soon after, the President comes to the guest room, thinking Mrs. Coulter attacked Dr. Cooper. The President orders that she be taken and put in chains.

The next day, during a storm, the President takes the bomb, along with Mrs. Coulter, in a zeppelin to a power station high in the Alps. Lord Roke comes along, hiding in Mrs. Coulter's coat. Lord Roke manages to unlock Mrs. Coulter's handcuffs, and she is determined to get back the piece of Lyra's hair that has been taken and placed in the resonating chamber of the bomb. Mrs. Coulter steals away in the darkness while Lord Roke stays near the zeppelin. A witch is sent in search of Mrs. Coulter and Lord Roke.

Lord Roke's leg is broken, and he is captured by a seagull, the daemon of the witch. The witch attacks Lady Coulter, and then flies off to join her daemon. Lord Roke uses his spur to kill the witch, who hurtles to the ground, and Lord Roke is killed in the fall. The president prepares to set off the bomb. He fights with Mrs. Coulter, and while they fight, her monkey daemon takes the lock of hair from the bomb but leaves a single hair clinging to it.

Dazed, Mrs. Coulter sees Lord Asriel. He picks her up and puts her inside the intention craft. Lord Asriel fires on the zeppelin, which begins burning and falls onto the men and the bomb. All the debris is swept down the mountainside and into the cataract.

In the land of the dead, two ghosts, Lee Scoresby and Will's father, find Will and tell him to find the spot where a lock of hair has been cut from Lyra's head. Will trims this hair right down to the scalp, cuts a hole into another world, and drops the hair there before closing the window up again. Immediately afterward, the bomb hits where the hair is in the adjoining world. The ground begins to shake and stones begin to fall. Lyra, Will, and the others find themselves clinging to the edge of an abyss. Very slowly, they begin to make their way around the abyss.

At one point, Lyra slips and begins to slide, but one of the harpies, called No-Name, swoops her up in her talons and returns Lyra to Will. They finally reach the point where Will can cut a hole into another world. Before they leave, Will's father gives them some information about what he and Lee Scoresby will do next and about where their daemons are. He explains that although you can travel in other worlds, your daemons will die if they stay too long in another world. Will then cuts a hole, and he and Lyra rest while all the ghosts come tumbling out of the land of the dead.

In the land of the mulefa, the platform in the canopy of the trees had been built, and Mary lives there, trying to find out what to do to save the trees. She wonders what happened 300 years ago to cause the scraf to begin blowing in this pattern. Mary experiences a few moments of being outside her body, swept along in the Dust. She realizes unless she halts what is going on, everything will be swept into oblivion.

Father Gomez, who is also in the land of the mulefa, sees great white birds and water at a distance and walks toward them. The birds see him, and one attacks. Father Gomez shoots and kills it. The other birds drop back. Father Gomez realizes that if these birds fear him, he can make them do exactly as he asks.

Lord Asriel returns to his base and goes off to consult with King Ogunwe while Mrs. Coulter talks to the alethiometrist, Mr. Basilides. He tells her that Lyra is alive and that the bomb did not kill her, but that she is in the land of the dead. From the watchtower, Lord Asriel sees the Chariot with the Regent, Metatron, in the distance. He seems to have an army of angels with him.

All of Lord Asriel's supporters begin to arrive from every world. Among them are Iorek and his bears. Mr. Basilides tells Lord Asriel that the daemons of Will and Lyra are in this world and that Metatron will try to capture them in order to control Will and Lyra. Lord Asriel gives orders: King Ogunwe is to protect the fortress. The Gallivespians, now under the control of Madame Oxentiel, will look for Will and Lyra and their daemons. Lord Asriel will destroy Metatron. Mrs. Coulter again slips away.

After spending a night resting in the beautiful world, Will and Lyra step back into the dark again and walk with Lee Scoreby, the remaining ghosts, and the harpy to a spot where Lyra says Will must cut through to another world where their daemons are. Will cuts his way into Lord Asriel's world, where a great battle is going on and Specters are just arriving. The ghosts from the land of the dead begin fighting the Specters. Amidst the battle, Will and Lyra feel pain and know that their daemons are nearby and in danger. A great storm breaks over the whole scene.

Mrs. Coulter and her daemon fly the intention craft straight to Metatron. She sees a group of men carrying the Authority on a litter. Mrs. Coulter goes to Metatron and tries to win him over by saying that she will betray Lord Asriel.

Lord Asriel has gone through a crack in the mountainside down long caverns and is watching at the abyss as ghosts are flowing steadily through the opening to another world. Following him are Mrs. Coulter and Metatron. Everything is covered in falling Dust. Further down the trail, Will and Lyra stumble along. They come upon cliff-ghasts attacking something in the mud that looks like a glittering cage.

Mrs. Coulter persuades Metatron to let her go ahead to Lord Asriel. She tells him Metatron is coming. When he gets to them, Lord Asriel and Mrs. Coulter and their daemons fight with Metatron, forcing him off the edge and into the abyss. At the same time, Will fights off the cliff-ghasts. On the litter is the Authority, almost dead, and the winds blow his ghostly form away. In the fight with the cliff-ghasts, Chevalier Tialys dies. Lady Salmakia dies, too. A hawk swoops down carrying Madame Oxentiel.

Troops arrive, and among them is the bear-king, Iorek. He orders the children onto his back. The Gallvespians, cavalry, ghosts, Specters, and bears engage in battle. Will cuts his way into another world, and he and Lyra slip into it, carrying their two daemons with them. Their daemons quickly run away.

In the new world, Will and Lyra bury Tialys and Salmakia, then fall asleep. When they wake in the morning, their daemons are gone. They wash in a nearby stream and see something at a distance coming toward them. They are mulefa, and two of them give Will and Lyra a ride down a smooth road. They arrive in the village and meet Dr. Mary Malone. Soon they are seated in the shade and are given food and drink. Exhausted, they fall asleep to awaken in the early evening.

In the evening, a group of mulefa come and Mary goes off with them, leaving Will and Lyra behind. The mulefa lead her to a spot where Will cut the window with the subtle knife. They watch a stream of ghosts stepping into the world and then dissolving within a few seconds. One ghost pauses long enough to say, "Tell them stories."

The next morning, Will and Lyra wake. They bathe in the river and spend a quiet day with Mary, mending nets, gathering food, and talking. Mary tells them how she was once a nun but stopped believing in God. She says people do good or evil deeds but are too complicated to be called good or evil persons. She says she feels loose in the universe without a purpose.

That night Mary can't sleep, and she gets up and walks toward her tree. The wind is blowing, and as she watches, her special tree topples down. Through the spyglass Mary can see the Dust flowing in the opposite direction. It occurs to her that maybe the Dust is escaping through the holes that the subtle knife has cut. She realizes that her purpose is to hold back the Dust flood.

Mary starts back to the village, and sees one of the big white birds, a tualapi, coming closer. She watches as a man carrying a rifle climbs off of its back and searches through the village. The man goes into her house, and finally turns and leaves without ever seeing Lyra and Will asleep beneath a tree.

In the morning, Lyra and Will leave the village and walk out in search of their daemons. Their daemons don't come right to them, but hide and follow Lyra and Will. Unknown to them, Father Gomez is also following them, hoping to get close enough to get a good shot at Lyra without hurting Will. His daemon, a green-backed beetle, flies ahead, leading Father Gomez toward them. Suddenly, Father Gomez feels pain and hears a voice say that it has captured his daemon. It is the ghost, Balthamos.

In a quiet grove near a stream, Will and Lyra stop for lunch. They kiss and profess love for each other. Balthamos goes through the wood, holding the beetle, and is followed by Father Gomez. When Father Gomez attacks, he falls into the stream, cracks his head on a rock, and Balthamos holds him under the water until he drowns.

Back in the village, there is excitement. For as Will and Lyra discovered their love, the Dust has stopped flowing away. It is now falling like snowflakes. The Dust pouring down from the stars has found a living home again, and the love of the children for each other is the cause of it all.

That night, the two daemons come to Will and Lyra but do not wake the sleeping children. Serafina Pekkala comes and takes the daemons a distance away and talks with them. She names Will's daemon Kirjava. She tells Kirjava and Pantalaimon that in most respects, Will and Lyra are witches now. The two daemons will soon settle on a form, and their job is to guide Will and Lyra and encourage them toward wisdom. Serafina flies back to the village and wakes Mary Malone and talks to her.

The next day, Will and Lyra walk in the woods again, and that night they go down to the sea where they watch and listen to birds. Two birds land and change into a white ermine and a cat. Pantalaimon and Kirjava come to Lyra and Will and tell them what Serafina had shared with them. When Will and Lyra realize they must close all the windows so that Dust does not escape, and that a new Specter is created every time a hole is cut, Will and Lyra are in despair. They realize each must live in a different world and there will be no way to pass between them. Lyra decides to consult the alethiometer but finds she can no longer interpret it.

The angel Xaphania comes and wants Will to show her how to close all the openings. She tells Lyra that after a lifetime, she will be able to read the alethiometer again. She also says that one window may be left open. Will and Lyra wish it would be a window that they could move through, but they realize that the one window left open must be the one from the land of the dead. Reluctantly, Will and Lyra accept the fact that they will live their lives apart from each other.

In the morning, a ship comes, and Serafina leads it to shore. The mulefa invite all the visitors to join them that night for a meal. The next morning, they leave. Will and Mary will go to their world, while Lyra and Serafina go into Lyra's world.

Three weeks later, Lyra is having dinner at Jordan College with Dame Hannah and the Master. They want to hear of her adventures, and she promises to tell them the truth if they will promise to believe her story. They discuss Lyra's future. Dame Hannah suggests that she study at a boarding school, St. Sophia's, and that her object of study be the alethiometer. The hope is that if people in all the worlds work at it, they'll be able to build the Republic of Heaven.

List of Major Characters: Will Parry and his father, John Parry; Lyra Silvertongue; Mrs. Coulter, Lyra's mother; two angels, Balthamos and Baruch; Ama, a village girl who lives near the cave where Lyra is kept prisoner; Iorek Brynison, the bear-king; Chevalier Tialys and Lady Salmakia, tiny Gallivespian spies; Lord Roke, leader of the Gallivespians; Lord Asriel, Lyra's father; Mary Malone, a researcher; and Roger, a friend of Lyra's who has died.

Vocabulary: The numbers in parentheses after the words below indicate on what page the word appears in the book. Look up each word in a dictionary and find its synonyms. Choose one that is appropriate and rewrite the sentence from the book, substituting the synonym for the vocabulary word.

petulant (24) _____

fastidiously (25) _____

disdain (26) _____

malevolence (29) _____

abashed (48) _____

noxious (55) _____

postern (56) _____

heretical (74) _____

enigmatic (81) _____

gesticulating (106) _____

turbid (114) _____

luminescence (159) _____

Comprehension Questions

1. How was Sir Charles Latrom killed?
2. Why isn't the body of Lee Scoresby simply a skeleton when the bear-king finds it?
3. What guides Pagdzin tulku to know which powders and herbs to gather in what order to make a medicine to combat sleeping sickness?
4. How does the small spy captain, Lord Roke, often move about?
5. What was strange about the deer- and antelope-like creatures that Dr. Mary Malone found in the new world she entered?
6. On what sort of activity do the mulefa spend a lot of their time?
7. Why did Mary Malone only use one hand sometimes in tasks she did with the mulefa?
8. Out of what material did Salmakia fashion the saddle that she put on her dragonfly?
9. The mulefa had something similar to a pair of wedding rings. What did the mulefa "wedding rings" look like?
10. Before she leaves the land of the dead, Lyra gives a name to the harpy called No-Name. What is it?

Answers: 1) Sir Charles was poisoned. 2) The witch had laid on a spell to preserve him. 3) Pagdzin tulku's daemon, a bat, flies about and determines what goes into the medicine. 4) Lord Roke flies on a small blue hawk. 5) The legs of these animals were arranged in a diamond pattern with one in front, two in the middle, and one behind. 6) The mulefa spend a lot of time maintaining their wheels. 7) By using one hand, Mary could work with a mulefa that used its trunk, and feel more connected to it. 8) The dragonfly saddle is made from hummingbird skin. 9) Mulefa "wedding rings" were strips of bright copper that were bent around the base of one of their horns. 10) Lyra names the harpy "Gracious Wings."

Discussion Questions

1. The reader learns that the bear-king has esteemed very few humans, but that one of these is Lee Scoresby. Yet when the bear-king, Iorek Brynison, finds his old friend dead after a battle, the bear eats the body. The text says he "accepts the man's last gift to him." Does this eating of the body seem appropriate? Why, or why not?

2. In one of the worlds, each of the characters has a daemon. For example, Father Gomez has a large green-backed beetle. A sailor has a seagull for a daemon. The daemon of the President of the Court is a lizard. Lord Asriel's daemon is a snow leopard. The concept of daemons comes from Greek mythology. Do you think that the choice of these various daemons is appropriate? What is the role of the daemons in the story?

3. On page 193, Will says, "Maybe sometimes we don't do the right thing because the wrong thing looks more dangerous, and we don't want to look scared, so we go and do the wrong thing just because it's dangerous." Do you think Will is right in saying this? Can you think of an instance where it was hard to make a right decision because you thought it might make you look scared? Discuss.

4. Lyra tells her friend, the bear-king, that we must keep promises no matter how difficult they are. Encourage a discussion about promises. When should they be made? Must all promises be kept? Should any promise ever be broken?

5. Pantalaimon is Lyra's daemon. Sometimes it is a mouse, sometimes a polecat, sometimes a bird, sometimes a wolf. With ESL students and other students in the class interested in different cultural backgrounds, explore whether there are works of literature from other countries in which animals change shape. What are some of these stories? Share what you learn with classmates.

6. In *The Lion, the Witch and the Wardrobe* there are many Christian symbols and messages. In *The Amber Spyglass* there is an indictment of organized religion and the authority of the church. Bring together students who have read both books and discuss their religious aspects. One useful resource is *The Horn Book* of July–August 2002, which contains an article by John Rowe Townsend called "Paradise Reshaped."

7. People who have studied *The Amber Spyglass* have said that there is an overall supporting structure of "a myth of creation and rebellion" and a struggle against "the old forces of control and ritual and authority." In a discussion group, ask students to discuss the book in these terms, and on the chalkboard to list those characters who are on each side of the struggle.

8. Lyra is not told what happened to her mother and her father, nor does she think to ask the witch about them. Similarly, no one knows that the ghost, Balthamos, destroyed Father Gomez. Do you think that the major characters should have been given this information? Why, or why not?

Research Activities

1. At one point, Will learns that Lyra is in the Himalayas. The most famous mountain in the Himalayas is Mt. Everest. It is the highest peak in the world. Invite a pair of students to

research this topic and give an oral report to the class in which they explain where Mount Everest is, how high it is, who first scaled it and when, and other pertinent information. Possible sources include *Sir Edmund Hillary: Modern Day Explorer* by Kristine Brennan (Philadelphia: Chelsea House, 2001), *Triumph on Everest: A Photobiography of Sir Edmund Hillary* by Broughton Coburn (Washington, DC: National Geographic Society, 2000), and various Internet sites including http://aleph0.clarku.edu/rajs/mountains.html and http://www.time.com/time/time100/heroes/profile/hillary_norgay01.html.

2. The arctic fox is mentioned in Chapter 3 of the book. Invite a pair of interested students to prepare a written report on the arctic fox using at least three sources of information and sharing it with classmates. Resources on the Internet include http://www.cws-scf.ec.gc.ca/hww-fap.cfm?ID_species=50&lang=e and http://www.mnh.si.edu/arctic/html/arctic_fox.html. Additional information may be found in *Polar Animals* by Paul Hess (New York: De Agoslini Editions, Ltd., 1996) and in *Arctic Foxes* by Jenny Markert (Mankato, MN: Child's World, 1991).

3. The power station near where the bomb is be launched is located high in the Alps. Ask a small group of interested students to research the Alps and write a report on the topic to share with the class. Sources of information on the Internet include http://agciwww.bio.ns.ca/schools/EarthNet/english/geology/qa/land/q5.html and http://www.btinternet.com/~nigelspencer/alps-title.htm. Useful books on the subject are *The Alps and Their People* by Susan Bullen (Toronto: Thomson Learning, 1994) and *100 Hikes in the Alps* by Vicky Spring (Seattle: Mountaineers Books, 2nd edition, 1992).

4. Bats are mentioned several times in this book. Invite a small group of students to research different kinds of bats, taking notes on note cards. Using these note cards, let them be prepared to be "bat experts" during a panel discussion in front of the class. Ask one student to be the emcee and to call on the others to share information. Possible sources include *Bats: The Amazing Upside-downers* by Phyllis J. Perry (Danbury, CT: Franklin Watts, 1998) and *Bats* by Sue Ruff (New York: Benchmark Books, 2001). Useful information on the Internet can be found at http://members.aol.com/bats4kids/ and at http://www.cccoe.k12ca.us/bats/welcome.html.

5. On page 83 of the book, Dr. Mary Malone mentions going to a conference in California and seeing the magnificent redwoods. Invite a pair of students to research the California redwoods and make an oral report to the class on what they learn. Where are these redwoods located? How big are they? How old are they? Possible sources of information include *Giants in the Earth: The California Redwoods* by Peter Johnstone, ed. (Berkeley, CA: Heydey Books, 2001); and *Coast Redwoods: A Natural and Cultural History* by Michael G. Barbour, John Evarts, and Marjorie Popper, eds. (Los Olivos, CA: Cachuma Press, 2001). Information is available on the Internet at http://www.nps.gov/ redw/ and at http://www.humboldtredwoods.org/.

6. One of the vehicles used in *The Amber Spyglass* is the zeppelin. A very famous event in American history involved a zeppelin called the Hindenburg. Invite a group of students to research this topic and write a paper, using at least three sources of information, which they share with the class. Possible sources of information include *Golden Age of the Great Passenger Airships: Graf Zeppelin and Hindenburg* by Harold G. Dick (Washington, DC: Smithsonian Institution Press, 1992); *When Giants Roamed the Sky: Karl Arnstein and the Rise of Airships from Zeppelin to Goodyear* by Dale Topping (Akron, OH: University of Akron Press, 2000). Information is available on the Internet at

http://www.vidicon-tv.comn/tohiburg.htm and http://www.ciderpresspottery.com/ZLA/greatzeps/german/Hindenburg.html.

Extension Activities

1. There is a description on page 88 and another on page 130 of some strange animals seen by Dr. Mary Malone. Invite interested students to draw these animals and incorporate them into posters advertising *The Amber Spyglass* and encouraging others to read the book. With permission, place the posters in the school library media center.

2. Dr. Mary Malone sees interesting trees, seedpods, butterflies, animals, and birds when she steps into a new world. Invite interested students to write several pages as they might appear in a science notebook if Dr. Malone were making scientific notes of her discoveries. In addition to descriptions, sketches might be included. Have the students share their notebook pages with other class members.

3. Have a group compare two of the couples in the book, Lady Salmakia and Chevalier Tialys with Mrs. Coulter and Lord Asriel. Have the students list on a chart ways in which these couples are similar and ways in which they are different. In either couple, are there designated feminine roles or actions that are different from the masculine roles and actions? Does their station in life make a difference?

4. Ask a pair of students to write a short article about mulefa under the name of Father Gomez to circulate among members of the Consistorial Court of Discipline, and have another pair of students write a short article about mulefa under the name of Mrs. Malone to be circulated among graduate students in her research division at Oxford. Compare the two articles on the same subject.

5. Invite a pair of students to write a short new chapter for the book in which Lyra is told how her parents died. Who will tell her? What is her reaction to this news? Have the students share their new chapter with the class.

6. Philip Pullman's *The Amber Spyglass* won the Whitbread Book of the Year Award in 2002. There are many awards given in the United States, England, and throughout the world for outstanding books. Invite a small group of students to research this topic with the help of the school or public library media specialist. The students should use a variety of sources for their information including the Internet and journals and magazines such as *The Horn Book,* which each summer includes in the July–August issue the acceptance speeches for the prestigious Newbery Medal and Caldecott Medal. The students should make and display in the classroom a chart listing the awards and a few of the recent winners' names and titles of their books.

How does reading *The Amber Spyglass* and engaging in the various activities suggested above help students meet the 12 NCTE/IRA English Language Arts Standards?

1. *The Amber Spyglass* meets Standard #1 by serving as an example of outstanding fiction.

2. *The Amber Spyglass* meets Standard #2 because it is a representative work of the broad genre of fantasy.

3. Discussion questions #1 through #8 help students to comprehend and interpret text, and the vocabulary exercise increases knowledge of word meanings, helping students to meet Standard #3.

4. Research activity #4, which suggests that students write information on note cards and participate as an "expert" on bats in a panel discussion in front of the class, addresses Standard #4, which asks students to adjust written language and style to communicate effectively for different purposes.

5. Extension activity #4, which suggests that students write about the mulefa society from two points of view for two different sets of readers, helps meet Standard #5, which requires that students use different writing processes for different audiences and for a variety of purposes.

6. Extension activity #5, which suggests that students write a new chapter showing how Lyra reacts when she is told the truth about the death of her father and mother, helps to meet Standard #6 by requiring students to apply their knowledge of language structure and language conventions to create a print text.

7. Extension activity #6 requires students to gather, evaluate, and synthesize data about book awards from a variety of sources and to communicate their discoveries. It helps to address Standard #7.

8. Research activity #3 involving the Alps helps to meet Standard #8 by encouraging students to use a variety of technological and information resources to carry out research and to communicate their knowledge.

9. Extension activity #3, which compares two couples playing major roles in the story, helps to address Standard #9 by allowing students to develop an understanding of and respect for diversity in social roles.

10. Discussion question #5 asking ESL students and others to examine the literature of other countries for examples of animal characters that change shapes and to compare and contrast these with the daemons in this story helps address Standard #10, which asks students to use their first language that is not English to develop a deeper understanding of the curriculum.

11. Discussion question #6 allows students to pool their information knowledge in the form of a book discussion group and compare and contrast the religious aspects of *The Amber Spyglass* with *The Lion, the Witch and the Wardrobe*. It helps meet Standard #11, which asks that students participate as knowledgeable, reflective, creative, and critical members of a literary community.

12. Extension activity #1 allows students to creatively select and prepare a means of sharing their enthusiasm for this book with other potential readers. It addresses Standard #12, in which students are asked to use spoken, written, and visual language to persuade others.

Harry Potter and the Goblet of Fire

J.K. Rowling

New York: Scholastic, 2000, ISBN 0-439-13959-7

Detailed Synopsis

Harry Potter and the Goblet of Fire is the fourth book in a projected seven-book series. Book 1 is *Harry Potter and the Sorcerer's Stone*. It is followed by *Harry Potter and the Chamber of Secrets* and *Harry Potter and the Prisoner of Azkaban*.

When the fourth book in this series begins, there is a recounting of events that occurred long ago in the village of Little Hangleton at a manor home called the Riddle House. Three people were murdered there, and the gardener, Frank Bryce, was arrested for the crimes. Frank insisted on his innocence. The police report showed no cause of death but said each victim looked frightened to death. Frank was released by the police and stayed on as gardener for the next inhabitants of the Riddle House.

A wealthy man currently owns the house but does not live in it, and Frank continues to tend the garden, often harassed by neighbor boys who play tricks. One night Frank sees lights in the big house and goes to investigate. Frank finds two men inside sitting by a fire and talking about spending a week in the house. The two men, Lord Voldemort and Wormtail, talk about having killed one woman, and they are planning another murder. Frank decides to sneak away and go to the police to report what he has heard, but before he leaves, Nagini, a gigantic snake, comes slithering toward him. The snake reports Frank's presence, and he is ushered into the room and killed by the wizard with a stroke of his wand.

Far away on Privet Drive, Harry Potter wakes up in bed from a bad dream he can only half-remember. The lightning-bolt scar on his forehead is stinging, which he fears may mean Lord Voldemort is near. He decides to write his godfather Sirius a letter, and then Harry goes down to breakfast.

While at breakfast, the postman brings a letter to the Dursleys from Mrs. Weasley inviting Harry to come and spend the remainder of the summer vacation with them and to go see the World Cup Quidditch match. Harry's uncle agrees and Harry sends off a note via owl saying that he'll be ready to be picked up tomorrow. Harry also sends off his note to his godfather, Sirius.

Harry packs his things and is ready to go with the Weasleys the next day. They arrive by floo powder in the fireplace and astonish Uncle Vernon, Aunt Petunia, and Cousin Dudley. For the brief period they are in the house, the Weasleys raise havoc. At the Burrow, there is lively mischief before everyone finally sits down to a good dinner cooked by Mrs. Weasley.

The next morning, everyone gets up early to go to the World Cup Match. Because so many are coming, arrival times are staggered. Mr. Weasley and his group head for Stoatshead Hill, the closest spot to find a Portkey, which will transport them from one spot to another at a prearranged time. The Weasley group meets Amos and Cedric Diggory. They all touch the Portkey, which is an old boot, and are swept away.

They land in a moor and are directed to their campsites. A Muggle in charge of tents becomes suspicious and is given a memory modification. They pitch their tents and some go to get water while others search for firewood. All of them explore the big camp area filled with wizards. Ludo Bagman comes along and takes bets on the Quidditch match from Mr. Weasley and from Fred and George Weasley.

Salesmen are selling souvenirs, and Harry buys three pairs of omnioculars, one for himself, one for Ron, and one for Hermione. These allow you to replay action of the game. They all walk through the wood to the stadium, where 100,000 witches and warlocks are taking their seats. The Weasley tickets are for the top box at midfield. Also sharing the box is a house-elf named Winky who says she is saving a seat for her master, Mr. Crouch. Draco Malfoy and his parents also arrive.

The festivities begin and the game is fast and furious. It ends when Krum gets the Snitch, making the final score Bulgaria 160 and Ireland 170, and causing Fred and George to win their bet. In the middle of the night, everyone is awakened. Some Death Eaters, supporters of Lord Voldemort, have caught the Muggles who run the campsite and are marching around with them. Mr. Weasley, Bill, Charlie, and Percy try to help restore order, while the others run into the woods until things have been sorted out.

In the woods, the group becomes separated. Harry, Ron, and Hermione are in one group and Fred, George, and Ginny are in the other. Harry loses his wand. They wander about until someone conjures up the sign of the skull, or the Dark Mark, in the sky. People are terrified. Several members of the Ministry of Magic accuse Harry, Ron, and Hermione of conjuring up the skull. When they discover the limp form of the house-elf Winky, she is accused of making the sign, and Winky is fired by her master.

Early the next morning, Harry and friends return to Mrs. Weasley's house. She has been worried and holds a newspaper filled with news about the Quidditch Match and the Dark Mark that appeared in the sky. It was written by Rita Skeeter, a reporter who is critical of the Ministry of Magic.

During the days that follow, Mr. Weasley and Percy work late hours at the Ministry. Mrs. Weasley shops for school supplies for the new term, and everyone prepares to return to Hogwarts. Just before the children are ready to leave, Mr. Weasley is summoned on important business. Mad-Eye Moody, a retired dark wizard catcher, reports someone trying to break into his house during the night. Mr. Weasley goes off to take care of that while

Mrs. Weasley orders taxis to take the children to the Hogwarts Express. Hints are dropped that something very special will be happening at the school this year. After departing the train, the children ride in carriages to Hogwarts.

In the Great Hall, the Sorting ceremony is held for the first-year students. Then plates fill, and the feasting begins. All have a good dinner except for Hermione, who loses her appetite when she finds the food has been prepared by house-elves who work like slaves. A strange-looking man called Professor Moody is introduced as the new Defense Against the Dark Arts teacher. The headmaster announces that a Triwizard Tournament will be taking place at Hogwarts this year.

The Triwizard Tournament was established 700 years ago and involves the Hogwarts, Beauxbatons, and Durmstrang schools of wizardry. The last tournament was held over a century ago. Each school sends a champion to compete in three magical tasks. Contestants must be 17 or older.

At breakfast, owls appear with letters, but nothing comes for Harry. Then classes begin. On the way to dinner, Malfoy makes unpleasant comments about another newspaper article and throws something at Harry. Before Harry can touch his wand, Professor Moody changes Malfoy into a ferret and marches him off to speak to the head of his house.

Two days later, Harry is in Moody's class. Mad-Eye Moody explains that he is to teach them curses for one year only. He begins with the Unforgivable Curses: Imperius, Cruciatus, and Avada Kedavra. Hermione rushes through dinner in order to go to the library. Ron and Harry do homework, and when Hermione returns she tells them about forming a new group, the Society for the Promotion of Elfish Welfare (S.P.E.W.). She wants the boys to join. Hedwig, Harry's owl, finally brings a note from Sirius saying that he is coming. Afraid that some harm might come to him, Harry quickly sends another note stating that all is well and Sirius doesn't need to come.

Classes continue, there is notice of the Triwizard Tournament, and a week later a flying carriage delivers some foreign students to Hogwarts. A huge woman the size of Hagrid steps out of the carriage. She is Madame Maxime. A dozen students are with her, and they all go inside to warm up. A few minutes later, Professor Karkaroff and his students arrive on the lake in a masted ship. Among these students, they recognize the famous World Cup Quidditch player, Krum. In addition to the foreign guests, two others arrive for dinner: Mr. Crouch, Head of the Department of International Magical Competition, and Mr. Bagman, Head of the Department of Magical Games and Sports.

Professor Dumbledore explains that the three tasks for the three champions will be spread throughout the school year and will involve magical prowess, daring, powers of deduction, and ability to cope with danger. Those wishing to represent a school must put their names and their school names on a piece of paper and drop it in the Goblet of Fire. An age line will be drawn around the goblet, so that no one under the age of 17 will be able to cross it, preventing underage students from entering.

The next morning, George and Harry, having first taken a drop of aging potion, try to cross the age line around the goblet and enter their names in the Triwizard contest. Both boys are zapped right out of the circle. Ron, Harry, and Hermione go to see Hagrid. Hermione tries to get him to join S.P.E.W., but he insists that very few house-elves would want be to independent. Later, all dressed up, Hagrid comes to dinner in the dining hall, walking with Madame Maxime.

Everyone sits down to Halloween dinner in the Great Hall, and there is excitement waiting for the announcement from the Goblet of Fire as to which three champions will enter the Triwizard Tournament. The Goblet spits out bits of parchment with the names: for Durmstrang, Viktor Krum; for Beauxbatons, Fleur Delacour; and for Hogwarts, Cedric Diggory. Then the Goblet spits out a fourth name: Harry Potter.

The four selected students gather in a room with a large group of adults. Some think it is unfair that Hogwarts will have two champions. Others insist that every name that comes out of the Goblet of Fire must compete in the tournament armed only with their wands. It is decided that Harry will compete, and Mr. Crouch gives instructions. He does not describe the first task because it is designed to test daring and courage in the face of the unknown. It will take place on November the twenty-fourth.

Harry goes upstairs, and all the Gryffindors are cheering him on. Everyone wants to know how he crossed the age line and managed to enter. No one believes that he didn't put his name in the Goblet. Even Ron doesn't believe him. Next morning in the common room, Harry is cheered again. He feels miserable. Hermione comes, bringing a stack of toast, and invites Harry to go for a walk. She insists that he write Sirius and tell him what has happened.

The next few days are difficult for Harry. His friend, Ron, still isn't speaking to him because he thinks he's lying about the contest, and most of the students don't believe that Harry hadn't put his own name in the goblet. Outside of Professor Snape's classroom, Malfoy and Harry attack one another using their wands. Goyle and Hermione are hurt in the attack. Goyle looks like a fungus and Hermione's teeth have grown long, like a beaver's.

Class begins, but Harry is rescued from it by being called upstairs for a photograph session and a testing of the challengers' wands to see that they are all in good working order. When Harry finally returns to his room, he finds the owl has brought him a message from Sirius arranging a meeting.

In the painful days ahead, Harry continues to miss Ron, and he has to deal with the fall-out from a Rita Skeeter article that appears in the *Daily Prophet*. One afternoon, wearing his invisibility cloak, Harry goes with Hermione into the village of Hogsmeade to the Three Broomsticks Pub. Hagrid and Professor Moody are there. Professor Moody can see through the invisibility cloak and tells Hagrid that Harry is there. Hagrid makes an appointment to see Harry later that night.

Harry slips out to keep his appointment. Hagrid takes him to Madame Maxime's place first, and then they go for a short walk, with Harry still wearing his invisibility cloak. They look at the four dragons that will be part of the Triwizard's first task. Harry goes back and talks with Sirius, who appears in the flames in the fireplace and warns him to be on the watch against Karkaroff, who was once a Death Eater and had been in Azkaban. Before Sirius has a chance to tell Harry what spell might work on a dragon, they are interrupted by Ron. Harry storms up to his room, still at odds with Ron.

Worried about the first test, Harry tries to think of what spell he might use on the dragon. Seeing Cedric, Harry decides to tell Cedric what the other challengers already know: that the first test will involve dragons. Moody hears him tell Cedric and talks with Harry. He tells him to use his strength, which Harry realizes is flying, and to use a spell to get what he needs, which Harry realizes is his broom. Harry then practices summoning spells with Hermione.

On the day of the first test, the challengers each draw out of a bag a miniature dragon with a number on it. Harry gets number 4, the Hungarian Horntail. One by one, the challengers go out of a tent to face the dragon and try to collect the golden egg. At Harry's turn, he summons his broomstick and succeeds in getting the golden egg with only a mild injury to his shoulder. Afterwards, Ron and Hermione come to see Harry, and Harry and Ron make up again. When scores are announced, Harry and Krum tie for first place.

The champions are told to open their golden eggs, which contain clues that will help them prepare for the second test to take place on February 24. Harry sends Sirius a letter by owl telling him he survived the first test, and a party is held in Harry's honor.

The next day in the Care of Magical Creatures class, Rita Sikeeter appears and sets a date to interview Hagrid for the newspaper. In Divination class, Professor Trelawney speaks about death getting closer. Harry ignores this. After he and Ron leave, they meet Hermione, and she makes them go downstairs with her. Harry learns that the house-elves, Dobby and Winky, are now working at Hogwarts in the kitchen.

In Transfiguration class, Professor McGonagall tells the students about the Yule Ball that is approaching. It is open to fourth-year students and above. The champions and their partners traditionally open the ball, so Harry is expected to get a date. Hermione reminds Harry that he should also be trying to figure out what his golden egg contains, but Harry puts off trying to decode his clue or inviting anyone to the Yule Ball. By the time Harry asks Cho Chang to go to the ball with him, she's already agreed to go with Cedric. So Harry asks Parvati Patil to go with him.

On Christmas morning, Harry wakes when Dobby, the house-elf, comes to give him a present. Harry unwraps gifts, eats lunch, and takes a walk in the snow, and then Hermione says she must start getting ready for the ball. The champions and their partners go to the head table, and to everyone's astonishment, Krum's partner is Hermione, hair smoothed, and dressed in blue, looking lovely. The champions and their partners begin the dance, and then Ron and Harry avoid further dancing. Ron picks a fight with Hermione, clearly annoyed that she came to the ball with Krum.

Harry and Ron go out into the garden to walk and talk. They come upon Hagrid and Madame Maxime. Madame Maxime becomes incensed when Hagrid suggests she is a half-giant like him. Ron explains later to Harry that giants are considered vicious, and that's why Hagrid usually keeps this information about himself secret.

When the ball ends, Cedric stops Harry and tells him that he owes him a favor. He suggests that to get the secret from his golden egg, Harry should take a bath with the egg. Harry does not act on this advice, which seems very strange to him.

When the new term begins and the students go to Hagrid's for their Care of Magical Creatures class, they have a substitute teacher. Malfoy produces an article written by Rita Skeeter denouncing Hagrid as a half-giant. Malfoy says that this article is the reason Hagrid is absent. Hagrid does not appear all week. On the weekend, the students go into Hogsmeade where Harry hopes to see Hagrid, but he is not there.

Harry bumps into Ludo Bagman, who is talking with a group of goblins. They want to know where Mr. Crouch is. It seems that Mr. Crouch has stopped coming in to the office altogether. Then Rita Skeeter appears, and Harry and Hermione both accuse her of trying to ruin Hagrid's life. Ron, Hermione, and Harry go to Hagrid's cabin and find Professor Dumbledore there. Together, they convince Hagrid to start back to work again and pay no attention to Rita Skeeter's article.

Harry finally decides to solve the egg mystery. Using his invisibility cloak, he takes the egg and sneaks to the prefect's bathroom in the middle of the night. When he opens the egg, it makes an awful wailing sound. Moaning Myrtle appears and tells Harry to put the egg underwater and to duck under, too, and listen to it. After listening several times, Harry decides that the clue means he will be searching for merpeople in the lake. This worries him, because Harry is not a good swimmer.

On his way back to his room, Harry consults the Marauder's Map and sees that Mr. Crouch is in Snape's office. He decides to go see what Mr. Crouch is up to. Harry gets his foot caught in the trick step and is almost discovered by Filch and Snape, but he is rescued by Professor Moody, who is very interested to learn that Mr. Crouch was in Snape's office.

The days until the second Triwizard task rush by, and Harry still doesn't know how to survive for any length of time underwater. He searches for some kind of spell that might work. Ron and Hermione help but are summoned away and never come back. Harry spends the night in the library searching for a spell. In the morning, he is awakened by Dobby, who tells him the task will begin in ten minutes. He gives Harry some gillyweed to eat and explains that the object he must find in the lake is Ron. Harry runs down just in time to join the other champions. He wades out into the lake, eats the gillyweed, feels fins and gills form, and dives deep.

Harry sees Moaning Myrtle in the water, and she points the way for him to go. Harry swims by many merpeople and finally comes to a spot where four hostages are tied with seaweed. He frees Ron but is prevented from helping the others. Harry waits while Hermione and Cho are rescued. Then he cuts Fleur's sister free and takes her and Ron to the top. Because he waited, Harry is the last to surface, but since he showed "moral fiber" by staying until all hostages were rescued, he is given high marks and ties with Cedric for first place in this event. The judges announce that the final event will be scheduled for June 24.

Harry receives a message from Sirius to meet him at two o'clock on Saturday afternoon near Hogsmeade. In Potions class, Snape reads aloud another article written by Rita Skeeter. This one makes fun of Hermione and Harry. Professor Karkaroff comes into class and insists on talking to Professor Snape. Snape makes him wait until class is over. Karkaroff points to something on his inner forearm and shows it to Snape. Then he leaves.

On Saturday, Harry, Ron, and Hermione go to Hogsmeade. They meet Sirius, who has taken the form of a black dog, and he leads them to a cave. He tells them that Mr. Crouch sent his own son to Azkaban because he had associated with Death Eaters, and that his son died there. After a short visit, Ron, Harry, and Hermione return to Hogwarts.

They send food to Sirius by owls. The next day, Hermione receives four nasty letters all saying she is not good enough for Harry Potter. Handling one causes her hands to break out in boils. Harry goes to Herbology and then to the Care of Magical Creatures class, where they work with treasure-seeking nifflers. Hate mail continues to arrive for Hermione, and she is determined to find a way to get even with Rita Skeeter.

At Easter, Harry begins to worry about the third task of the Triwizard Tournament, which will be to get through obstacles in a maze grown up on the Quidditch field and to touch the cup that will be hidden in the center of the maze. The champions meet on the field and are shown the maze. On their walk back to Hogwarts, Krum and Harry see Mr. Crouch staggering out of some bushes and talking to himself. Harry approaches him. Crouch wildly asks to see Dumbledore. Harry leaves Krum with Crouch and goes to get Professor Dumbledore.

When Harry and Professor Dumbledore return to the forest, they find Krum unconscious and Mr. Crouch missing. Hagrid is summoned, and he brings Karkaroff to Dumbledore and takes Harry back to Gryffindor Tower. Professor Moody comes and goes searching for Crouch. The next morning, Harry sends an owl to Sirius telling him what has happened. Harry, Hermione, and Ron talk to Professor Moody, who says that Mr. Crouch disappeared last night and is nowhere on the grounds.

Harry begins practicing stunning and banishing spells to use in the maze against animals that may lurk there. In Divination class, Harry goes into a sort of dreamlike trance in which he sees Lord Voldemort, Wormtail, and Nagini. He wakes up screaming and rolling on the ground.

Harry goes to see Professor Dumbledore. Professor Moody and Mr. Fudge are with him. Dumbledore asks Harry to wait in his office for a few minutes and goes out with the others. While Harry is waiting, he notices in a case a basin filled with a strange substance. He looks into the liquid, touches it, and falls into someone else's thoughts. Harry find himself in a room with about 200 wizards. Two dementors bring in Karkaroff and put him in a chair in the center of the room. He gives up the names of several death eaters. Then, in another scene, Ludo Bagman is brought in, placed in the chair, and accused of passing information to the enemy. But a jury acquits him.

In the next memory scene, Harry sees four people sitting in chairs in the middle of the underground room. One is the son of Mr. Crouch. The jury finds them guilty and sentences them to life in Azkaban prison. Two people they are accused of torturing are Neville Longbottom's parents. Harry is awakened in Professor Dumbledore's office and speaks with him about all these memories he has seen.

Harry continues to master spells to use for the third task. On the day of the last task, another article by Rita Skeeter appears in the newspaper maligning Harry Potter. The champions are called to meet their families. Harry is delighted to find that Mrs. Weasley has come to watch him.

Finally, the champions enter the maze and begin to confront the obstacles that are designed to keep them from reaching the center of the maze. In the maze, it seems that Krum puts a spell on Cedric, so Harry stupefies Krum and sets up red sparks so that the judges will come and rescue him. Then he and Cedric split up and continue to try to reach the center of the maze. Harry meets a Sphinx, who offers him a riddle to solve. Close to the cup, a giant spider appears. Harry and Cedric stupefy the spider, and together they take hold of the Triwizard Cup.

Once they touch the cup, they are zipped away, miles from Hogwarts. They find themselves in a graveyard. A figure approaches, carrying something in its arms. Harry's scar begins to hurt terribly. He hears the words "Avada Kedavra." When Harry looks up, his pain weakens, but Cedric lies dead beside him. Before he fully realizes what is happening, Wormtail ties Harry to the headstone of Tom Riddle.

Harry watches a snake come slithering up. Wormtail reappears with a cauldron of liquid and lights a fire under it, and then reveals a creature in the bundle he has been carrying earlier. Wormtail drops the creature into the cauldron, calls up dust from the grave that falls into the cauldron, takes a dagger, cuts off his own hand, and drops it into the cauldron. Last of all, Wormtail makes a cut in Harry's arm and takes a vial of blood that he also drops in, and Lord Voldemort steps from the cauldron.

Slowly, Death Eaters begin arriving. Each one falls to his knees and kisses the hem of Lord Voldemort's robe. Voldemort attaches a silver hand to Wormtail's arm. Lord Voldemort goes around the circle noting who is present and absent among his Death Eaters. Voldemort puts the Cruciatus spell on Harry, but then stops the pain and orders that Harry be untied and allowed to fight him, one on one.

A circle is formed around them, and the duel begins. Harry is immediately hit again briefly with the Cruciatus spell and is in an agony of pain. Both Harry and Voldemort cast spells. They are lifted in the air to another spot in the graveyard, and their wands remain connected as a sort of golden web envelopes them. Harry hears the song of the Phoenix. Shades of people Voldemort had killed begin coming out of Voldemort's wand: Cedric, Frank Bryce, Bertha Jenkins, and Harry's father and mother. Harry's mother tells him when the wand connection is broken, he must get to the Portkey, which is the Triwizard Cup, and it will take him to Hogwarts. Harry breaks the wand connection, grabs Cedric's wrist and the cup, and flies back to Hogwarts.

Harry starts to tell Professor Dumbledore and Cornelius Fudge what has happened, but Professor Dumbledore leaves to talk to Cedric's parents. Moody takes Harry to his office and confesses he was the one who put Harry's name in the Goblet of Fire and who raised the Dark Mark in the sky at the Quidditch World Cup match. Just before Moody can kill Harry, the door of the office breaks open and Professors Dumbledore, Snape, and McGonagall enter the room.

Dumbledore explains that this man is not really Alasdair Moody. Dumbledore sends Snape for a truth serum and sends McGonagall to bring a black dog from near Hagrid's house to Dumbledore's office. While they go on their errands, Dumbledore unlocks a special trunk and reveals the real Moody weak and unconscious, in a dungeonlike room within the depths of the trunk.

Slowly, before their eyes, the false Moody begins changing and is revealed as the young Barry Crouch. Given the truth serum, Barry Crouch explains that he and his mother drank a potion and changed places in Azkaban prison. She was the one who died in prison and was buried. Winky, the house-elf, was Barry Crouch's keeper at his home. The only other person who knew he still lived was Bertha Jenkins, who dropped in unexpectedly one day and saw him, so Mr. Crouch put a memory spell on her.

Winky took Barry Crouch to the World Cup game, where he sat under an invisibility cloak in an empty seat everyone thought was being saved for Mr. Crouch. Barry Crouch stole Harry's wand at the game and put the Dark Mark in the sky, but his father found him in the wood and took him home. Voldemort learned all this when torturing Bertha Jenkins and came for his faithful servant, Barry Crouch. Voldemort placed Mr. Crouch, Sr., under the Imperius Curse and turned Barry Crouch into Professor Moody. Barry Crouch goes on to confess how he killed his father and turned the Triwizard cup into a Portkey.

After Barry Crouch is tied up, Professor Dumbledore takes Harry to his office, and Harry tells the professor and Sirius all that happened that night. He is then taken to the hospital, where his friends are waiting for him. Professor Dumbledore sees that Harry goes to bed, and he tells the others to save their questions for later.

In the morning, Harry is awakened by angry voices. Cornelius Fudge brought a dementor in to see Barry Crouch, and the dementor gave Crouch a fatal kiss. Fudge does not believe anything Harry says, nor does he believe Lord Voldemort has returned. Dumbledore tells him what he thinks must be done about dementors, Azkaban prison, and the giants, but Fudge refuses to listen. Fudge leaves, and Dumbledore sets everyone to work. Harry is given a potion and falls asleep again.

At the end of the term, Professor Dumbledore gives a final speech about the bravery of Cedric Diggory and Harry Potter. He tells the students of Lord Voldemort's return and urges then to unite against that dark power.

On the train ride home, Hermione tells Ron and Harry she discovered how Rita Skeeter got her news. She is an unregistered Animagus, and in the form of a beetle, she eavesdrops to get her stories. Hermione captured her as a beetle and keeps her in a bottle, planning to release her back in London. Malfoy, Goyle, and Crabbe come into Harry's train compartment, and Fred, George, Ron, Hermione, and Harry all put a hex on the three boys.

Back in town, Uncle Vernon meets Harry, and Harry decides to try not to worry over the summer but to accept what will come and meet it as best he can.

List of Major Characters: Harry Potter, a student at Hogwarts; Sirius, Harry's godfather; Harry's friends at school—Hermione Granger, Ron Weasley, and Neville Longbottom; the Weasley family—Mr. and Mrs. Weasley, their twin sons Fred and George, Bill, Charlie, Percy and Ginny; staff members at Hogwarts—Professor Dumbledore the headmaster, Snape the potions master, McGonagall the transfiguration master, and Hagrid the gamekeeper; Madame Pomfrey, who runs the Hogwarts hospital; Draco Malfoy, Crabbe, and Goyle, unpleasant students at Hogwarts; Viktor Krum, Cedric Diggory, and Fleur Delacour, the other Triwizard Champions; Lord Voldemort, a dark wizard; Peter, nicknamed Wormtail, Lord Voldemort's servant; Hedwig, Harry's snowy owl; and Harry's relatives—Uncle Vernon, Aunt Petunia, and Cousin Dudley.

Vocabulary: The page numbers below in parentheses indicate where the word was used in the book. Look up each word in a dictionary. Rewrite the sentence in which it was used, using a synonym in place of the vocabulary word.

incoherently (9) _____

tremulous (26) _____

foreboding (40) _____

diatribe (40) _____

sanctimoniously (64) _____

impeccably (90) _____

feinting (108) _____

vindictiveness (209) _____

colluding (238) _____

imperiously (275) _____

exacerbated (295) _____

incredulously (411) _____

Comprehension Questions

1. What did Frank Bryce, the old gardener, think was the cause of the light he saw upstairs in the empty Riddle House?
2. Instead of owls, what delivered Sirius's letter to Harry during the summer?

3. What happens to Dudley when he eats a piece of Ton-Tongue Toffee dropped by the Weasleys in his living room?
4. What kind of racing broom for Quidditch did Harry own?
5. What does "apparating" mean?
6. What sorts of objects can serve as Portkeys?
7. The grandfather clock belonging to Mrs. Weasley doesn't tell time. What does it tell?
8. Describe Buckbeak.
9. After Harry has faced the dragon, Rita Skeeter wants "a word" with Harry for her next newspaper article. What word does Harry give her?
10. Why does Malfoy refer to Hermione as "the long-molared Mudblood"?

Answers: 1) Frank thought some neighborhood boys had broken into the house. 2) Tropical birds delivered the letters. 3) Dudley's tongue swells up, dangles out of his mouth, and turns purple. 4) Harry owns a Firebolt. 5) "Apparating" means disappearing from one place and reappearing almost instantly in another. 6) Almost any object can be a Portkey, including an old boot, a punctured football, or an old newspaper. 7) The clock tells where each member of the Weasley family is—at home, traveling, work, and so on. 8) Buckbeak is a hippogriff, half gray horse and half giant eagle. 9) The word Harry gave her was "Goodbye." 10) Hermione has rather long front teeth, and both of her parents are muggles.

Discussion Questions

1. Which of the various classes that Harry takes at Hogwarts (Charms, Potions, Care of Magical Creatures, Divination, Herbology, Defense Against the Dark Arts, Transfiguration, and History of Magic) would you most like to take, and why? Which would you least like to take, and why?
2. Professor Dumbledore has a Pensieve. It is a basin into which he pours his thoughts and then, later on, can look through them and reflect about them. Do you think this is a useful device? Why, or why not?
3. Gather together students who have read both *Harry Potter and the Goblet of Fire* by J.K. Rowling and *Dragonflight* by Anne McCaffrey. Ask them to picture the scene in each book where there is high interest in a dragon's golden egg. How are the dragons portrayed in each book? How are the two authors able to achieve such different impressions of dragons?
4. Hagrid showed Harry the dragons before the first test. He also showed them to Madame Maxime. Karkaroff snooped about at night and saw the dragons. Harry told Cedric about the dragons. So all of the champions learned about the dragons being part of the first test before the day of the test. Professor Moody said that cheating was always part of the tournament. Do you think cheating should be part of the tournament? Since other people told them about the dragons, do you think the champions were cheating? Would the test have been any more difficult if they had not known about the dragons?
5. If Lord Voldemort had not been involved, which of the three tests that Harry faced in the Triwizard Tournament do you think was hardest? Why?
6. Harry and Ron did not invite Cho and Hermione to go with them to the Yule Ball, nor did they treat their dates well that night. Hermione spent a lot of time getting ready for the ball, but the boys spent very little preparing for it. Do you think the reactions of the boys and girls at Hogwarts were typical of the ways boys and girls at your school behave before, during, and after a big dance or party?

7. Professor Dumbledore thinks that the giants that have been driven out of England should be asked to return before Voldemort enlists them on his side. Hagrid says he is going on a summer mission. Do you think Hagrid will be going to try to bring giants back to England? What problems might that pose?

8. Why do you suppose Cornelius Fudge allows dementors and Azkaban prison to remain instead of replacing them with a more humane penal system?

Research Activities

1. Hedwig is a snowy owl. Invite a pair of students who are interested in this topic to research and write a paper using at least three sources of information. They should report their findings to the class. Possible sources of information can be found at http://www.owlpages. com/species/nycleas/scandiaca/Default.htm and at http://www.cws-scf.ec.gc.ca/hww-fap/ hww-fap.cfm?ID_species=45&lang=e. Useful books are *Snowy Owls* by Wendy Pfeffer (Parsippany, NJ: Silver Press, 1997) and *Living in a World of White* by Tanya Lee Stone (Woodbridge, CT: Blackbirch Press, 2001).

2. One of the competitors in the Triwizard Tournament, Viktor Krum, is from Bulgaria. Invite a small group of students to research the topic of Bulgaria. Each person should have one or two areas, such as natural resources, industries, foods, arts, and so on, about which to become the expert. Information should be written up on note cards. When everyone in the group is ready, they should present their report to the class in the form of a panel discussion, referring to their note cards as needed. A moderator should be designated to call on the others to question panel members on such topics as the country's location, flag, cities, major crops and products, outstanding geographical features, and the like. Class members might ask additional questions. Possible sources of information are http://www.cia/gov/cia/ publications/factbook/geos/bu.html and http://www.1uptravel.com/international/europe/ bulgaria/index.html Useful books on the topic include *Bulgaria* by Kirilka Stavreva (New York: M. Cavendish, 1997) and *Bulgaria* by Abraham Resnick (Chicago: Children's Press, 1995).

3. The snake, Nagini, plays a role in the story. She is described as being 12 feet long and the sort of snake that is "milked." Snakes are milked in the making of certain antivenoms. Invite a pair of students to do some research on the topic of poisonous snakes and snake venom and to report to the class what they learn. Possible sources of information include *Snakes* by Deborah A. Behler (New York: Benchmark Books, 2002) and *Snakes* by Maria Mudd-Ruth (New York: Marshall Cavendish/Benchmark Books, 2002). Information is also available on the Internet at http://ca.news.yahoo.com/o202529/5/mpho.html and at http://ntri.tamuk.edu/vietnam/trip_snake_turtle_farm.html.

4. In the maze, Harry is faced with a Sphinx that insists he solve a riddle. Ask two students to do some research on the Sphinx and to report to the class in an oral report what they learn. Sources of information available on the Internet include http://www.arab.net/ egypt/tour/et_sphinx.htm and http://www.unmuseum.org/sphinx.htm. Other sources of information include *Africa Close-up: Egypt/Tanzania* (Maryknoll, NY: Maryknoll World Productions, 1997, one videocassette, 28 minutes) and *The Sphinx* by Bernard Evslin (New York: Chelsea House, 1991). The students should engage the assistance of the school media specialist in helping them to locate current magazine articles concerning any recent archeological digs in Egypt.

5. Harry's magic wand has a Phoenix feather in it. The Phoenix is a mythical bird that has been associated in many cultures with immortality. There are stories about the Phoenix in ancient Egyptian and Greek mythology, in Christian writings, and in Chinese mythology. Students from various cultures may wish to explore the topic of the Phoenix together, research information, and compare the function of the Phoenix in various myths. They may find myths in other languages. Their findings should be shared with the class. Possible sources of information include http://lrca.gilead.org.il/phoenix.html and at http://www.mythicalrealm.com/creatures/phoenix.

6. The judges of the Triwizard Tournament did not always agree on their scoring. During the last Olympic games, a big controversy arose over the judging of ice skating. Have a pair of interested students, with the help of the school or library media specialist, research this topic by using newspaper and magazine archives. They should write a short report on what they learn, using at least three sources of information, and share it with the class.

Extension Activities

1. Ask interested students to imagine that Rita Skeeter has decided to write an article for the *Daily Prophet* about the Weasley family and particularly about Ron Weasley. Students should use the information known from reading the book and, like Rita, feel free to invent gossip to make their stories more interesting. Study and imitate the same style and voice as the articles attributed to Rita that are published in the book. Post these stories on a bulletin board in the classroom.

2. Remember that the people of Little Hangleton still talk about the three strange deaths that occurred long ago at the Riddle House. Invite students to be reporters for the *Little Hangleton Gazette* and write a story titled "Death Strikes Again at Riddle House" describing the strange death of Frank Bryce. Make this a factual article based on data from the book, but play up the unsolved mystery angle and speculate as to the cause of death. Post these stories on a classroom bulletin board.

3. Harry's favorite candies are Chocolate Frogs and Fizzing Whisbees. What are the current favorite candies in your class? Invite a small group of students to conduct a poll in which they ask classmates to name their two favorite candies. Do further research to find out the names of some of the largest candy manufacturers in the United States. Are these big names represented in your class favorites? Armed with this information, the students should prepare and share with the class a graphic, showing the results of the candy poll.

4. Invite an interested group of students to look carefully through the book and note the way that Hagrid speaks. Keeping that style firmly in mind, write a letter from Hagrid, sent during the summer vacation after the action in this book ends, telling Harry Potter about what Hagrid has been doing in searching for giants in Europe and promising Harry an introduction to some real giants when he returns to Hogwarts for the new term. Post the letters on a bulletin board.

5. Using any preferred media and choosing any scenes from the book, interested students should make a poster that will encourage others to read *Harry Potter and the Goblet of Fire*. With permission, hang these posters in the school media center.

6. Invite a small group of interested students to come up with a task that they think would have been a good one for the Triwizard Tournament. Have them write down the rules for this task, and then share it with the class.

How does reading *Harry Potter and the Goblet of Fire* and engaging in the various activities suggested above help students meet the 12 NCTE/IRA English Language Arts Standards?

1. *Harry Potter and the Goblet of Fire* meets Standard #1 by serving as an example of outstanding fiction.

2. *Harry Potter and the Goblet of Fire* meets Standard #2 because it is a representative work of the broad genre of fantasy.

3. Discussion questions #1 through #8 help students to comprehend and interpret text, and the vocabulary exercise increases knowledge of word meanings, helping students to meet Standard #3.

4. Extension activity #1, which suggests writing an article about the Weasley family in the manner of a Rita Skeeter article for the *Daily Prophet,* addresses Standard #4, which asks students to adjust written language and style to communicate effectively for different purposes.

5. Extension activity #2, which suggests that students write up the strange death of Frank Bryce as a factual newspaper article for the *Little Hangleton Gazette,* helps meet Standard #5, which requires that students use different writing processes for different audiences and for a variety of purposes.

6. Extension activity #4, which suggests that a student write a letter in Hagrid's style to Harry Potter telling him about his summer search for giants, helps to meet Standard #6 by requiring students to apply their knowledge of language structure and language conventions to create a print text.

7. Research activity #3 requires students to gather, evaluate, and synthesize data from a variety of sources to communicate their discoveries, and it helps to address Standard #7.

8. Research activity #4 involving researching the Sphinx helps to meet Standard #8 by encouraging students to use a variety of technological and information resources to carry out research and to communicate their knowledge.

9. Discussion question #6 about the conventional roles played by the boys and girls at Hogwarts, especially those surrounding the events of the Yule Ball, help to address Standard #9 by allowing students to develop an understanding of and respect for diversity in social roles.

10. Research activity #5 asking students interested in many cultures to compare and contrast the use of the Phoenix in various mythologies helps address Standard #10, which asks students to use their first language that is not English to develop a deeper understanding of the curriculum.

11. Discussion question #3, bringing together students who have read both *Dragonflight* and *Harry Potter and the Goblet of Fire,* allows students to pool their information knowledge in the form of a book discussion group and compare and contrast aspects of these two fantasy novels. It helps meet Standard #11, which asks that students participate as knowledgeable, reflective, creative, and critical members of a literary community.

12. Extension activity #5 allows students to creatively select and prepare a means of sharing their enthusiasm for this book with other potential readers. It addresses Standard #12, in which students are asked to use spoken, written, and visual language to persuade others.

The Hobbit or There and Back Again

by J.R.R. Tolkien

New York: Ballantine Books, 1988, ISBN 0-345-33968-1

Detailed Synopsis

The Hobbit is a quest fantasy. Bilbo Baggins, a hobbit, lives in a comfortable hobbit-hole. One day, Gandalf, the Wizard, pays a visit. Galdalf wants to send the hobbit on a daring adventure, but Bilbo Baggins isn't interested. He does, however, politely invite Gandalf to tea the next day.

At tea time, a stream of dwarves as well as Gandalf appear at the hobbit-hole. The dwarf, Thorin, leads the discussion, and Bilbo learns he has been chosen to be the 14th member of an expedition. Using a map to a faraway mountain and a special key, they will attempt to go through a secret entrance and confront Smaug, the dragon.

Bilbo learns that long ago, Thorin's family was driven out of the far North and came to live and mine on the mountain where they built the town of Dale. Then Smaug, the dragon, came, robbed them, and killed most of the people in Dale. Only a few got away, and these few now want to go back and reclaim their treasure.

The next day, Bilbo and the dwarves set off on their quest. They travel some distance until one night they are taken captive by trolls and tied into bags. Gandalf appears in time to cause the trolls to quarrel among themselves for such a long time that they are caught out in daylight and turned to stone.

Bilbo and the dwarves find treasure and food in the troll's cave, which they take. They continue until they meet some friendly elves, and they stay and feast at the Last Homely House in the valley. After three weeks, they finally set off into the mountains again, only to be caught in a huge thunderstorm. They take shelter in a cave, spread out their things to dry, and fall asleep.

During the night, goblins appear and snatch all of them except for Gandalf, who escapes. They are taken to Goblin-town far underground. Just when it appears that the goblins will kill them, Gandalf reappears and puts the cave in darkness. He kills the Great Goblin, and in the confusion Bilbo and the dwarves try to escape. As they flee, Bilbo is knocked unconscious. When he awakes, Bilbo makes his way along through the tunnel. As he travels, he finds a golden ring, which he puts in his pocket.

Bilbo continues until he comes to a lake and sees a slimy creature called Gollum. The two of them play at riddles. But it is more than a game. It is understood that if Bilbo can't answer a riddle, he'll be eaten. If Gollum can't answer, he'll show Bilbo the way out. After riddling for a time, when Gollum slips back to his island, Bilbo runs away. He puts on the golden ring he found and becomes invisible. When Gollum comes back, he can't find Bilbo and unknowingly leads the invisible hobbit to the back door, allowing Bilbo to escape.

Outside again, Bilbo meets up with Gandalf and the other dwarves. In telling about his escape, he does not mention his ring of invisibility. That night, wolves, called wild Wargs, come out to howl at the moon in the clearing where the dwarves are resting. The dwarves climb up into trees. Gandalf throws flaming pinecones at the wolves, and a fire breaks out. The goblins come to help the wolves catch the dwarves, but a group of eagles appears and rescues them.

The Lord of the Eagles takes Bilbo, Gandalf, and the dwarves to the Great Shelf on the mountainside, where they spend the night. In the morning, the eagles fly them from the Misty Mountains to a hilltop called the Carrock. Gandalf says he must leave them soon but first will try to arrange a meeting for them with someone he knows. They meet with Beorn, a skin changer, who sometimes appears as a strong man and at other times appears as a huge, black bear.

They stay at Beorn's house for a time. Beorn offers them ponies and food for their journey, but he warns them that going through Mirkwood will be difficult and that they must not stray from the path.

When they reach Mirkwood, Gandalf leaves them. Since there is no safe way around the wood to the Lonely Mountains where Smaug lives, Bilbo and the dwarves enter Mirkwood. It is a dark and frightening place. In crossing a river, Bombur slips into the water and afterward falls into a deep sleep. They carry him for days before he awakes, remembering nothing of his journey.

They leave the path to investigate some elves, and Bilbo becomes separated from the others. He falls asleep, and when he wakes, he finds himself being wrapped by a huge spider. Bilbo uses the sword that he found in the goblin cave to kill the spider. He puts on his invisibility ring and learns that all the dwarves have been captured by the spiders, wrapped in bundles, and hung from a tree branch to be stored until eaten.

Bilbo leads the spiders away from the dwarves and then slips back to rescue them. Only after they escape do they realize that Thorin is missing. He had stepped into a circle of elf light and been carried off by the Wood-elves before the spiders caught and wrapped up the others.

The elf-king lives in a great cave some miles within the edges of Mirkwood. His elves capture the dwarves as they flee the spiders, but Bilbo slips on his invisibility ring and is not taken captive. In the dungeon of the elf-king, Bilbo finds Thorin and all the other dwarves.

Bilbo carries out a plan to get the keys, unlock the cells, stow the dwarves into empty barrels, and float away after dropping through a trapdoor into the stream.

When the barrels reach a shallow shore, elves pole and push the barrels together and rope them for the night. In the morning, they are towed to Lake-town. That night, when it is dark, Bilbo releases the dwarves from the barrels. They go to see the Master of the town. They are fed and housed and spend a week here before they finally leave Lake-town in three large boats with horses, ponies, and provisions.

After two days of rowing, they go ashore at a spot that is in the shadow of Lonely Mountain. Scouts report seeing the ruins of Dale but no sign of the dragon. They find the door shown on Thorin's map but cannot open it until one night, just as the sun sinks, a gleam of light falls right on the rock-face, and a hole appears. Thorin puts the key into the hole, and the door opens.

Bilbo sets off alone down into the dark cave, where he finds Smaug, the dragon, sleeping on a pile of treasure. Bilbo takes a golden cup from the treasure and makes his way back to the dwarves. That night, the dwarves tremble when Smaug awakes, realizes a cup is missing, and begins bellowing and trampling underground.

Bilbo and the dwarves spend the night in the cave. The next day, Bilbo goes down to see Smaug again, using his invisibility ring. They talk, and Bilbo observes and tries to discover the dragon's weakness. He notices a patch on the dragon's breast that is unprotected. When Bilbo tells his companions of his day's adventures, a wren listens to his story.

Later that night, as the dwarves hide in the cave, Smaug comes and tries to smash through the door. He can't get through, so he goes off to attack Lake-town. While Smaug is gone, Bilbo and the dwarves visit the dragon's lair. They explore the tunnels and spend the night in the lookout post at the southwest corner of the mountains.

While Smaug is attacking the village of the Lake Men, Bard, their leader, is told by a bird to aim at the hollow of the left breast where the dragon is unprotected. He does, and a well-placed arrow kills Smaug, but by this time, much of Lake-town is in ruins. The elf-king and his people hear the news of the attack and come to help.

The master of Lake-town stays and begins to build a new town. The men of arms, including Bard and the elf-king, march toward the mountain. The dwarves learn that Smaug is dead and that many are headed their way seeking the gold and treasure. The dwarves send for their kin in the mountains to come and help them, and they fortify the entrance to the caverns.

When the elf-king and Bard come, they ask Thorin for part of the treasure since Bard is the heir of Giron of Dale. Thorin refuses this reasonable request. Bilbo slips out at night and takes the Arkenstone of Thrain from the treasure horde to Bard to use in his bargaining. Then he sneaks back again.

When Bard and the elf-king appear with the Arkenstone, Thorin still won't bargain, and they are about to go to war when the goblins and wolves come marching upon them. This attack unifies the others. Just when it looks as if the goblins will win the battle, the eagles swoop in, and then Beorn, in bear's shape, appears and joins the fight. Three fourths of the goblins warriors are killed, and the others leave.

Thorin has also been killed in the fierce battle. He is buried deep in the mountain with the Arkenstone. Dain becomes king under the mountain. Ten of the original dwarves on the quest also survive and remain. A fourteenth share of the treasure is given to Bard.

Bilbo takes a small chest of gold and silver and heads home. He returns from his adventure in the spring at the very moment when all of his things are being auctioned off since he had been thought lost forever. Bilbo settles back in his comfortable home, no longer quite as respectable as he once was, but quite content.

List of Major Characters: Bilbo, the hobbit; Gandalf, the wizard; Thorin, leader of the dwarves; Bard, leader of the Lake-men; Smaug, the dragon; Gollum, a slimy creature who lives in a lake in the goblins' caverns; the Great Goblin, head of the goblins; Beorn, a skin changer; the Lord of the Eagles, who rescues them from the wolves; and the elf-king, who lives near the edge of Mirkwood.

Vocabulary: The page number where each word below was used in the story is indicated in parentheses. Look up each of these words in the dictionary, and write two synonyms that might be used in its place.

depredations (9) _____ _____

obstinately (22) _____ _____

defrayed (29) _____ _____

reeking (48) _____ _____

tongs (60) _____ _____

benighted (94) _____ _____

pinnacles (111) _____ _____

lamenting (145) _____ _____

abominable (154) _____ _____

runes (204) _____ _____

lintel (205) _____ _____

pallid (235) _____ _____

Comprehension Questions

1. According to the old stories told by the dwarves, when Bullroarer attacked in the Battle of Green Fields, he is credited with inventing the game of golf. Explain how this happened.
2. In addition to a map of the mountain, what else does Gandalf hand over to Thorin?
3. Why do you think Gandalf doesn't find a mighty warrior instead of Bilbo Baggins to go on the expedition with the dwarves?
4. What happens to the three trolls that captured all the dwarves?
5. Why do the travelers stay so long with the elves in the Last Homely House?
6. Describe how to go about reading moon letters such as those that were on the map of the mountain.
7. Why are the goblins particularly enraged when they see the sword that Thorin carries?
8. When they finally open the door that leads into the mountain, why do the dwarves expect Bilbo to enter it alone?

9. How does Smaug describe himself?
10. What prevents the battle from happening between the dwarves and the Lake-men and the elves?

Answers: 1) King Gofinbul's head was knocked off with a wooden club, sailed a hundred yards, and went down a rabbit hole. 2) Gandalf also gives Thorin a silver key. 3) The warriors are all busy fighting one another in distant lands. 4) They are turned to stone because they were not underground before dawn. 5) They stay to enjoy food, drink, and stories and to mend clothes and stock up on supplies. 6) You can see moon letters when the moon shines behind them if the moon is the same shape and season as it was on the day when the letters were written. 7) The sword, taken from the cave of the three goblins who had turned to stone, is called Orcrist, Goblin-Cleaver, and Biter. It had killed hundreds of goblins when the elves of Gondolin hunted them. 8) Bilbo had been brought on the journey and promised a share of the reward to perform just this sort of service for the dwarves. 9) Smaug says, "My armour is like tenfold shields, my teeth are swords, my claws spears, the shock of my tail a thunderbolt, my wings a hurricane, and my breath death." 10) The sudden attack of the goblins from the north and of the wolves unites the others.

Discussion Questions

1. Many works of fantasy involve both a journey and a quest. With this in mind, why do you think that Tolkien's title for this book is *The Hobbit or There and Back Again?*

2. By the time Bilbo goes to bed after feeding all the dwarves, listening to their stories, and finding them all places to sleep in his Hobbit-hole, he is very tired. The Tookishness is wearing off, and he is not planning to leave on a journey in the morning. When he wakes in the morning, he is relieved to find them gone. Why, then, does Bilbo go running off to join the adventure?

3. During the chapter called "A Short Rest," the author points out that "things that are good to have and days that are good to spend are soon told about, and not much to listen to; while things that are uncomfortable, palpitating, and even gruesome, may make a good tale." Do you agree with this statement? Why, or why not?

4. This story is set in a number of different locations. Discuss the various locations as they occur chronologically in the story and how each influences the overall design of the story.

5. The wizard, Gandalf, is very unpredictable yet unfailingly helpful to Bilbo and the dwarves. What elements does his unpredictability add to the story?

6. One of the statements in the story is that "every worm has its weakness." What does that statement mean in the context of this story? Does the statement have broader application?

7. Each of the dwarves on the journey with Bilbo is distinct and has his own personality. As part of a discussion group with others who have read the story, give reasons for your answers to the following two questions. If you had to choose just one of the dwarves for a friend, which would it be? If one of the dwarves was to be your enemy, which would it be?

8. On his quest, Bilbo meets many dangers: trolls, goblins, Gollum, the spiders of Mirkwood, the woodland elves, and Smaug, the dragon. Which of these was most frightening to you, and why?

9. Thorin Oakenshield gains the disrespect of many characters in the story by the time the Battle of Five Armies begins. How does he earn this disrespect? Why do you think he acts the way he does? If he had lived through the battle, do you think he would have changed?

10. Bilbo is in Hobiton at the end of the novel, and he seems happy and content. But because of his adventures, he is regarded differently from the way he once was. What has changed? Does Bilbo belong back at home?

Research Activities

1. The spiders in Mirkwood were ten feet across and almost ate the dwarves. In real life, how large is the largest spider, where does it live, and what does it eat? Are any videos on different types of spiders available that could be borrowed and shown to the class? You might also want to visit some web sites, including http://giantspiders.crosswinds.net. For information on tarantulas, see *Tarantulas* by Peter Murray (Mankato, MN: Child's World, 1993). Ask students to prepare a short oral report on this topic to share with the class.

2. Although they are imaginary, much has been written about elves, dwarves, goblins, and trolls and how they are alike and different from one another. Invite interested students to do some research on this topic. ESL students and class members with strong backgrounds in other cultures can perhaps share information about similar folk story creatures from their countries. Ask the students to make an oral report in which they discuss these various groups of "little people." Possible sources of information include *Kids Draw Angels, Elves, Fairies, & More* by Christopher Hart (New York: Watson-Guptill, 2001) and *The Barefoot Book of Giants, Ghosts and Goblins* by John Matthews (New York: Barefoot Books, 1999). An Internet site of interest is http://rom.mud.de/info/world/races.html.

3. Do some research about Middle Earth and draw a map of the region, which you might share by posting it on a bulletin board. One of the Internet sites you might consult is http://www.glyphweb.com/arda/g/goblins.html. After reaching this site, click on "maps."

4. Bard, the bowman, is one of the heroes of *The Hobbit*. Using information that Bilbo obtained and that was shared with him by a bird, Bard kills Smaug, the dragon, by shooting an arrow into his vulnerable spot. There are many types of bows and arrows used for different purposes. In some states, bow and arrow hunting still takes place. Perhaps someone in your community uses a bow and arrow and would be willing to answer questions. Invite a pair of students who are interested in this topic to research it, find pictures of various bows and arrows, and make a brief presentation to the class. Sources of information include *Charge!: Weapons and Warfare in Ancient Times* by Rivka Gonen (Minneapolis, MN: Runestone Press, 1993) and http://www.reshafim.org.il/ad/egypt/weapons/missiles.htm.

5. The Arkenstone of Thrain was very significant to the dwarves. Thorin said, "It is beyond price." Even today, kings, queens, and other wealthy people value some jewels above all others. Ask that a pair of students who are interested in gemstones do some research on this topic. What are some of the best-known jewels or jewelry collections in the world? One source for information on the Hope diamond is http://www.si.edu/resource/faq/nmnh/hope.htm; another site, to learn more about the Emerald Dagger in the Topkapi

Museum in Turkey, is http://www.ee.bilkent.edu.tr/~history/Ext/emerald_20.html. Ask the students to share what they learn in a written report to the class and, if possible, to show pictures of some of these famous jewels.

6. Part of the story line in *The Hobbit* depends upon unusual birds that can listen and speak to humans. In the real world, there are a few birds that can be taught to speak. Ask a pair of interested students to research this topic. Perhaps a pet store owner can be of help or can refer the students to someone in the community who has a "talking bird" and might be willing to make a school visit. A source of information on the Internet is http://www.alexfoundation.org/research/articles/birdsusa.html, and a book of interest is *Talking Birds* by Alice K. Flanagan (New York: Children's Press, 1996). Ask the students to share what they learn with class members.

Extension Activities

1. Bilbo and Gollum tell one another complex riddles. Ask a group of interested students to make up some original riddles and try them on the class. Can they stump their friends?

2. Smaug is but one of a very large number of storybook dragons. Choose another dragon from literature and compare it with Smaug. How are they alike? How are they different? Ask students to make drawings using whatever medium they prefer and share with their class information about these two storybook dragons.

3. The dwarves are always making up stories to tell or songs to sing about their adventures. Bilbo makes up a song to tell to draw the spiders away from the dwarves so that he can slip back and rescue them. Invite students to make up an original verse about some part of the hobbit's adventure that they think would add to the story. Share the verses made up by classmates and decide on what pages they would place them in the book.

4. Tolkien's stories lend themselves to great visual interpretations. Invite interested students to design and make a mural featuring scenes from *The Hobbit*. Use whatever media you prefer. Hang the mural in the library with information about the title and author of the book in an attempt to persuade other readers to read the book.

5. Choose a scene from *The Hobbit* that you thinks lends itself well to dramatization. Cast class members in various roles. It would be helpful if an adult volunteer would serve as director. Use very simple costumes and props. Rehearse the scene, and when it is ready, have the cast present the scene to their classmates.

6. Ask students to study their local newspaper to see how staff members report exciting major events. What information comes in the first paragraph? What sorts of verbs and descriptive language are used? What supporting details are included in later paragraphs? Then, in this style, have students write up a report of Smaug attacking Lake-town and being shot down by Bard. When it is complete, have them share their news stories with their classmates.

How does reading *The Hobbit* and engaging in the various activities suggested above help students meet the 12 NCTE/IRA English Language Arts Standards?

1. *The Hobbit* meets Standard #1 by serving as an example of outstanding classic fiction.

2. *The Hobbit* meets Standard #2 because it is a representative work of the broad genre of fantasy literature.

3. Discussion questions #3 and #6 help students to comprehend and interpret text, and the vocabulary exercise and extension activities #1, #3, and #6 all help to increase knowledge of word meanings, helping students to meet Standard #3.

4. Extension activity #3, which suggests that students make up an original verse in the style of Bilbo's song to the spiders, addresses Standard #4, which asks students to adjust written language and style to communicate effectively for different purposes.

5. Extension activity #6, which suggests that a student write up the exploits of Bard in slaying the dragon in the form of an article for a modern newspaper, helps meet Standard #5, which requires that students use different writing processes for different audiences and for a variety of purposes.

6. Research activity #5, which suggests that students prepare a written report on famous jewels using print and nonprint resources, helps to meet Standard #6 by requiring students to apply their knowledge of language structure and language conventions to create a print text.

7. Research activity #4, which deals with the past and present use of bows and arrows in warfare and in hunting and which suggests the use of a personal interview as well as print and Internet resources, helps to address Standard #7 by requiring students to gather, evaluate, and synthesize data from a variety of sources.

8. Research activity #1 involving different types of spiders helps to meet Standard #8 by encouraging students to use a variety of technological and information resources to carry out research and to communicate their knowledge.

9. Discussion questions #2 and #10 about how society views Bilbo Baggins before and after his adventures with the dwarves help to address Standard #9 by allowing students to develop an understanding of and respect for diverse social roles.

10. Research activity #2 asking students from other cultures to share information of "little people" from their cultures that are similar to the elves, trolls, and goblins in *The Hobbit* helps address Standard #10, which asks students to use their first language that is not English to develop a deeper understanding of the curriculum.

11. Discussion question #7 allows students in the form of a book discussion group to pool their thoughts about which of the dwarves would make good friends and which might be dangerous enemies and compare and contrast their opinions with others who have read the story. It helps meet Standard #11, which asks that students participate as knowledgeable, reflective, creative, and critical members of a literary community.

12. Extension activity #4 allows students to prepare scenes from the book in the form of a mural to both share their enthusiasm for the story and to entice other potential readers. It addresses Standard #12, in which students are asked to use spoken, written, and visual language to persuade others.

The Castle in the Attic

Elizabeth Winthrop

New York: Bantam Skylark, 1985, ISBN 0-533-15433-8

Detailed Synopsis

The Castle in the Attic is a quest fantasy. As the story opens, 10-year-old William learns that Mrs. Phillips, his friend and caregiver since birth, has decided to return to her home in England. She feels that William is now old enough to care for himself and that her leaving will result in his parents, Mr. and Mrs. Lawrence, spending more time with him.

William tries to think of ways to convince Mrs. Phillips to stay. When arguments fail, he takes and hides two of her favorite possessions, her husband's picture and a pearl pin that had been left to her by her mother. He is sure that she would never leave without them. Eventually William returns the picture and pin, but says he will think of some other way to keep her with him.

Mrs. Phillips gives William a farewell gift. It is an enormous stone and wooden castle that has been in her

family at least as far back as her great-great-grandfather. She places the castle in the attic. It comes with a two-inch-tall lead knight. When William unwraps the knight, it comes alive. The Silver Knight, Sir Simon, explains that a wizard has taken over his kingdom, and that when all conditions are right, he will return to claim it.

William continues with the regular activities of his life. He practices gymnastics, attends school, and continues to try to think of a way to keep Mrs. Phillips with him. But whenever he can, he visits the Silver Knight in the attic. Sir Simon shows him that he has a token, taken from the wizard's necklace, which shrinks things down to his size. This gives William an idea. Using the token from the wizard's necklace on the day that Mrs. Phillips has packed her suitcase and is leaving for good, William shrinks her and then takes her up to the castle to live with the Silver Knight.

William continues his daily routine, spends more time cooking with his father, and even regrets his hasty action, but he knows he cannot restore Mrs. Phillips to her normal size unless he goes with the Silver Knight back to his kingdom and gets a second piece from the wizard's necklace. William allows himself to be miniaturized and practices to be the knight's squire. When all is ready, William and the Silver Knight leave the castle and start on their quest to take the knight's kingdom back from the wizard, Alastor, and to get the second piece from the necklace.

Going through a dangerous wood, William and the Silver Knight become parted. When William reaches the kingdom, he finds the land dried and shriveled up. A young boy directs him toward the wizard's castle. William stops long enough to perform a good deed for a man who has been placed under enchantment. Learning that the wizard is looking for a jester, William goes to the castle to apply for the position. He confronts the dragon guarding the castle and is taken on as the court jester.

He soon learns that the Silver Knight has again been turned into lead and is in the castle. An old crone, Calendar, assists William, and the boy is able to snatch the necklace, turn Alastor to lead, bring the statues back to life, turn the kingdom free of enchantment back to Sir Simon, and return home. Using the magic piece from the necklace, William restores Mrs. Phillips to her normal size, and she departs, promising to throw the leaden wizard and the tokens from the necklace into the ocean as she sails across the sea to England.

List of Major Characters: William Lawrence; his parents, Mr. and Mrs. Lawrence; Jason, his friend; Mrs. Phillips, his caretaker; Sir Simon, the Silver Knight; Alastor, the Wizard; and Calendar, an old woman who lives in Alastor's castle.

Vocabulary: Look up in a dictionary each of the following words that is used in *The Castle in the Attic*. Then write an original sentence that demonstrates that you understand the word's meaning.

acrid _____

armory _____

chided _____

edict _____

illusions _____

portcullis _____

raucous _____

rituals _____

scullery _____

troubadour _____

vaulted _____

windlass _____

Comprehension Questions

1. Why does Mrs. Phillips change William's gymnastics routine to the front flip instead of the dive roll?
2. Mrs. Phillips said that in the world of magic, every person is given the right weapon. What is her weapon?
3. What is pictured on Sir Simon's coat of arms?
4. What keepsake does Lady Elinore give Sir Simon to take with him on the quest?
5. What is the name of the Silver Knight's horse?
6. William is hungry and thirsty and is tempted to take a bite from the apple he picks from the very top of the tree. What stops him from eating it?
7. What secret does Calendar share with William about the eyes of the dragon that guards the castle?
8. What part of the dragon is vulnerable to a dagger blow?
9. Why didn't the old crone, Calendar, try to stop the wizard when he first came to power?
10. What happens to the land in the kingdom as soon as the wizard is defeated?

Answers: 1) The front flip is another weapon and allows William to get back on his feet a little faster. 2) Her weapon is the needle and thread. 3) Sir Simon's coat of arms contains a lion flanked by a cross. 4) Lady Elinore gives Sir Simon a long silk scarf. 5) Sir Simon's horse is named Moonlight. 6) Birds stop William from eating the apple. 7) If you look directly into the dragon's eyes, his fire cannot harm you. 8) The dragon is vulnerable in its right thigh. 9) The wizard sucked out Calendar's heart and replaced it with a stone. 10) After the wizard is defeated, the land springs back to life again.

Discussion Questions

1. William does not take Bear with him on his quest, but he does take him up to the attic. What is Bear's function in the story?
2. Both Jason and William are unhappy with their parents. William doesn't like being asked questions about school. Jason doesn't like his mother concentrating on whether or not he has practiced the piano or taken the garbage out. Do you think these parents concentrate on the wrong things? Discuss. What should parents concentrate on?
3. Before he leaves on the quest, William wishes that he could tell Jason all about the castle and Sir Simon, but he doesn't. He thinks that when he comes back, he will tell Jason about it. Do you think William ever does tell Jason? Why, or why not? If he does tell, will Jason believe him? Why, or why not?
4. There is a time complication in this story. Sir Simon explains that if you willingly allow yourself to be miniaturized and enter the castle (as William did), when you return you will not have lost any time from real life. But if you enter it unwillingly (as Mrs. Phillips did), the time spent being only two inches high is time that is lost from one's normal life. Why do you think the author included this complication? Explain how if William comes

back on the same day that he left, and Mrs. Phillips loses a week, they can both be together on the front walk waiting for the bus.

5. When William touches the statues in the castle, they come back to life. Mrs. Phillips is afraid that if William touches the wizard after he had been turned to lead, he would come back to life, too. Do you think this would have happened? Why, or why not?

6. In *The Castle in the Attic,* the characters follow conventional social roles. Mrs. Phillips, as Lady Elinore, stays at the castle and sews while William and the Silver Knight go forth to win the kingdom back from the evil wizard. Would you have preferred that the story defied these conventional roles and have had Mrs. Phillips go back in disguise as a knight to the kingdom? Discuss the difference that changing conventional roles would have made in the story.

7. With other students who have read *The Castle in the Attic,* discuss it as an example of fantasy literature. In what ways is it unique? In what ways does it resemble other fantasy stories? How does the dragon in this story compare with the dragon, Smaug, in *The Hobbit* or with the dragons in *Dragonflight?* How does this quest story compare with other quest stories such as *The Hobbit?*

8. William and his father begin to plan dinner menus and to cook together. In many families, there is a special meal that some member of the family likes to cook and that becomes known as his or her specialty. Invite students to talk about their favorite family dinners and why they are special. They might even want to bring in and share a recipe. These could be gathered into a recipe book of class favorites.

Research Activities

1. The wizard, Alastor, wears a strange necklace. It has two tokens on it that fit together. The token has the image of Janus, and its magic works when one says, "Saturn." One of these tokens causes a person to shrink, and the other token returns a person back to normal size. Do some research. Who was Janus? Who was Saturn? What is their history? How does this fit in with their function in this story? In doing your research, consult the Internet as well as print sources. Share the information that you glean in a written report to the class that includes a bibliography. Possible sources of information include *Greek and Roman Mythology A to Z: A Young Reader's Companion* by Kathleen N. Daly (New York: Facts on File, 1992), http://www.gwydir.demon.co.uk/jo/roman/, and http://www.dl.ket.org/ latin1/lesser/roam/saturn.htm.

2. There is a dragon in this story. Dragons appear in many stories about the Middle Ages. They also appear in Asian literature. If there are Asian ESL students in the classroom, they may wish to prepare and share with the group stories that they know in their native language or stories that they can find through research from their background and traditions that involve dragons. It would be interesting to compare and contrast the role of the dragon from one of these Asian stories with the dragon in *The Castle in the Attic.*

3. Encourage a small group of interested students to visit Elizabeth Winthrop's web site at http://www.absolute-sway.com/winthrop/message.html. Elizabeth Winthrop is the author of many books for children, including *The Castle in the Attic.* She shares the fact that her great-great uncle, President Theodore Roosevelt, wrote 38 books. Ask these students to research Teddy Roosevelt and prepare a report to share with the class. They should use at least three sources of information. Possible sources include *Bully for You, Teddy Roosevelt* by Jean Fritz

(New York: G.P. Putnam's, 1991), *Young Teddy Roosevelt* by Cheryl Harness (Washington, DC: National Geographic Society, 1998), and http://www.theodoreroosevelt.org as well as http://www.whitehouse.gov/history/presidents/tr26.html.

4. Mrs. Phillips sews a tapestry while she waits for William and the Silver Knight. There are many famous tapestries, including the Bayeux Tapestry, which is an embroidery that is about 230 feet long. It depicts the Battle of Hastings that took place on October 14, 1066. At http://sjolander.com/viking/museum/bt/bt.htm, students can see pictures of this tapestry. Invite a group of interested students to learn more about tapestries and to share what they learn with the class in an oral report. In doing their research, they should consult at least three sources of information.

5. Ask a small group of students to research coats of arms. There are several Internet sites that offer to sell heraldic items to customers but also offer free information about coats of arms. One is http://www.coatofarms-shop.coj/coatofarms/html. Ask these students to make a coat of arms and display it on a bulletin board. It can be an authentic coat of arms of some member of their family or simply one that they invent. Ask them to explain the various symbols on the coat of arms to their classmates.

6. Some students will be particularly interested in armor and weapons. Encourage these students to choose some aspect of weaponry, such as the history of swords, and to share their information with the class. One source of information is http://www.castles. org/armor_and_weapons/history.htm. They might want to include drawings of significant weapons from the past. Other possible sources of information are *Arms & Armor of Medieval Knights: An Illustrated History of Weaponry in the Middle Ages* by David Edge (Collingdale, PA: Diane Publishing Co., 1993) and *A Knight and His Armor* by R. Ewart Oakeshott, second edition (Chester Springs, PA: Dufour Editions, 1999).

Extension Activities

1. Sir Simon and Lady Elinore try to help William understand the rules of conduct that a knight, squire, or page must follow. This discussion takes place in Chapter 10. Write out the rules that you think are important in the form of calligraphy on a piece of paper, making it as elegant as possible and tying it with a ribbon like a scroll. You may use the rules mentioned in the book and add others that you think might be important. Share with your classmates the rules you come up with.

2. With the help of interested classmates, act out the scene from the book when the Silver Knight and Mrs. Phillips discuss with William the rules of conduct that guide a knight, squire, and page. (You might use the scroll from extension activity #1, above, as a prop in the play.) Perhaps a parent volunteer might serve as director. With the help of a music educator, students might select appropriate period music to play before and after the scene.

3. Ask a pair of students to study the style used in your local newspaper for front-page stories of exciting events. Have them use this as a model as they write about William's exploits in saving the kingdom in the form of an exciting news article for a modern newspaper or magazine. The students should post their finished article on a bulletin board to be shared with others who have read *The Castle in the Attic.*

4. Draw a floor plan for a castle. Include a scale of size. Label the various rooms that it contains. Be sure to show the specific rooms mentioned in William's castle, including the

armory, buttery, chapel, portcullis, and drawbridge, and add as many additional rooms as you would like. Post your "blueprints" on a classroom bulletin board.

5. Write a short Chapter 18 to be added to *The Castle in the Attic*. Be sure to use correct spelling and punctuation throughout. In this chapter, have William participate in the long-anticipated gymnastics meet. Try to use the same language and tone as is used in the rest of the novel. Does William find that the time he spent in practice to serve as a squire and in being a jester for the wizard help him in his gymnastics meet? Who appears on the day of the event to watch him compete? Ask others who have read the book to read your new chapter and discuss it with you.

6. Ask students who have read *The Castle in the Attic* to prepare an advertisement for the book to encourage others to read this novel. The presentation could take the form of a short TV commercial or of a print advertisement that might appear in a magazine. Allow time for these presentations to be shared with the class.

How does reading *The Castle in the Attic* and engaging in the various activities suggested above help students meet the 12 NCTE/IRA English Language Arts Standards?

1. *The Castle in the Attic* meets Standard #1 by serving as an example of outstanding fiction.

2. *The Castle in the Attic* meets Standard #2 because it is a representative work of the broad genre of fantasy.

3. Discussion questions #1 through #6 help students to comprehend and interpret text, and the vocabulary exercise increases knowledge of word meanings, helping students to meet Standard #3.

4. Extension activity #1, which suggests writing out the rules of conduct that guide a knight and preparing these rules in the form of an elaborate scroll, addresses Standard #4, which asks students to adjust written language and style to communicate effectively for different purposes.

5. Extension activity #3, which suggests that a student write up the exploits of William in the form of an article for a modern newspaper or magazine, helps meet Standard #5, which requires that students use different writing processes for different audiences and for a variety of purposes.

6. Extension activity #5, which suggests that a student write a new chapter to be added to the book, helps to meet Standard #6, by requiring students to apply their knowledge of language structure and language conventions to create a print text.

7. Research activity #5 about coats of arms helps to address Standard #7 by requiring students to gather, evaluate, and synthesize data from a variety of sources.

8. Research activity #1 involving the history of Saturn and Janus helps to meet Standard #8 by encouraging students to use a variety of technological and information resources to carry out research and to communicate their knowledge.

9. Discussion question #6 about the conventional roles played by men and women in this book helps to address Standard #9 by allowing students to develop an understanding of and respect for diversity in social roles.

10. Research activity #2 asking ESL students to compare and contrast the use of dragons in Asian literature with the dragon in this story helps address Standard #10, which asks

students to use their first language that is not English to develop a deeper understanding of the curriculum.

11. Discussion question #7 allows students to pool their information knowledge in the form of a book discussion group and compare and contrast it with other fantasy novels. It helps meet Standard #11, which asks that students participate as knowledgeable, reflective, creative, and critical members of a literary community.

12. Extension activity #6 allows students to creatively select and prepare a means of sharing their enthusiasm for this book with other potential readers. It addresses Standard #12, in which students are asked to use spoken, written, and visual language to persuade others.

❖ Author–Title Index

❖ About the Author

Phyllis J. Perry has over thirty years of service as an elementary school teacher and administrator, as well as teacher training and supervisory experience, and has taught college and university courses. She earned her doctorate from the University of Colorado in education, majoring in curriculum and instruction. Her undergraduate work was at the University of California, Berkeley.

Dr. Perry is the author of over forty children's and professional books, as well as numerous articles, reviews, and research reports. In recognition for her achievements, she has received the Governor's Award for Excellence in Education from the State of Colorado, as well as the Distinguished Leadership Award for Outstanding Contributions to Education. She has won three awards for her writing from the Colorado Authors' League and is a member of the Society of Children's Book Authors and Illustrators. A resident of Boulder, Colorado, Dr. Perry now devotes full time to writing and consulting.